Public Pension Fund Management

Governance, Accountability, and Investment Policies

*Proceedings of
the Second Public Pension
Fund Management Conference, May 2003*

Public Pension Fund Management

Governance, Accountability, and Investment Policies

*Proceedings of
the Second Public Pension
Fund Management Conference, May 2003*

Edited by

Alberto R. Musalem

Robert J. Palacios

THE WORLD BANK

Cover design and photo manipulation: James E. Quigley, World Bank Institute.

Original cover photo: Getty Images.

Contents

Chapter 1
A Framework for Public Pension Fund Management. . . . 1

Jeffrey Carmichael and Robert Palacios

Chapter 2
Governance of Public Pension Funds:Lessons from Corporate Governance and International Evidence 49

David Hess and Gregorio Impavido

Chapter 3
Transparency and Accountability of
Public Pension Funds. 91

Anne Maher

Chapter 6
Key Differences in Public Pension Fund Management between Ireland and Poland. **151**

Krzysztof Pater

Chapter 7
Governance of Public Pension Funds: New Zealand Superannuation Fund **157**

Brian McCulloch and Jane Frances

Chapter 8
Investment Policies, Processes and Problems in U.S. Public Sector Pension Plans: Some Observations and Solutions from a Practitioner 211

John H. Ilkiw

Chapter 9
The Norwegian Petroleum Fund 241

Knut Kjær

Chapter 10
Governance and Investment of Provident and Pension Funds: The Cases of Singapore and India. . . . 259

Mukul G. Asher

Chapter 11
Supervision of a Public Pension Fund: Experience and Challenges in Kenya 281

Edward Odundo

Tables

Figures

Boxes

Foreword

Public pension fund management is an important practice in a great number of countries and represents about one-third of worldwide pension schemes. In addition, in many countries public pension funds represent an important share of the financial system's assets. Special issues concerning these funds include fund governance, fund managers' accountability, investment policies, the exercising of shareholders' rights, and corporate governance; and fund management has an impact on fiscal policy and financial markets.

Proper management of public pension funds contributes to fulfilling the promise of providing adequate retirement income while developing financial markets. The issue of management has only recently attracted the attention of policymakers, practitioners, and development agencies. Most important, countries that do not pay sufficient attention to the management of public pension funds often discover that these funds have been mismanaged and failed to contribute to financial markets' development. Government intervention is then required to deal with ensuing problems. In this context, the World Bank through the World Bank Institute, the Financial Sector Vice-Presidency, and the Human Development Vice-Presidency decided to organize the public pension fund management conferences. Participants addressed initial experiences with best international practices in public pension fund management and challenges confronted by emerging economies to implement them.

This is the second conference on the topic, bringing together about 150 senior policymakers, practitioners, academics, and staff of multilateral agencies to address issues of governance, accountability, and investment policies. This conference aims to foster ongoing dialogue and exchange of experiences across regions and between emerging and developed economies.

Thanks are due to many individuals who contributed to the success of the conference and to this volume, including the authors and discussants of the paper presented herein. Special thanks are owed to Ms. Demet Cabbar of the World Bank, who helped to organize the conference and coordinated the effort to consolidate conference proceedings into this book. We also acknowledge the editorial, proofreading, and indexing assistance of Grammarians, Inc. Funds for the conference and this proceedings were generously supplied by the World Bank.

CESARE CALARI
Vice-President, Financial Sector

FRANNIE LÉAUTIER
Vice-President, World Bank Institute

JEAN-LOUIS SARBIB
Senior Vice-President, Human Development

Contributors

Mukul G. Asher is Professor in the Public Policy Programme at the National University of Singapore. He was educated in India and the United States. In addition to these countries and Singapore, he has also taught or researched in Australia, Malaysia and Sweden. From June 1997 to December 1997 he was a Visiting Professor at the Fiscal Affairs Department of the International Monetary Fund. He specializes in Public Finances of developing countries. He is regarded as the leading authority on social security arrangements in Southeast Asia. He is also involved in researching social security issues in India. He has authored or edited several books, and has published numerous articles in national and international journals. He has been a consultant to the World Bank, International Monetary Fund, Asian Development Bank, UN-ESCAP, Asian Development Bank Institute, and Oxford Analytica. He has addressed many academic conferences and business and professional gatherings. His contacts with the print and the radio and the TV media have been extensive.

Jeffrey Carmichael's career experience includes 20 years in senior positions with the Reserve Bank of Australia, 7 years as Professor of Finance at Bond University and appointment to a number of Government inquiries and Government and private sector Boards. In 1996/97 he served as a member of the Wallis Inquiry which recommended sweeping changes to Australia's regulatory structure. He was Chairman of the Australian Prudential Regulation Authority until June 2003. He is a private consultant to the World Bank, the Asian Development Bank and a number of countries in the area of regulatory structures and policies. Dr Carmichael has a PhD from Princeton University and has published in a number of the world's leading journals, including the *American Economic Review* and the *Journal of Finance*. In 1995 he was awarded an Officer in the Order of Australia for service to education, finance and the community.

David Hess is an Assistant Professor at the Rutgers Business School. His research focuses on issues in the areas of corporate governance, corporate social responsibility, and business and government. He has contributed articles to such publications as the *California Management Review, Business Ethics Quarterly, Cornell International Law Journal, Journal of Corporation Law,* and *Northwestern Journal of International Law & Business.* Professor Hess received a J.D. from the University of Iowa, M.A. and Ph.D. degrees in management from The Wharton School of the University of Pennsylvania, and a B.A. in economics from Grinnell College.

John Ilkiw was named director, global consulting practices of Frank Russell Company in May 2000. He is responsible for the quality and consistency of Russell's global consulting advice. In addition, he is senior consultant to a limited number of U.S. consulting clients. Prior to assuming his current role, John was director of consulting for Russell's London office. He was responsible for the reputation and profitability of Russell's London-based consulting operations. He was also senior consultant to clients in the U.K., Jersey and Switzerland. John joined Frank Russell Company in Canada in 1989 as a consultant and was director of consulting in the Toronto office from 1994 to 1997. He specialized in trustee education, fund governance, asset-liability management and structured investment strategies. From 1986 to 1989, John was an asset-liability management consultant with William M. Mercer Limited. From 1983 to 1986, he was Ontario's director of the Pension and Income Security Policy Branch. Before that time, John served as a senior advisor on pension issues for Ontario's Ministry of Treasury and Economics. He joined the Ontario civil service in 1974 to research Canada Pension Plan financing and benefit issues. John is a former Chair of the Investment Advisory Committee to the Pension Commission of Ontario. He is a CFA Charterholder of the Association for Investment Management and Research and the author of *The Portable Pension Fiduciary: A Handbook for Better Fund Management*, published by Maclean-Hunter in 1997. John holds a B.A. in economics from York University (1972) and an M.A. in Economics from the University of Toronto (1975).

Gregorio Impavido has worked as a Financial Economist in the Financial Sector Development Department of the World Bank since 1998. His areas of expertise are pension funds and pension reforms, insurance markets, supervision of insurance and private pensions markets. Prior to 1998 he was a consultant to the European Investment Bank and worked at the European Bank for Reconstruction and Development (EBRD). He has researched and analyzed insurance and pension markets, supervision, and regulation in numerous countries and has researched contractual savings and financial markets development in Eastern and Western Europe, Asia, Africa and Latin America (i.e. Philippines, Mozambique, Gambia, Senegal, Mexico, Armenia, Georgia, Lithuania, Luxembourg, United Kingdom). Mr. Impavido is the author and co-author of number of essays on the effects of contractual savings development on financial markets. He holds a Ph.D. in Economics and an M.Sc. in Quantitative Development Economics from the University of Warwick, UK; and a B.Sc. in Economics from Bocconi University.

Knut N. Kjær is the Executive Director of the Norges Bank Investment Management/The Norwegian Government Petroleum Fund since 1997 to the present. From 1994 to 1997, he served as the Executive Vice-President of Storebrand, Norway's largest insurance company. Mr. Kjær is also a founding member of the Economic Analysis Centre, ECON, where he was a senior partner and researcher from 1986 to 1994. From 1983 to 1986, he worked as a Research Fellow at the Department of Economics at the University of Oslo and then as a Researcher in Economic Analysis Group, Statistics Norway.

John MacNaughton is the first President and Chief Executive Officer of the Canada Pension Plan (CPP) Investment Board. Prior to joining the CPP Investment Board Mr. MacNaughton had a distinguished career in the investment industry in Canada and abroad. In the spring of 1999, he retired as President of Nesbitt Burns Inc., one of Canada's largest investment dealers, after 31 years with that company and predecessor firms such as Burns Fry and then Nesbitt Burns. He served as President from 1989 until his retirement. Mr. MacNaughton is presently a Trustee of the University Health Network which operates three teaching and research hospitals: Princess Margaret, Toronto General and Toronto Western. He has served previously as Chairman of the Princess Margaret Hospital Foundation, Chairman of the Investment Dealers Association of Canada, President of the Empire Club of Canada, National Secretary of Progressive Conservative Association of Canada, Vice President and Director of the Canadian Stage Company, and Governor of Ryerson Polytechnic Institute (now University).

Anne Maher is Chief Executive of The Pensions Board, Ireland. She is a board member of the Review Board established by the Accountancy Foundation in the UK, of the Irish Accounting and Auditing Supervisory Authority and of the Irish Health Insurance Authority. She is also a member of the Advisory Council to the Eircom ESOP Trustee and a Governor of The Pensions Policy Institute (UK). She holds a law degree from University College Dublin.

Brian McCulloch is Principal Advisor in the Asset and Liability Management Branch of the New Zealand Treasury. The Asset and Liability Management Branch advises Treasury Ministers on managing and financing the Crown's assets and liabilities. The branch is responsible for giving advice on financial policy on the Crown balance sheet, public sector financial management systems and managing commercial, contractual and litigation risks on behalf of the Crown. This includes advice on the Crown's ownership interests and obligations in State Owned Enterprises, Crown companies, and Crown financial institutions. The branch also includes the New Zealand Debt Management Office, which manages the Crown's debt portfolio, overall cashflows and interest-bearing deposits. Since joining the Treasury in 1990, Brian has undertaken various management and advisory roles in the general area of financial management policy. He recently led the policy development for the establishment of the New Zealand Superannuation Fund. His experience prior to joining the Treasury included auditing and management consulting. Dr. McCulloch is also a Chartered Accountant and holds a Ph.D. in accounting and finance from the School of Business at the University of Washington.

Alberto R. Musalem has been an adviser on contractual savings (pension and life insurance) and the tax treatment of financial instruments in the Financial Sector Development Department at the World Bank since January 1998. He pioneered the work on contractual savings at the Bank including research and analysis of the effects of contractual savings on financial markets. Previously, Mr. Musalem lead the dialogue on macroeconomics, trade and financial sector policies in several countries of Latin America, Middle East and Eastern Europe. His experience prior to joining the World Bank includes work for the Rockefeller and Ford Foundations as a visiting professor in graduate economics programs in South America and the United States. He also worked as a staff of the Harvard Institute of International

Development in a capacity of advisor to the Government of Colombia on macroeconomics, trade and financial sector policies. He received a Ph.D. in Economics from the University of Chicago. He is the author of numerous publications and working papers. Mr. Musalem led the team that organized the first and second Public Pension Fund Management and Contractual Savings Conferences in Washington, DC.

Edward Odundo is the Chief Executive Officer of Retirement Benefits Authority (Kenya). Mr. Odundo has held various high level responsibilities such as The Commissioner of Value Added Tax, Kenya Revenue Authority and Founder and First Chairman of the Forum of VAT Administrators in Africa for Kenya, Uganda, Tanzania, Malawi, Rwanda, Ghana and Zambia, with its headquarters in Accra, Ghana; First Financial Controller Kenya Revenue Authority, General Manager, East Africa Reinsurance Company Limited and Finance Manager, Kenya Reinsurance Corporation. He is a founder of the Pan Africa Pensions' Forum for Eritrea, Ghana, Kenya, Namibia, Senegal, Tanzania and Zambia. He is a well-accomplished Accountant who holds a B.S. degree in Finance and Accounting and an M.B.A. degree in Strategic Management and Marketing. Mr. Odundo is a Finalist Ph.D. degree student in Strategic Management at the University of Nairobi. He also holds membership in several professional bodies including; Fellow of the Institute of Certified Public Accountants (FCPAK), membership of the Institute of Certified Public Secretaries (CPS), Member of the Institute of Management (MKIM), former Deputy Chairman of the Certified Public Accountants of Kenya (ICPAK), former Board Member of the Registration of Accountants of Kenya (RAB).

Robert Palacios is Senior Pension Economist at the World Bank. As a member of the team that produced *Averting the Old Age Crisis* in 1994, Mr. Palacios has written extensively on topics of pension reform. He has also been involved in pension reform operations in various countries in Africa, Eastern Europe, Latin America and Asia. Mr. Palacios is currently working in India, Nepal, Senegal and Cape Verde. He also manages an applied research project known as the Pension Reform Primer (www.worldbank.org/pensions).

Krzysztof Pater was appointed Minister of Social Policy in Poland in May 2004. He was involved in the reform of the Polish pension system as the advisor to the Minister of the State Treasury since 1995, being responsible for the creation of the concept of the funded pillars in the new pension system. In 1997–1998, he was the Deputy Executive Director of the Office of the Government Plenipotentiary for Social Security Reform. He created the detailed concept of the funded part of the new Polish pension system and managed the legislative process, aimed at the implementation of the new system. In 1998–1999, he worked as Vice President of Managing Board in PKO/Handlowy Universal Pension Society, managing one of the Polish mandatory pension funds. After that he worked as independent advisor for public, scientific and private institutions. In November 2001, he was nominated as Under-secretary of State in the Polish Ministry of Labour and Social Policy. Since January 2003, he works as Under-secretary of State in the Ministry of Economy, Labour and Social Policy. He is responsible for all social insurance problems, including the old age and disability pension system. He is also Vice Chairman of the Insurance and Pension Funds Supervisory Commission. In early 1990s, he worked on the strategy of the State involvement on the Polish capital market as the Advisor to the Minister of Privatization. He has been also the member of the task group, preparing the concept of the OTC market in Poland, the Secretary of the Supervisory Board in the National Depository of Securities and the representative of the Minister of Privatization and the Minister of the State Treasury, working in the Committee Coordinating the Development of the Warsaw Stock Exchange System. In 1994, he has earned the securities broker's license, granted by the Securities Commission. He is an active member of the Polish Scouting and Guiding Association (ZHP). In 1997–2001, he was the Deputy Chairman of ZHP.

Introduction

The World Bank in recent years has been increasing its participation in the international debate on public pension reform. Its reasons for doing so are twofold: to improve the advice it gives to its clients, and to improve the design of its programs in this area. One of the most important components of this effort, and one in which the Bank has some claim to comparative advantage, is the bringing together of country experiences to establish what policies work and which do not. To this end the Bank has sponsored workshops and conferences to bring together practitioners in pension fund management, policymakers, academics, and international development institutions.

The Bank hosted its first major conference between 24 and 26 September 2001, at which it became apparent that reforms in this area were at an early stage and that there was clear demand for more information and advice. Between 5 and 7 May 2003, the Bank therefore hosted the Second Public Pension Fund Management Conference, in Washington, D.C. Where the first conference had brought together about 75 participants, the second conference was attended by 150 senior policymakers, practitioners, academics, and staff of multilateral agencies. The delegates addressed issues of governance, accountability, and investment policy.

This interest in the management of public pension reserves is motivated by several factors. Central among these is the social concern of the financing of pensions—the sustainability of pension funds in countries as diverse as Sweden and China depends to some extent on how these funds are administered. In many countries the public pension fund furthermore is the largest domestic source of long-term savings, raising important policy questions about the bearing that pension reserves have on national savings, fiscal policy, the financial sector, and, ultimately, growth. This influence will be of the greatest significance in countries in which a large proportion of the population is not covered by formal retirement savings programs.

It is important to recognize that this discussion of reserves management is taking place against the backdrop of the continuing international debate about the reform of public pension systems. The nature of this debate has shifted significantly since the publication of *Averting the Old Age Crisis: Policies to Protect the Old and Promote Growth*, World Bank, New York: Oxford University Press, 1994. Where the debate once was about whether or not to increase the level of prefunding, it is now about how best to achieve this. One approach to prefunding is to license private asset managers, under close supervision, to manage individual accounts that are fully funded and subject to at least limited competition. The more common approach, however, remains the public management of reserves, guided by the imperative of smoothing out the demographic effects of a population aging.

Large unfunded pension liabilities have serious implications, and for the most part it is the growing awareness of these implications that is driving recognition of the need to set aside assets to cover at least part of future pension payouts. While this implicit pension debt may not be reported on a government's balance sheet, it does impose an intertemporal fiscal constraint, and financial markets will punish sovereigns that let the debt get out of control. Increasing recognition of the need to set aside assets also is partly due to the fact that the younger workers who will bear the brunt of the intergenerational transfer implied by this liability are starting to protest.

There are three ways of increasing the 'funding ratio' (that is, the size of reserves relative to the size of the liability): by reducing the liability (for example, by cutting benefits); by increasing the revenues earmarked for the reserves (usually, by raising payroll taxes); or by improving the investment returns of an existing fund. A reform package may include two or even all three elements.

Politically, the most popular approach is to increase investment returns, but the history of public pension funds shows that this is not readily achieved. Measured by most reasonable standards, public pension funds typically perform poorly, and the evidence suggests that this is because of a conflict of interest borne by the government or parastatal officials appointed to determine asset allocation. Reserves in partially funded public schemes have been used to subsidize housing, state enterprises, and various types of economically targeted investments; they have been used to prop up stock markets; and, as a captive source of credit, they have allowed governments to run larger deficits than would have otherwise been the case. This is in large part possible because the decisions to allocate pension reserves typically occur in a regulatory vacuum and with little public accountability or transparency. Minimum standards for reporting and accounting often are absent.

Proponents of centralized fund management (as opposed to decentralized and competitive management) argue that new governance designs and investment policy can shield public pension funds from the kind of political interference that has plagued them in the past, and that it is possible, even in the absence of competition and independent supervision, to ensure that trustees make prudent investment decisions. While it is too early to draw conclusions, the new systems and policies implemented in Canada, New Zealand, and Ireland and by the Norwegian Petroleum Fund certainly appear to be much more robust than those operated in the past. Commercial investment policies and the use of professional boards, combined with modern principles of governance codified in statutes, in particular represent major advances.

These experiments promise much, but the vast majority of countries with public pension reserves continue to operate as they have for decades. The cases of India and Kenya highlight the inertia that has inhibited the reform of funded schemes in Asia and Africa. Even Singapore, with its modern financial markets and high country rankings for governance, has failed to deliver adequate returns to the members of its retirement system—on the contrary, it continues to tap its massive pension funds for purposes other than income security in old age.

These experiences, whether positive or negative, all enrich the policy debate. The challenge facing policymakers is to draw out the general lessons of these experiences and to tailor them to country-specific conditions.

The paper by David Hess and Gregorio Impavido applies the logic of corporate governance to this problem, and attempts to establish a general framework from which to view the problem. The paper by Jeffrey Carmichael and Robert Palacios similarly attempts to create a preliminary generic framework, and offers a checklist of questions to be addressed when assessing the robustness of a particular case.

The first paper by Anne Maher highlights the need for transparency and accountability in the management of public funds. If public funds do not have the confidence and support of those for whom they are established they are unlikely to succeed; Maher points out that public awareness of and interest in the fund is probably the best discipline for such funds, and that transparency and accountability in themselves can create demand for good overall governance. Her paper is a rich discussion of the key components for the successful design of transparency and accountability schemes.

The paper by John McNaughton discusses the implementation of the governance, accountability, and investment policy model adopted by the Canada Pension Plan (CPP) Investment Board. McNaughton highlights the way in which this model protects against political risks, ensures the integrity of the organization, and describes the unencumbered investment mandate and practice. He emphasizes that the success of the Canadian model is in great part due to the fact that it is fully transparent: The CPP board has a strong commitment to robust public reporting and accountability, and it is this that underpins the credibility of its governance model. The paper additionally explains the CPP's investment philosophy and practices and details the progress and performance made since the CPP became operational in October 1998.

Maher's second paper deals with the establishment of the National Pensions Reserve Fund of Ireland. The paper discusses the governance structure, transparency, accountability, and investment policy model used, and documents the early performance of the fund. Poland's practices are described by Krzysztof Pater, who details in particular the environment under which the Poland pension fund was established. Pater also highlights the importance of a gradual approach to change, specifically for its ability to ensure that reforms gain the trust and support of the public.

The paper by Brian McCulloch and Jane Frances discusses the establishment of the New Zealand Superannuation Fund, which was created in part to support the management of Crown finances through future demographic changes. Crucial to the underlying policy of the fund are governance arrangements that aim to ensure the efficient management of the fund. The fund is to be a clearly defined portfolio of Crown financial resources, managed by an independent governing body with explicit commercial objectives and clear accountability; the paper describes the legislation that seeks to ensure that these principles are fully realized.

The paper by Knut Kjær discusses the model of governance, accountability, and investment policy adopted by the Norwegian Petroleum Fund. Kjaer provides some background information about the fund and explains what he believes is special about the management model used. He also discusses the investment strategy and addresses the issues of how the fund managers create excess return, how they select external managers, and what they see as being most important to the investment process.

The paper by John H. Ilkiw discusses the generic investment policy process followed by most private and public sector pension plans in the United States, Canada, and the United Kingdom. Ilkiw also discusses the impact that ineffective governance structures and procedures have on pension fund investment performance, and continues by identifying the organizational and behavioral impediments that public sector funds often face, such as inadequate understanding by governing fiduciaries of the principles of financing and investment; the inability of governing fiduciaries to separate policy approval from policy implementation; and an overreliance on past performance when making decisions. These impediments obviously are not unique to public sector pension plans, but usually are more visible here than among private sector plans. The paper concludes by introducing a performance report designed explicitly for governing fiduciaries.

Mukul G. Asher's paper examines the governance and investment issues relating to provident and pension funds in Singapore and India. In Singapore, the key governance challenge facing the Central Provident Fund (CPF) is how to secure the services of competent, independent board members—a task that is complicated by the country's monocentric power structure and by the fact that information tends to be regarded by those in power as a strategic instrument rather than a public good. Asher recommends that changes be made to give much higher priority to the fiduciary responsibility of the CPF board, greater transparency of the investment process and outcome, and lower transaction costs. He additionally recommends that consideration be given to the formation of a separate asset management company with statutory requirements for fiduciary responsibility and transparency. The board of such a company should comprise independent, competent members regulated by the newly constituted Provident Fund Authority.

Regarding India, Asher describes the five components of the pension system and identifies as a key reform issue the question of how to de-link from the fiscal operations of the central and state governments the direct and nonaccountable use of funds generated by the five components. He stresses that pension and provident funds must be able to operate on their own. Asher also recommends the harmonization of investment guidelines (that is, that the Employees Provident Fund Organization investment guidelines move toward the Insurance Regulatory and Development Authority guidelines for pension funds). He concludes that the design of pension and provident schemes in India is not consistent with international good practices in key areas such as benefit and contribution formulas, actuarial studies, administration and compliance, portability, investment policies and management, and stakeholder relations, particularly as regards the provision of information, transparency, accountability, and corporate governance. He does, however, identify a growing awareness of the need to reform the system—the establishment of the Pension Fund Regulatory and Development Authority is in particular an important advance.

Finally, the paper by Edward Odundo discusses the experience and challenges of supervising the public pension fund in Kenya. Odundo explains the importance of the 2000 establishment of the Retirement Benefits Authority, which was charged with implementing the Retirement Benefits Act and overseeing the industry's management and development. Control of the authority's operations is vested in an independent board of directors that has a majority private sector representation and the autonomy to run the industry without undue government interference. The Retirement Benefits Act was introduced with the objective of supporting the introduction of international fund management practices. The key compliance requirements of the act include the timely preparation and wide publication of audited annual accounts; the outsourcing of investments to independent professional fund managers; the placing of assets with reputable and stable custodial institutions; and, in the long term, the diversification of the investment portfolio according to guidelines provided in the law. Perhaps the most important lesson from the Kenyan experience is the need for support from stakeholders, and particularly from politicians. As Odundo argues, stakeholder backing can be a catalyst for the successful regulation of a public pension fund.

The countries examined in this book are of all sizes and at all levels of development. They are all, however, facing the same problem of how to manage public pension funds. Despite the huge stakes involved, the reform agenda has moved slowly and there is little cross-country research available to guide policymakers. There is also no clear and accepted standard of best practice in the field. This book, with contributions from every part of the globe, hopes to be a first step toward the establishment of guidelines to ensure the secure and effective management and use of the retirement savings of workers around the world.

ALBERTO R. MUSALEM
ROBERT PALACIOS

A Framework for Public Pension Fund Management

Jeffrey Carmichael and Robert Palacios

Public pension schemes, or social security schemes, as they are known in some countries, have long been recognized as having major economic and social implications. In addition to their obvious social welfare objective of providing adequate retirement incomes for the aged, public pension schemes can influence economic performance and capital accumulation through their effect on taxes and intergenerational transfers. For many countries, the implicit liability to finance public pensions is by far the most significant unrecognized liability in their public accounts.

The debate over public pensions was in the 1970s and 1980s predominantly about whether or not such schemes should be funded; by the 1990s it had shifted to how best to organize the funding. Given the adoption by many countries of a funding program, it is appropriate that the focus should now shift to how public pension funds should be managed. The debate at this point is largely about governance, broadly defined.

There is no single set of governance principles that can be applied universally, but there are many principles that have wide application. This paper outlines a framework for considering these principles and their place in public pension fund management. In some cases we have based our assessments on actual examples. In other cases, where we could find no adequate

1

precedents, we have identified what we regard as the appropriate outcome based on criteria of equity and economic efficiency.

The first section provides an overview of the growth of public sector pension funds throughout the world and the extent of funding. The following section summarizes the general principles of public sector governance and their application to public pension funds. The section after that focuses on accountability issues. The fourth section discusses investment policies and the final section provides a brief concluding statement.

The Growth of Public Sector Pension Funds

Pension provision in most countries is a combination of public (unfunded) schemes, publicly mandated contributory schemes, and voluntary private retirement savings. In some countries publicly mandated pension contributions are privately managed, but in others the government retains management of these funds either directly or through a specially created management agency. For the purposes of this paper we will treat both public unfunded schemes and publicly managed mandatory schemes as equivalent: in both cases the government is responsible for the provision of retirement incomes from the scheme.[1] The lines of distinction between the different schemes generally can be unclear: even some privately managed mandatory schemes carry explicit or implicit government guarantees and/or operate under government rules that are, in practical terms, tantamount to government management.

Given the widely held belief that providing for the retired generation is, at least in part, a responsibility of government, it is not surprising that of the different models of mandated retirement income provision public pension schemes have by far the longest history. Initially, many of these schemes intended substantial prefunding of their obligations. In the post-Second World War period, however, there was increased acceptance of pay-as-you-go financing, with little concern expressed over poor rates of return on pension fund investments. It has only been in recent decades, as populations have aged and the liabilities of public pension schemes have exploded, that many governments have shifted the focus of their attention to private pensions, both voluntary and publicly mandated, as a means of reducing their future liabilities and mitigating increasingly obvious intergenerational transfers.

1

There is no international standard for reporting this liability (sometimes referred to as the implicit pension debt). This is an important point, since stating the extent to which accumulated reserves should cover the liability is one way of introducing discipline to the process. Despite the lack of consistent reporting, there have been several attempts to provide preliminary estimates across a range of countries.

Figure 1.1 shows the unfunded liabilities of public schemes, as at 1994, as a percentage of GDP for selected Organisation for Economic Co-operation and Development (OECD) countries. The estimates are calculated by taking the net present value of expenditures between 1994 and 2070, using a 5 percent discount rate. Even in countries such as the United States that have well-developed and actively encouraged private sector pension schemes,

Figure 1.1: Implicit Public Pension Debt in Selected OECD Countries, 1994

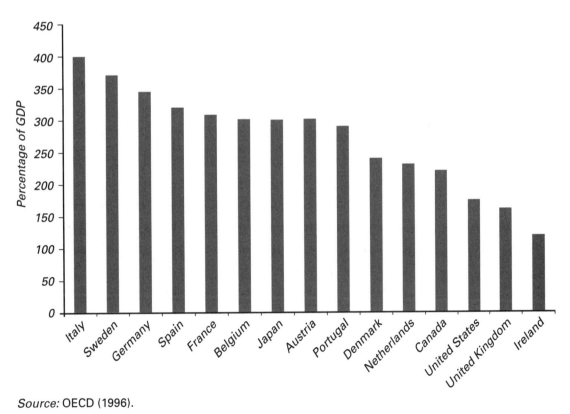

Source: OECD (1996).

Table 1.1: Implicit Public Pension Debt of Low- and Middle-Income Countries

Country	Public debt 1999–2000	Pension spending as share of GDP	IPD by discount rate		
			2%	4%	5%
Brazil	33	9	500	330	275
Macedonia, FYR	41	9	441	291	244
Slovenia	25	11	429	298	255
Romania	18	6	386	256	214
Poland	43	12	379	261	220
Ukraine	59	9	365	257	220
Portugal	55	5	358	233	193
Malta	56	5	356	234	194
Slovak Republic	31	8	304	210	179
Hungary	59	9	300	203	171
Uruguay	45	14	295	214	187
Kyrgyz Republic	135	7	282	185	154
Croatia	33	11	274	201	175
Estonia	7	9	268	189	163
Moldova	78	8	229	159	136
Lithuania	28	7	221	155	134
Nicaragua	109	2	220	131	104
Turkey	65	5	217	146	123
Costa Rica	34	2	203	121	97
Philippines	71	1	185	107	81
Iran, Islamic Rep. of	10	2	146	89	72
Bolivia	56	4	111	73	62
Argentina	53	5	106	85	78
Ecuador	209	1	103	63	51
Mexico	19	1	101	65	54
Colombia	24	2	88	56	46
Dominican Republic	23	1	80	49	40
Cape Verde	52	1	78	47	38
Chile	9	7	77	60	53
Senegal	78	2	73	51	44
Mauritius	35	3	63	47	42
El Salvador	22	2	60	43	37
Peru	43	2	57	40	34
Korea, Republic of	33	1	57	33	26
Morocco	79	1	50	32	26

Sources: Authors' calculations and public debt data based on SAVEM tables (World Bank), At-a-Glance tables prepared for the Annual Meetings (World Bank), and various IMF statistics on Article IV consultations.

implicit pension debt is shown to be much larger than the level of outstanding government debt and larger than private pension assets.

A cross-country study by Holzmann, Palacios, and Zviniene (2003) reports the implicit pension debt for low- and middle-income countries. A concept similar to a projected benefit obligation is applied (see Table 1.1). Their findings show a huge range of magnitude of implicit pension debt (IPD). The former Soviet republics and Eastern European countries have IPDs in excess of 150 percent of GDP, while demographically younger countries with low coverage, such as El Salvador and Senegal, and countries with relatively immature schemes, such as the Republic of Korea, have IPDs of less than 50 percent of GDP.[2] It should be noted that even the lowest of these are still very high, especially when compared with the tax base that will have to finance the liabilities. Many of these countries have engaged in an explicit policy of accumulating reserves to offset part of these liabilities. In many cases, a scaled premium approach has been used to smooth contribution rates over time and mitigate intergenerational transfers. In other cases the reserves serve only as a buffer fund, aimed at avoiding short-term liquidity problems.

Palacios (2002) estimates that at least 65 countries worldwide have significant reserves in their publicly managed pension schemes. Table 1.2 shows the regional distribution of these funds. Together, these assets represent approximately one-quarter of global GDP.[3] They are often the single largest institutional investor in the country.

Despite their size, public pension reserves, both individually and in the aggregate, represent only a fraction of liabilities. Changing this key ratio

Table 1.2: Regional Distribution of Public Pension Funds

Region	Number of public funds	Percentage of countries in region	Average share of GDP (%)
High-income OECD	10	45	10.8
Latin America and Caribbean	11	44	8.4
Sub-Saharan Africa	22	47	8.7
East Asia	5	56	7.0
South Asia	9	90	16.6
Middle East and North Africa	7	33	12.3

of reserves to liabilities is the goal of pension reforms that are now being implemented around the world. After a long period of expansion, many countries are cutting benefit promises by a series of parametric reforms that are redefining the defined benefit promise and in consequence reducing the IPD. After decades of poor performance and a perception that pension reserves may have led to increased government consumption rather than increased public savings, a handful of countries are attempting to increase investment returns and ensure that real savings are being generated. Finally, a few countries, such as China, are beginning to build up significant public pension reserves in anticipation of the rapid ageing of the population.

The desire to increase the ratio of assets to liabilities in public pension funds has a parallel in the emergence of mandatory fully funded plans in some countries. Whether or not it is feasible to achieve a certain funding ratio through the accumulation of reserves in a public or quasi-public scheme depends on the interlinked matters of governance, investment policy, and accountability. Strict actuarial rules and regulations often cover the funding arrangements and management of private sector defined benefit pension schemes, but typically no such rules apply to governments. In most countries the accountability of private sector plans is exerted through competition under the rules applied by a supervisory agency, but in the public monopoly context the same effect is difficult to achieve. And when a large pool of public pension fund assets are involved it can be difficult to separate the investment policy of the public pension fund from other government objectives. This paper is an attempt to frame an approach to these dilemmas.

Governance of Public Pension Schemes

Governance of public pension schemes is a specific application of the more general subject of public sector governance.

The literature on public sector governance is relatively new. That corporate governance has been a major focus of attention in recent years is hardly surprising in view of the spectacular corporate collapses of companies the size of Enron and WorldCom. The lower profile of public sector governance arises from the fact that poor governance in the public sector is more likely to lead to slower growth, economic inefficiency, and corruption than to spectacular collapses. The costs of poor public sector governance, however, are at least as great as those of poor corporate governance, and arguably are even greater.

This section looks first at the general issues of public sector governance, then applies the relevant principles to public pension management.

Public Sector Governance: General Issues

There is no universally agreed definition of public sector governance, nor is there a straightforward translation of the accepted definitions of corporate governance to the public sector.[4] Most of the definitions of corporate governance are oriented toward shareholders and are therefore not strictly appropriate in the public sector context. For that reason we suggest the following working definition for the purposes of this paper—one that is flexible enough to cover both public and private sector governance:

Governance refers to the systems and processes by which a company or government manages its affairs with the objective of maximizing the welfare of and resolving the conflicts of interest among its stakeholders.

Defined in this way, governance can be seen to include issues such as transparency, resolution of conflicts, and the overall way in which the business in question is run.

As noted by Carmichael (2002), the need for high standards of public sector governance arises from the same types of issues that give rise to the need for strong corporate governance. Namely, in acting on behalf of its citizens the government creates a principal/agent problem for its citizens. The difficulty in resolving the public sector principal/agent problem is that, in most instances, there is no ready metric by which the agents can measure the performance of the principals. However, provided there is adequate transparency for the scheme, this should be much less of a problem in the case of public pension schemes than it is in areas such as regulation, public policy, or law enforcement.

A second difficulty in resolving the principal/agent problem is the hiatus between elections. Unlike corporate shareholders, citizens are between elections effectively disenfranchised of their political vote. Again, this should be less important in the case of public pension schemes than in other areas of public policy and management, provided there is adequate transparency and accountability.

Carmichael suggests that government involvement in the financial sector is particularly prone to conflicts of interest and therefore, from a governance perspective, in need of special attention. These conflicts arise from the extensive participation of some governments in their financial systems:

- as the regulator of financial institutions;
- as an owner of financial institutions;
- as a market participant;
- as a fiduciary agent; and
- through direct intervention in the operations of the market.

To address these conflicts, Carmichael suggests a set of principles for public sector governance. These principles, which draw on and expand the International Monetary Fund (IMF) Code of Good Practices on Fiscal Transparency and the Code of Good Practices on Transparency in Monetary and Financial Policies, cover the following four main areas:[5]

- transparency and accountability;
- the independence and accountability of financial regulatory agencies;
- the effectiveness of financial regulatory agencies; and
- anticorruption measures.

Of these four areas, the first and the fourth are particularly relevant in the case of public pension schemes. Anticorruption and good management issues are discussed in the following subsection, and accountability and transparency issues in Section 4.

Laying a Foundation for Public Pension Scheme Governance

Before examining the governance measures that may be appropriate for different public pension schemes it is necessary to identify the risks to stakeholders from public involvement.

Stakeholder risks fall into four main categories:

- failure of the government to meet its retirement income promises;
- use (or misuse) of contributors' funds by the government to meet social policy objectives other than retirement income objectives;
- underperformance of the fund due to the use of contributors' funds for directed lending or as a captive source of finance for the government; and

- loss of funds due to corruption or mismanagement.

Not all of these risks apply equally to every form of public pension scheme. For example, the major risk in an unfunded public pension scheme is that the government's retirement income promises may grow beyond the budget's capacity to fund them, usually as a result of demographic changes such as an increase in longevity, a reduction in fertility, or a reduction in the tax base.

The ease with which a government can change the terms of a scheme is partly a function of the precision of the promises made by the scheme and partly a function of the legal tradition involved. Where the pension scheme is unlinked to earnings during employment, governments have mostly found it easy (legally, if not always politically) to reduce the scheme's liabilities by cutting benefits or tightening eligibility requirements. Where the promise is more explicit, adjusting the scheme has been less straightforward. In the United States, for example, the courts have ruled that the terms of the scheme can be changed by the government at its discretion. In several European countries, in contrast, the courts have ruled against certain changes.[6]

The risk that a government will fail to deliver on its promises is more explicit in government-managed mandatory contribution schemes. While funded public defined benefit schemes usually are guaranteed by the government against underperformance due to the theft or misuse of contributors' funds, the guarantors ultimately are the taxpayers themselves.[7] With taxpayers as the ultimate guarantors, there is thus a distinct temptation for some governments to use those funds for political and even personal purposes. The temptation is increased by the fact that the payoff to members of the funds is usually far in the future (and the unpalatable increase in tax rates therefore the responsibility of a future government), whereas the benefits from exploiting the available resources usually are immediate.

The existence of contributors' funds also introduces the risk of misuse of funds, underperformance due to directed lending, and mismanagement. The existence of a government guarantee does not entirely remove the risk of promissory failure. Indonesia is a good example of the risks involved. The Indonesian government mandates that Indonesian workers contribute to the publicly managed fund JAMSOSTEK. Following a period in which previous governments often directed contributed funds to

1

favored projects and uses, there are serious concerns about the adequacy of the fund to meet its promises. While the full extent of the funding gap is unclear, there is a widespread perception among Indonesians that they are at risk given the severe budgetary constraints under which the Indonesian government is operating.

The primary defenses against each of these risks are good governance structures and transparency. The governance provisions of public pension schemes should be aimed at establishing good business practices, avoiding corruption, avoiding mismanagement, and avoiding abuses by the government itself.

Drawing partly on the IMF Code of Good Practices on Fiscal Transparency and Code of Good Practices on Transparency in Monetary and Financial Policies, we suggest the following as a starting point or foundation set of best practice principles for the governance of publicly managed pension schemes.

There should be clarity of roles and responsibilities within the pension fund.

Clarity of roles, objectives, and responsibilities is fundamental to transparency and accountability.

The objectives should be set down by government, preferably in law, along with an explicit statement about the promises being made and any government guarantees involved.

The objectives and responsibilities of the agency established to manage the scheme should also be clearly stated—again, preferably in law—and made available to the public.

An example can be found in the Canadian pension reforms carried out between 1995 and 1998.[8] Under the Canadian Pension Plan (CPP) Investment Board Act of 1998, the board has a clear fiduciary duty (a) to manage CPP funds in the best interests of contributors and beneficiaries, and (b) to invest its assets with a view to achieving a maximum rate of return, without undue risk of loss, having regard to the factors that may affect the funding of the CPP and the ability of the CPP to meet its financial obligations.

The act goes on to spell out the roles and responsibilities of government and the investment board.

Canada is by no means unique: there are any number of countries in which roles and responsibilities are clearly established.

The law establishing the management agency should provide unambiguous conditions under which members of the governing body of the agency can be appointed and removed.

1

Some public pension schemes are managed within the government, effectively as departments, while others are managed by specially established agencies. In some countries these agencies operate as statutory authorities, while in others they operate as trusts. In general, we regard the departmental model as too open to abuse and therefore not best practice. Whatever the precise legal form, the members of the governing body of the management agencies operate with a fiduciary responsibility to the members of the scheme, and that single consideration should dictate the terms according to which appointments and dismissals can be made.

While the independence from government of directors and trustees is important in some respects, it is less critical than in the case of a regulatory agency. The more critical requirement is that directors and trustees act honestly, diligently, and effectively in the interests of members. A fit-and-proper test for staff appointments thus is likely to form the centerpiece of appointment conditions. The test should include explicit prohibitions, such as of persons with a criminal record, as well as general skill requirements. Directors and trustees should operate under strict rules to minimize conflicts of interest, and penalties for the abuse of their position should be harsh.

The practice in some countries of appointing representative boards rather than professional boards, while admirable in intent, is unlikely to provide the level of expertise and commitment needed for good governance.[9] Nevertheless, where this tradition is strong there may be ways of mitigating the problems associated with this practice, for example through the training of trustees or the creation of independent advisory committees made up of professionals.

Dismissal provisions should strike a balance between the need to remove a director or trustee quickly in the event of a breach of fiduciary responsibility and the need to prevent arbitrary dismissal, for example, should a trustee resist improper attempts by the government to use the fund in ways that are explicitly prohibited by the terms of the scheme. Natural justice considerations suggest that where a director or trustee has been accused of impropriety he or she should stand aside from the management agency while the matter is dealt with.

Unlike those public sector agencies in which the need to preserve the independence of the agency requires a higher level of protection against dismissal, the directors and trustees of a public pension scheme should be subject to dismissal if their performance is not up to the standard required by the fund's objectives (provided the assessment of performance is not arbitrary). For example, poor strategic decisions that result in consistent underperformance of benchmarks over a period of years should be adequate grounds for replacing a director or trustee. Of course, dismissal on such grounds can only happen if information on performance is reliable and available in a timely fashion.

Again, Canadian law provides a good example of some of these issues. In Canada, the Finance Minister, in consultation with provincial governments, appoints the 12 members of the CPP board. The appointment process involves a nominating committee that recommends qualified board candidates to the federal and provincial governments. The board and the appointment process are subjected to close public scrutiny and candidates for the board, in addition to having suitable qualifications, are required to meet demanding skill and character requirements.[10]

Similar types of provisions can be found in the public pension schemes of a number of other countries, including Ireland and New Zealand. Reflecting the greater attention given in recent years to matters of governance, these considerations are much more likely to be found in schemes that have been reformed in the past five or so years than they are in older schemes.

The managing agency should be free from inappropriate interference from the government in pursuing its objectives and meeting its responsibilities.

Ideally, the government should remain at arm's length from the investment decisions of the fund manager. In the event that government wishes to retain the right to direct lending to particular sectors or activities, including financing its own budget deficits, it should do so openly and transparently. Best practice suggests that the law establishing the scheme should identify what is "inappropriate interference" and the director and trustees should be protected from dismissal for resisting such interference. This naturally is a difficult area: few governments like the idea of having their hands tied or of otherwise being forced to publicly disclose when they choose to use their hand.

New Zealand has chosen the disclosure route. Under New Zealand law, the minister has explicit power to give directions to the governing board of the public pension fund. However, these must be in writing, must be presented to the Parliament, and must be published in the official gazette[11].

Ireland takes a slightly different approach, instead directly restricting one possible avenue towards misuse of the public pension fund for the Government's its own purposes. This is achieved via an explicit prohibition on investment by the fund in Irish Government securities.

The Canadians considered addressing the potential for directed lending by limiting the fund's equity investments to the market index, on the grounds that removing the scope for the management agency to pick individual stocks would also remove the government's ability to interfere with investment policy. Ultimately, however, they decided that this would be unnecessarily restrictive from an investment management perspective. The clear direction in law to invest in the members' interests was considered to be sufficient protection from government interference. (In other countries this may not be sufficient, and more explicit protections may need to be considered.)

The Netherlands is explicit in its investment policy for its public employees' pension scheme (see Annex 1.A). They state that:

> "The fund's board is to resist all investment compulsion and investment restrictions that have a negative effect on an optimal investment return. There is no room for socially initiated investments, or for economically targeted investments, if such investments do not meet the return requirements formulated by the board."

The processes for formulating and executing scheme policies should be open and transparent.

The policy framework and its process of implementation should be disclosed and adequately explained. The different roles of the government and the managing agency in establishing and executing policy should be clearly distinguished.

In cases where a fund is managed by a complex combination of committees it may be difficult to achieve the desired level of transparency. For example, under the pension reforms carried out in Japan in 2001, responsibility for managing the public pension fund reserves shifted from the Ministry of Finance to the Ministry of Health, Labor, and Welfare. Under the new arrangements the minister sets the overall asset allocation, subject to a series of restrictions imposed by law. The allocation is subject to consultation with a group of experts from a subcommittee for funds management, appointed by the minister. The management of the fund is then delegated to a three-person board (appointed by the minister) and advised by an expert committee. Under a complex committee structure such as this it is often difficult to identify where ultimate responsibility for scheme policy lies.

The structure of delegations permitted within the scheme should be clearly defined.

If the manager of the scheme is established as a statutory agency, for example, the law establishing the agency should spell out the powers of the governing board of the agency as well as the powers of delegation within the agency. Where delegation to external operators is contemplated, this should be explicitly permitted by law and, where appropriate, circumscribed. For example, the law may permit the outsourcing of information technology (IT) and back office functions, but not of investment decisions; it may permit internal delegation of operational decisions but not of strategic decisions; and so on. The essential point is that the structure of delegation should be well thought out and transparent to stakeholders; it also should state clearly where responsibility lies in the event of delegation. Responsibility should include the explicit requirement for the governing body of the management agency to monitor and review delegated powers.

The management agency should be required by law to establish internal governance structures and processes to minimize corruption, mismanagement, and fraud.

Governance procedures should include (a) the mandatory establishment of a risk management and audit committee with appropriate reporting lines; (b) a code of conduct for staff and senior executives, detailing how to deal with conflicts of interest and establishing minimum standards of ethical behavior (including protection for whistleblowers); (c) detailed description of the roles and responsibilities of the different groups within the agency, such as the board, senior management, and audit committee, and how they are to account for their actions; and (d) a quality control process and rigorous documentation, review, and audit requirements on investment decisions and IT support systems. Many of the best practice governance requirements that have been developed for investment companies, including the requirement to establish a compliance committee, are applicable to public pension fund management agencies.

The government should require that the management agency be regulated and supervised by the same agency that is responsible for regulating private pension providers and, where feasible, that it should meet the same standards imposed on private providers.

This requirement is not only a matter of good governance but is also compatible with the objective of establishing competitive neutrality throughout the financial system. There may nevertheless be limited divergences in prudential standards. The most obvious of these is the minimum funding regulations typically imposed on the private sector. Given the role of the government as the implicit guarantor of the public scheme, and given the explicit partial funding nature of many public schemes, requiring the public scheme to meet the same minimum funding requirements as private pension schemes is somewhat redundant.[12] The same principle applies to the minimum capital requirements often imposed on private sector managers. Public pension schemes should, however, generally be expected to comply with the same governance, accountability, and investment rules as their private sector counterparts.

Canada has not placed its public fund under the jurisdiction of any of its private sector financial regulators, but it has imposed a similar set of standards, in terms of governance and investments, as those required of the private sector. In contrast, regulatory reforms proposed in Indonesia would see the Indonesian public pension fund come under the same regulator as private pension funds. This is already the case in Kenya, Morocco, and Costa Rica.

These governance requirements are onerous in no sense other than that they restrict the scope for government and scheme managers to use the funds to their own advantage. In 2000, many of these requirements were enshrined into legislation in Ireland with the passage of the National Pensions Reserve Fund Act.[13] The act provides for:

1

- The statutory obligation that the Irish Government pay the equivalent of 1 per cent of GNP into the fund each year until at least 2055.
- The establishment of an independent commission, the National Pensions Reserve Fund Commission, to control and manage the fund, with discretionary authority to determine and implement an investment strategy for the fund, based on commercial principles.
- The appointment of seven Commissioners by the Minister of Finance, subject to a statutory requirement for substantive expertise at a senior level in specified areas.
- The appointment of the National Treasury Management Agency as manager of the fund, to carry out such functions as are delegated to it for this purpose by the commission. The appointment of the agency is for a period of 10 years, with five-yearly options to extend or to appoint an alternative manager.
- A strictly commercial investment mandate for the fund, with the objective of securing the optimal return over the long term subject to prudent risk management. (The fund is explicitly prohibited from investing in Irish Government securities, to ensure that it is not used artificially to support government borrowing.)
- The appointment by the commission of investment managers to invest and manage portions of the fund, and of custodians to ensure the safekeeping and security of the assets of the fund.

A Governance Checklist

The following is a set of questions designed to help countries assess the extent to which their public pension schemes meet the intent of the best practice governance guidelines proposed above[14]:

- Are the roles of the respective parties in the public pension scheme clear? For example, is the government's promise clear, are the objectives of the managing agency clearly and publicly enunciated, and so on?
- Are the terms well understood under which the managing agency and its governing members are appointed and terminated?

- Are there adequate fit-and-proper-person protections to prevent the agency from being deliberately manipulated by the government or the board of the agency?
- Is the management agency open and transparent about its governance structures?
- Is the scheme open to periodic review? Do the government and/or the managing agency welcome constructive criticism?
- How well do the agency's internal and/or external governance systems compare with those imposed by the regulator of private pensions?

Accountability of Public Sector Pension Schemes

Central to the achievement of good governance is the establishment of structures to ensure that a business is well run. Central to the achievement of accountability is ensuring, by creating compatible incentives, that those governance structures are effective. There are many issues that exist in the gray area between governance and accountability. The preceding sections of this paper identify the structures that, according to best practice, should be in place for good governance. This section focuses on the disclosures and incentives that should be associated with the implementation of those structures for the achievement of full accountability.

The creation of compatible incentives requires that those who make decisions and business judgments be held responsible for those decisions. Not only should poor judgment be penalized, however; full accountability implies also that good judgment be rewarded.

Since (most) governments are ultimately accountable through the electoral system, the focus of this section is on the accountability to scheme members of the management agency.

Laying a Foundation for Public Pension Scheme Accountability

The central considerations for a best practice accountability framework are transparency and reward structures.

The main role of transparency in the case of unfunded schemes is to reveal to taxpayers the likelihood of their retirement being funded at a suitable level from the government's budget. This requires either explicit recognition of the pension liability in the government's accounts or periodic

1

disclosure by the government of trends in longevity and retirement incomes and their implications for future budgets. An example of such a disclosure is the analysis published by the Australian government in its 2003 budget papers projecting the impact of trends in longevity and fertility on public pensions and consequently on forward budgets.[15]

In the case of contributory schemes, transparency requirements should go well beyond budgetary projections, which provide information about the financial strength of the guarantor but not about the financial strength of the fund. The ultimate safeguard for pension investors in these cases is full disclosure of portfolio composition, investment decisions, and performance. Many funds are reluctant to disclose such information on the grounds of competitive disadvantage. While this reluctance is understandable, the risk to both the investors and the guarantor are such that the need for disclosure should dominate market sensitivities. Releasing detailed portfolio statistics with an appropriate time lag can reduce the competitive disadvantage incurred.

With these considerations in mind we suggest the following as a starting point for an accountability framework for public pension schemes.

There should be full and open disclosure about the governance structure of the scheme and the managing agency.

Some elements of the governance structure are likely to be disclosed as a matter of course in the law establishing the agency. Other governance features are more likely to be implemented as a result of the governance requirements imposed on the agency by the law (for example, the requirement to establish an explicit structure of delegations). Accountability requires that details about the governance structure are made public. In particular, there should be adequate disclosure of the arrangements put in place to detect and prevent fraud.

An example of the issues that might be covered in such a public governance document is included in Annex 1.B. This annex outlines the index of the governance document put together by the board of the Australian Prudential Regulation Authority (APRA). APRA is a regulatory agency rather than a pension management agency, but the governance issues are similar.

As part of its disclosure of governance arrangements the managing agency should be required to publish its formal delegations of powers and responsibilities.

Delegations are central to accountability. In the case of funded public pension schemes, the contributors to the scheme (the principals) delegate the management and safety of their investments to the government-appointed scheme managers (the agents). The managers in turn delegate certain decisions to various individuals within the agency. For example, the managers may employ specialist fund managers, back office processors, account managers, and so on. Some of these functions may be outsourced to private firms. Any such delegations should be made public and should be reviewed regularly.

Once the agency has formalized its structure of delegations it should make these available to all stakeholders (for example, through its website).

Funding shortfalls should be identified and disclosed, along with the government's proposed remedial actions.

The process for assessing and dealing with a funding shortfall should be transparent and preferably contained in law. The fund should be subject to periodic actuarial review and, unless the government has an explicit policy of partial funding, the government should be required to fund any actuarial shortfall that it has guaranteed. This is the practice in many countries with private sector defined benefit schemes. Where the government has an explicit policy of partial funding, the extent of the underfunding should be assessed and reported in the government's accounts.

Where the scheme is unfunded, there should be periodic actuarial assessment of pension liabilities under a range of scenarios for longevity and fertility. Should this assessment indicate a future problem, the government should identify a strategy to deal with it.

The management agency should be subject to regular governance and performance audit.

The agency should be subject to regular audit for performance by an independent and credible external auditor. In addition, there should be a periodic review of the governance procedures and their effectiveness within the agency. The findings of these audits should be laid open to public scrutiny, at least in summary form.

This practice is common in many countries. In Canada, in addition to the annual financial audit the minister is required to at least once every six years initiate a special examination of management practices.

The management agency should be required to report comprehensively on its decisions and performance.

This is arguably the key accountability issue. Full disclosure of performance in both absolute and relative terms is fundamental to protecting the interests of contributors.

To avoid causing undue market disadvantage, detailed reporting could be done annually and published with an acceptable time lag. The reporting should provide sufficient information to enable accurate scrutiny of the agency's performance, and on at least a quarterly basis should include a detailed breakdown of asset composition by investment type and sector. It should provide a full disclosure of fees paid and earned, full details of the cost of operations, including comparisons with industry benchmarks, and a breakdown of performance against a predetermined and public set of benchmarks. Quarterly summary reports should be made on overall performance, with an attribution analysis. If these reports are to be useful, best practice international accounting standards must be adopted for the valuation of assets and the calculation of returns and other figures. At a minimum, the accounting standards for the public pension fund should not be less rigorous than those applied to private pensions in the same country.

Both Canada and Ireland use publicly disclosed benchmarks for performance comparison. In the Canadian case the benchmark is private sector fund performance, while Ireland uses a predetermined set of benchmark indices. The Canadian fund managers additionally are required to hold public meetings at least every two years in each province to discuss performance. It is worth noting that since instituting public reporting of this type the Canadian administrative costs have fallen by more than 60 percent.

Where governments explicitly direct investments for social purposes (this is not our preferred model, but is one that for obvious political reasons must be considered) the impact of these decisions should be calculated separately and disclosed to members.

To the greatest extent possible, rewards for performance should be linked to delegated responsibilities and should be risk-based.

Those who make delegated decisions should be rewarded or sanctioned according to the way in which they exercise their delegations. The manager of the scheme should not enter into contracts that create the potential for expensive exits of staff or service providers who have failed to meet the expectations of their positions or contracts.

Since the primary purpose of a pension fund is to provide income replacement in retirement, the performance of the fund is central to meeting this objective. As discussed in the next section, achieving optimum performance involves a balancing of risk and return. A feature of best practice financial incentive structures is that they offer performance rewards for returns adjusted for risk. Put simply, a 10 percent return earned from lending to governments is not the same as a 10 percent return earned in trading derivative products. The financial markets convention in calculating performance is to measure either risk-adjusted return per dollar of capital or assets committed, or unadjusted returns per dollar of risk-adjusted capital or assets committed. Either is acceptable as a basis for calculating rewards.

Managers should be required to review periodically the exercise of delegations they have made.

When making delegations, managers should provide guidance as to how the delegated powers are to be exercised. For example, the delegation of investment authority in certain securities may be accompanied by explicit restrictions on the types of securities in which the funds may be invested, as well as a risk limit (such as an overall value-at-risk limit). Accountability reports should record the actual investment decisions made, the consequences of those decisions, and any breaches of the guidelines.

Efforts should be made to encourage the development of a compliance culture within the agency. Compliance should be rewarded and breaches of guidelines, either governance or investment, penalized—even where the returns are higher than expected.

An Accountability Checklist

The following is a set of questions designed to assist countries to assess the extent to which their public pension schemes meet the intent of the best practice accountability guidelines proposed above. While some of the issues covered may be requirements of law, a well-governed agency should provide much of this information simply as a matter of good practice.

- Does the public have access to adequate information about the governance structures of the public pensions scheme and its managing agency, through explicit laws, annual reports, publications, and/or websites?
- Is disclosure of potential conflicts of interest of board members required and imposed?
- Is the scheme subject to regular independent audit for both governance and performance?
- Are the financial performance and financial state of the scheme revealed publicly on a regular basis, and are they based on sound accounting standards?
- Is the scheme's financial performance reported against established benchmarks?
- Is the government open about its liabilities under the scheme and subject to independent actuarial reviews?
- Are the incentive structures within the scheme transparent to the public, linked to delegated responsibilities, and risk-based?

Investment Policies

As funding of public pension schemes grows, governments increasingly are finding themselves in the role of fiduciary agent for their citizens. This role carries with it an implied responsibility for the public pension manager to select an investment strategy that balances risk and return appropriately for the citizens on whose behalf it is investing.

Investment policy comprises three main components: the setting of long-term performance targets; defining an acceptable risk tolerance; and setting parameters for short-term asset allocation. These should be set out clearly in an investment policy statement. [16] In addition, procedures to be followed with regard to the implementation of the investment policy must be clearly defined. Setting long-term targets and selecting a tolerance for risk involve strategic decisions that are fundamental to the viability of the scheme as a source of income replacement in retirement. The long-term strategy should identify whether the risk tolerance and performance targets are capable of producing outcomes that will meet the objectives of the scheme. This part of the investment policy should establish the broad shape of the portfolio and the risk parameters that will govern investment decisions. The strategic part of the policy also should establish the board's position on nonfinancial issues such as shareholder activism, socially responsible investment, and economically targeted investment.

The need for internal consistency between the strategic objectives of the scheme and its investment policy cannot be overstated. For example, the objectives of the Canadian fund included increasing funding from 8 percent to 20 percent by the year 2017. The target long-term real rate of return consistent with this objective was 4 percent. One consequence of this ambitious strategy was that the board recognized that, for consistency, it needed to invest heavily in equities. Bringing the scheme's objectives explicitly into the investment strategy in this way can help identify any inconsistencies in the parameters of the scheme—as well as help identify the consequences of unrealistically ambitious objectives.

The New Zealand scheme also provides an interesting example in this respect. The New Zealand objectives include a partial funding target set in law, along with a formula determining the government's contribution each year. The formula specifies the government's contribution as "the percentage of GDP that, if projected over the next 40 years, would be sufficient to enable the fund to meet retirement income entitlements." The government's contributions accordingly are based on annually revised estimates of the assets and liabilities of the scheme, and are designed to ensure that the scheme meets its legislated funding objectives over a long time horizon.

Apart from the need for long-term consistency, the central considerations for a best practice framework for investment policies are that they be transparent and clearly designed to operate in the best interests of fund members.

In the case of a private sector investment fund the primary focus of investment policy is the balancing of market risks and returns. These risks include the risk of loss due to counterparty default (such as the bankruptcy of an issuer of debt or equity), the risk of loss due to movements in market prices (such as falls in equity prices, property prices, interest rates, and/or exchange rates), and the risk of loss due to operational failure (such as a failure of IT systems, settlement procedures, or legal documentation). The case of a public pension fund is more complex. In addition to these private sector risks, public pension funds must also contend with the potential for them to dominate markets, and the temptation for governments to direct the investment of funds for their own purposes (including not only the temptation to use the fund to finance the government's own deficit, but also the temptation to provide credit directly to members).

In the private finance sector, the market risk dimension of investment strategies increasingly is expressed in terms of comprehensive measures of risk, such as value-at-risk, rather than in terms of prohibitions, sectoral limitations, or target ratios. While diversification often is an explicit consideration in public sector investment policies, the modern approach of using a comprehensive measure of risk automatically incorporates diversification. This approach has yet to reach far into the public sector, where investments are often handicapped by limited mandates and restrictions that militate against modern risk management practices.[17] These issues, as well as the specific public sector risk issues, need to be addressed as openly as possible.

Laying a Foundation for Public Pension Scheme Investment Policy and Processes

The central considerations for a best practice framework for investment policies are that they be transparent and clearly designed to operate in the best interests of fund members. With these in mind we suggest the following as a guide to best practice in the design and implementation of investment policies and processes for public pension funds.

The investment policy should state that the purpose of accumulating and investing pension reserves is solely for the benefit of members of the pension plan.

Few public funds state this explicitly in practice;[18] in fact, many include objectives such as economic development or advancing social welfare in their mission statements.[19] While these objectives are laudable, and while there may be positive indirect effects arising from the accumulation of long-term savings in the economy, giving them equivalent status with the interests of members inevitably leads to conflicting objectives.

The policy should make a clear statement about the investment of fund assets in government securities. While some funds expressly prohibit investment in government securities,[20] they may in many instances be viewed on both safety and liquidity grounds as an integral part of a balanced portfolio. An alternative to prohibition is to set limits on such investments to prevent their being improperly tapped, at the government's initiative, as a source of funding. Like all such limits these should not be regarded as immutable; however, they should be changed only by an explicit decision of the governing board of the fund and should be announced publicly, along with the reasons for making the change. Perversely, many countries take the approach of imposing minimum holding requirements for government securities, rather than maximum requirements. From the contributors' perspective, this is totally inappropriate.

Similar considerations apply to lending from the fund back to members. This practice raises difficult issues, the first of which involves risk diversification. If public pension funds are to provide income replacement in retirement they ideally should be exposed to a diversified set of risks that are as different as possible from those that members face during their working lives. For the same reasons that many countries prohibit private pension funds from lending back to sponsor firms, there is a case for prohibiting the investing of pension fund assets back with members. This issue is by no means unambiguous, since investment with members may enable those members to better survive and prosper to retirement. Following this line of argument, some countries have encouraged their public pension funds to lend to members for housing.[21]

A more difficult issue involves equity among members. If a fund has a policy of lending to members, it must establish unambiguous and nondiscriminatory rules defining which members may borrow from the fund (that is, qualifying criteria for access to the fund) and the terms under which such borrowing will take place. This type of lending increases the potential for corruption. A third issue that is more difficult yet involves how to handle defaults. If one member borrows from the fund and defaults, the burden of the default may result in a lower payout to other members or, if the government guarantees the benefits of the scheme, a greater burden on taxpayers to make up the shortfall. The alternative of assigning the loss from default against the benefits of the individual member involved would resolve the equity issue but would run contrary to the intent of the public pension scheme of providing a secure source of income in retirement.

Ultimately, lending to members by a public pension fund is little different from directed lending by government and if possible should be avoided. Where it is contemplated, the role of such lending should be clearly stated in the investment policy, as should the way that the lending fits the risk–return profile and objectives of the fund. The policy also should have transparent rules as to how applications for such lending will be evaluated and the terms on which it will be made available.[22]

A policy that is directed solely to the interests of fund members will be characterized by few, if any, prohibitions on investments. The interests of fund members will be enhanced by sound diversification of risks. Rules that limit or prohibit investments, including investments in foreign securities, reduce the capacity of the fund to diversify and serve the interests of fund members. The one area of exception to this general rule is that of lending to related parties, either to the government or to members, as noted above.

In practice, avoiding restrictions can be extremely difficult. For a whole range of social and political reasons most countries still impose some restrictions, especially with respect to foreign investments. Even some of the countries cited here for their general good practice are restricted in this area. One exception is New Zealand, which deliberately avoids any such restrictions in law, instead leaving all investment policy to the fund board. Interestingly, the only restriction placed on the New Zealand fund is an ethical constraint that the fund's investments must not "prejudice New Zealand's reputation as a responsible member of the world community."

This type of ethical constraint, also imposed in the Netherlands, is to be applauded, especially where it leaves to the fund's board the responsibility of judging how the constraint should be implemented.

The policy statement also should identify the potential for the fund to be or to become a dominant force in the domestic market, and should specify how the fund would resolve such a situation, should it come to pass. There are several ways of dealing with this problem, including:

- ensuring that the fund can invest in foreign securities (where no single fund is likely to be dominant);
- dividing the fund among a range of fund managers (provided the external managers are given clear guidelines as to the range of investments they may make and also of the risk–return profile they are to establish); and

- using index investments to avoid individual companies becoming dominant.

A final aspect of investment policy that should be addressed by the governing board is its attitude to exercising its voting rights as a shareholder. Since the fund could potentially be a major shareholder (especially in small markets), it has a responsibility to exercise its governance rights wisely. The exercise of voice is important, but to avoid a situation in which the government de facto directs private business it is usually better to delegate this power to the fund managers. One way of minimizing the conflicts of interest that may arise from such situations is for the fund to publish, with a time lag, a summary of the way in which it voted in its various shareholder capacities. Some countries, fearing that the potential for pressure on the public fund to influence corporate governance for purposes other than those in the interest of the fund itself, have imposed concentration limits or have delegated voting rights to fund managers; others, such as Sweden, have put a cap on the effective voting power of the fund. The significance of this problem and the potential remedies are directly related to the size of the public pension fund relative to the markets in which it invests. In all cases, however, a policy for shareholder voice should be explicit and documented. The policy of the Netherlands (see Annex 1.B) provides a good example of how this can be done.

The investment policy should be set by the board of directors or trustees, should be fully documented, and should be available in summary form to members of the scheme.[23]

For obvious competitive reasons the publicly disclosed elements of the investment policy should be restricted to the broad strategic direction of the fund, the attitude toward risk, and the board's position on the nonfinancial aspects of investment. It should not include details of strategies with respect to individual sectors or investments. The investment strategy should be clearly identified with the objectives of the scheme. It should be free from political direction.

A key objective is the target funding ratio during a given time period. Many public, partially funded defined benefit schemes set this target in terms of the ratio of reserves to annual spending. It is instead the ratio of funds accumulated to liabilities that should be the anchor for investment policy and the basis for setting a target long-term rate of return.[24]

The investment policy should identify all relevant risks and the board's approach to measuring, monitoring, and managing each of them.

While market risk is the predominant risk in any public pension portfolio, it is by no means the only source of risk. Like any investment fund, pension investments are subject to credit risk, liquidity risk, and operational risk. The investment policy should identify each of these, how each potentially affects the performance of the fund in meeting the objectives of the scheme, and how the board proposes managing them.

For example, every public pension fund is unavoidably exposed to credit risk through its investments in fixed-interest securities and through counterparty exposures. The board should ensure that the agency has a system for assessing credit risk and for managing such exposures. Market price risk—interest rate risk and currency risk in particular—falls into the same category of unavoidable risks. The investment policy should make a clear statement about the role of these risks and how they will be managed. Where relevant and appropriate, modern market practices should be adopted.

Liquidity risk also is a particular problem for pension funds. One source of liquidity risk arises through the need to meet the income entitlements of retirees. The board should ensure that the agency has a comprehensive system for measuring and monitoring the cash flows into and out of the fund, for projecting these forward, and for ensuring that the fund has access to assured sources of liquidity at lowest cost. In this respect public pension funds should meet the same liquidity standards as are applied to private pension funds.

Illiquidity also arises from investments in nonmarketable assets. Not only do these investments reduce the liquidity of the fund, they also create accountability difficulties associated with their acquisition, disposal and ongoing valuation. Purchases of sub-standard investments from related parties at above-market prices or, equivalently, sales of valuable assets at below-market prices have long been recognized and exploited by unscrupulous fund managers. Even without overtly corrupt practices, the difficulties faced in revaluing illiquid assets means that losses may accumulate undetected over long periods of time.

In general, the investment policy should seek to minimize investment in illiquid assets. We recognize, however, that in many countries this may not be practicable, especially where funds are prohibited from investing in foreign assets. In these cases we recommend that investment in illiquid assets be limited to a benchmark maximum percentage set by the board based on a realistic assessment of the spectrum of investments available. A conservative benchmark would set the maximum percentage below that generally available to the community. Where such investments are permitted the board should establish a well-articulated policy covering their purchase, disposition and valuation. This policy should state clearly that such investments are to be transparent and at arms length. The policy could include provision for an independent assessment of each purchase or sale of illiquid assets to be carried out, or at least overseen, by the audit committee of the board and carried out before the transaction occurs (subject to reasonable materiality conditions). This assessment should evaluate the price at which the transactions are to take place, the independence of the parties involved, and the appropriateness of the transaction for the fund. To further reduce scope for corrupt practices, the prices and details of all transactions in illiquid assets should also be disclosed to the members and the public.

In terms of addressing the potential for the disposition of illiquid assets to generate significant, unanticipated losses, at a minimum, public pension funds should require annual valuations from independent valuers of all their nonmarketable investments. Ideally, a conservative adjustment factor should then be applied to reflect the difficulty and timeframe that may be involved in realizing such a position. The collateral "haircuts" recommended by the draft Basel II framework for bank regulation provide a useful starting point for such an approach. The details of the valuation process and its results should be disclosed publicly.

Illiquidity can arise in another form where the fund holds an excessively large position in an otherwise marketable instrument. In the same way that market and default risks are diversified for a single investor by spreading investment across a diverse portfolio of investments, so too for a single company, liquidity risk is diversified by spreading the holding of the company across a diverse portfolio of investors. Even where a fund is not a dominant force in the domestic market as a whole it may hold an excessive position in a single company, such that there is insufficient free trading stock to establish a proper market. This risk should be addressed explicitly by the board in its investment policy, possibly by setting exposure limits on company positions. The parallel market and default risks should also be addressed in the investment policy, either by setting an overall diversification requirement or by exposure limits to sectors as well as to individual issuers and groups of related issuers.

The investment policy should clearly delineate the role of managers and, where relevant, the criteria for selection and retention of external parties. These criteria should be based on objective benchmarks that are provided regularly to the board in a form that can be understood.

As discussed in the paper by John Ilkiw (2003) for this conference, objective criteria are necessary if conflicts over the retention of managers are to be avoided—especially when board members do not have adequate financial expertise to assess performance.

The Canadian, Irish, New Zealand, and Swedish schemes cited in this paper address all of these issues.

An Investment Policy Checklist

The following is a set of questions designed to help countries assess the extent to which their public pension schemes meet the intent of the best practice investment policy guidelines proposed above.

- Is the investment policy fully documented and publicly available?
- Is the stated purpose of the scheme to benefit the members of the scheme? If not, are there potential conflicts between stated objectives?
- Does the policy permit lending to government and/or members? If so, are there transparent guidelines identifying the issues involved and governing how such investments will take place?
- Is the target rate of return based on a long-term funding ratio objective, and is it consistent with this objective?
- Does the investment policy identify how it will deal with actual or potential market dominance?
- Have all major risks been identified and taken into consideration in forming the investment policy? Has the tolerable level of risk been defined by the board?

- Are the processes involved in delegating the implementation of the investment policy to managers clearly defined? Are benchmark criteria for hiring and firing managers clear, and is the information available that is needed by the board to act on them?
- Are the investment parameters defined in terms of restrictions and prohibitions or in terms of modern portfolio concepts?

Conclusion

This paper has attempted to draw together a set of principles that collectively define what we regard as best practice for establishing and operating a public pension scheme. The driving principles behind this framework are that the scheme should have clear objectives, that it should be free from conflicts of interest, that it should be operated in as transparent a manner as possible, and that the operators of the scheme should be accountable to its members for their decisions and for the extent to which they have met or failed to meet the objectives of the scheme. In short, public pension schemes should be operated in the best interests of those who bear the burden of their financial failings.

In defining these principles as best practice we are fully aware that the pension schemes in many countries do not satisfy the principles we have outlined. In many cases, the deviations from best practice are deliberate and are designed to meet other objectives of government. While we recognize the difficulty of affecting change in these situations, it is only through open discussion and public recognition of the issues involved that the members of public pension schemes can bring pressure on governments to change these schemes to better reflect their interests. Public debate in the 1980s and 1990s about the extent of the underfunding crisis in public pension schemes encouraged many countries to begin or increase funding. Hopefully, public debate now about the way in which this funding is managed will help prevent, in the coming decades, a different type of crisis in public pension funding.

References

Anusic, Z., P. Okeefe, and S. Madzarevic-Sujster (2003). "Pension Reform in Croatia", World Bank Pension Reform Primer Working Paper series

1

#0304. Washington, D.C.: World Bank. Available online at: www.world bank.org/pensions.

Australian Commonwealth Government. 2003. *Budget Paper No. 5: The Intergenerational Report.* Commonwealth of Australia.

Carmichael, J. 2002. "Public Sector Governance and the Financial Sector." In R. Litan, M. Pomerleano, and V. Sunderajan (eds.), *Financial Sector Governance: The Roles of the Public and Private Sectors.* Washington, D.C.: Brookings Institution Press.

Hess, D., and G. Impavido. 2003. "Lessons from Corporate Governance and International Evidence." Paper presented at the Second World Bank Conference on Managing Public Pension Reserves, May 5–7, 2003, Washington, D.C. Published in this volume.

Holzmann, R., R. Palacios, and A. Zviniene. 2003. "Implicit Pension Debt: Issues, Management, and Scope in International Perspective." World Bank Pension Reform Primer Working Paper series, forthcoming. Washington, D.C.: World Bank.

Iglesias, A., and R. Palacios. 2000. "Managing Public Pension Reserves: A Review of the International Experience." World Bank Pension Reform Primer Working Paper series. Washington, D.C.: World Bank. Available online at: www.worldbank.org/pensions.

Ilkiw, J. 2003. "Investment Policies, Processes, and Problems in U.S. Public Sector Pension Plans: Some Observations and Solutions from a Practitioner." Paper presented at the Second World Bank Conference on Managing Public Pension Reserves, May 5–7, 2003, Washington, D.C. Published in this volume.

Maher, A. 2003. "Public Pension Funds Accountability: The Case of Ireland." Paper presented to Second World Bank Conference on Managing Public Pension Reserves, May 5–7, 2003, Washington, D.C. Published in this volume.

McCulloch, B., and J. Frances. 2003. "Public Pension Fund Governance: The New Zealand Superannuation Fund." Paper presented at the Second World Bank Conference on Managing Public Pension Reserves, May 5–7, 2003, Washington, D.C. Published in this volume.

OECD (Organisation for Economic Co-operation and Development). 1996. *Ageing in OECD Countries: A Critical Policy Challenge.* Social Policy Studies 20. Paris: OECD.

———. 1999. *OECD Principles of Corporate Governance.* Ad Hoc Task Force on Corporate Governance. Paris: OECD.

————. 2001. "OECD Principles of Corporate Governance: Questions and Answers." Available online at: www.oecd.org/daf/governance.

Palacios, R. 2002. "Managing Public Pension Reserves, Part II: Lessons from Five Recent OECD Initiatives." World Bank Pension Reform Primer Working Paper series. Washington, D.C.: World Bank. Available online at: www.worldbank.org/pensions.

1

1

Annex 1.A: ABP Investment Policy Statement

Introduction

The Governing Board of the foundation "Stichting Pensionfonds ABP" (ABP) ensures that the assets of the pension fund are invested prudently. The Board sees to it that investments are made exclusively in the interest of the (former) participants in the pension fund. The Governing Board determines what risks ABP is prepared to accept in connection therewith. Subject to these risk parameters, ABP wishes to maximize return on its investments for the benefit of the (former) participants in ABP.

Each of the various ABP bodies (Governing Board< Board of Directors and Investment Committee) has its own duties and responsibilities in the investment process. These are set out in the Regulation on Investment Procedures. In broad lines, the Regulation on Investment specifies that policy and strategic decisions are the responsibility of the Governing Board. These decisions are prepared by the Board of Directors, which is advised by the investment Committee. The Governing Board has delegated the actual investment of the available funds to the Boards of Directors, the responsible body for ABP's day-today management.

The investment of available funds is carried out in accordance with the applicable requirements for the exercise of prudence. The Governing Board sees to it that these requirements—which are embedded in many parts of the ABP organization—are satisfied. The effect of these requirements is that no investment is based on coincidental decisions by ABP management, directors or employees. Instead, there is consistent and reasoned investment practice in all segments of the organization.

The characteristics of this investment practice are set out in this Code. They form the basis for a prudent ABP investment policy on behalf of the (former) participants in the pension fund and in relation to the society in which ABP operates.

ABP has an Advisory Council consisting of representatives of employers affiliated to ABP and representatives of the (former) participants. The Governing Board has asked the Advisory Council to advise on the intended resolution to formalize the Code. On December 1, 2000 the Advisory Council decided in favour of the resolution.

The text of the Code was formally accepted by the Governing Board of ABP on December 21, 2000.

I. The Investment process

1. The concept of investment process is of paramount importance to ABP in evaluating whether there is a prudent investment policy.
2. ABP understands 'investment process' to mean the entirely of rules governing the preparation, implementation and management of investments.[25]
3. ABP requires of all the managers in its organization that they see to it that all activities are carried out in accordance with the rules of the investments process. ABP can at all times hold them responsible for compliance with these rules.
4. The Governing Board and the Board of Directors ensure that in all stages of the investment process ABP avails itself of the professional expertise required for:

   - An optimal investment result;
   - An accurate management of the investments; and
   - The control of risks associated with investments.

5. ABP has an Investment Committee which advises the Board of Directors with regard to the organization of the investment process, the development of the investment policy and extraordinary investment intentions. The Investment Committee consists of members who are independent of ABP and who have proved to be experts in the area of investments or financial markets.
6. The Governing Board has delegated the organization and day-today management of the investment process to the Board of Directors. The Governing Board bears ultimate responsibility for the entire investment process.
7. The Governing Board presents the main lines of the investment process to the Advisory Council.

II. Investment plans

1. ABP makes a distinction between the strategic (multi-year) investment plan and the annual investment plan.
2. The aim of the investment plans is to secure that ABP's available funds are invested in accordance with the Dutch Pansion and Savings Fund Act, namely: in a solid manner, with due regard to the requirements of solvency, liquidity, return and the diversification of risk.
3. The investment plans are drawn up in accordance with the Regulation on Investment Procedures.[26]
4. The Board of Directors develops the investment plans and presents them to the Investment Committee for assessment.
5. The investment plans are laid down by the Governing Board.
6. The strategic investment plan spells out the relationship between ABP's assets and liabilities. It contains the major investment decisions which ABP has to make, i.e.

   a. The desired strategic asset allocation according to investment categories and countries (regions). The risk profile of this strategic allocation is analyzed in the light of all the rights and obligations at fund level, both on the short and the long term;
   b. The return target set for each asset class, expressed in one or more benchmarks;
   c. The extent to which ABP is prepared to accept the risk that investment results at fund level may deviate from the desired strategic allocation ("total risk");
   d. The currency policy.[27]

7. The investment plan describes the way in which ABP will implement the strategic investment plan in the year in question.
8. The Board of Directors presents the strategic investment plan to the Advisory Council.

III. Implementation of the investment plan

1. The Governing Board of ABP has delegated the implementation of the investment plan to the Board of Directors, in accordance with the Regulation on Investment Procedures.

2. In implementing the investment plan there is room for every investment category, every investment instrument and every investment technique, provided the defined criteria regarding risk and return, solidity and prudence are satisfied.[28]

3. In implementing the investment plan, one needs to guard against conflicts of interest. ABP's management and employees are therefore bound by a Code of Conduct.

4. The investments entered into, pursuant to the investment plan, are made by ABP employees and third parties contracted by ABP for that purpose. Among these third parties are investment managers, custodians and brokers.

5. The aforementioned third parties are selected and evaluated on the basis of objective criteria. Considerations taken into account and associated arguments applied are recorded in systematically built up selection and evaluation file.

6. The investments entered into, pursuant to the investments plan, the management of investments and the control of risks associated with investments, are effected with due regard to the on Manual of Market Risk Management.[29]

7. The Board of Directors reports to the Governing Board on a quarterly basis on the manner in which the investment plan is being implemented.

8. The results of the investment policy are presented to the Advisory Council annually.

9. The Governing Board and the Board of Directors render account of their management of the fund's assets in ABP's annual financial statement.

IV. Social responsibility

1. The aim of ABP's investment policy is to obtain a maximum return for the (former) participants in the pension fund, within the risk parameters established by the Governing Board. ABP requires from

all those involved in its investment process and undivided dedication to this investment objective.

2. In the light of this objective, ABP will resist all investment compulsion and investment restrictions which have a negative effect on an optimal investment return. There is no room for socially initiated investments or for economically targeted investments,[30] if such investments do not meet the return requirements, if such investments do not meet the return requirements formulated by ABP.

3. ABP is conscious of the social role it fulfils as a large investor. This role compels ABP to exercise great care in its actions. ABP is prepared at all times to account for the consequences of its investments practice for society, the environment, employees and human rights.

4. Naturally, ABP will not become involved in any investment transaction which would, for instance, contravene international law. Moreover, ABP will avoid and investment:

    -   If illegal or morally reprehensible behavior is thereby promoted,
    -   If the investment—were it to be made—is directly related to a violation of human rights[31] and fundamental freedoms. If it is likely there will be such a relationship and if ABP is aware of this, ABP will refrain from the investment

5. ABP will promote that criteria of a social, ethical and environmental nature will be integrated in its investment process. In this context one or more experimental investment portfolios may be created whereby investments are selected, managed and divested on the basis of special concern for these criteria. Of course, this leaves the goal of ABP's investment policy unaffected.

V. The role of the shareholder ("corporate governance")

1. Pension funds are closely involved in the discussion concerning corporate governance. They must be able to rely on stable and reliable corporate structures and in decision-making within companies which safeguards the interests of the investors. This allows pension funds to make large amounts of capital available to companies for a long period. For this reason ABP has an active corporate governance

policy in which it requires high standards of transparency, independent supervision, accountability and shareholders' rights.

2. ABP will evaluate the quality of corporate governance on the basis of principles which have been drawn up by authoritative international organizations.[32] At the basis of these principles is the theory that a company should be subjected to a well-functioning correction mechanism,[33] in case the management of the company fails to pay sufficient attention to the interests of the shareholders.

3. ABP will place developments in The Netherlands in this international context. This position relates to, and is a logical consequence of, ABP's internationally diversified equity portfolio.

4. Companies will be forced by international competition and the dispersal of their share capital t adapt their corporate governance according to international standards. In this way they can obtain the loyalty of investors.

5. ABP will promulgate that listed companies should aim at generating a sustainable maximum return for their shareholders.[34] ABP will evaluate the policy of the Board of Directors and Supervisory Board of a company in the light of this target.

6. ABP will manage and exercise its shareholder rights if this contributes to the risk and return profile of its investment portfolio.

7. It is explicitly not ABP's intention to concern itself with the strategy of, or the day-to-day state of affairs within the company. However, on the basis of financial risk and return criteria ABP will assess whether the company strategy has met its financial targets.

8. ABP emphasizes the legal separation of duties between the Board of Directors, the Supervisory Board and the General Meeting of Shareholders of a company. ABP adheres to its independent role as a shareholder. It does not pursue a seat in the Supervisory Board which might affect this independence.

9. ABP supports the non-selective disclosure by companies of all information relevant to investors. If the company discloses relevant information to certain participants in the securities markets,[35] it should publish the same information simultaneously or without delay to the public.

10. ABP will only in exceptional circumstances seek contact with the management of a company outside the framework of the general meeting of shareholders. If these contacts do take place, they have

the object of communicating what in the opinion of ABP is in the interest of the company and its shareholders.

11. As a long-term shareholder, ABP wishes to emphasize the long-term target of the company in relation to sustainable economic growth. The management of the company must be in a position to account publicly for possible contested investment decisions, to prevent the company from alienating itself from the society in which it carries on its business. This requires that the management of the company evaluates such investments in the light of a code of practice which it draws up and publishes to this end. The result must be: a prudently operating company which shows that it takes into account the environmental care, social stability, human rights and fundamental freedoms in its investment decisions and striving for profitability. ABP emphasizes that it is the task of the Board of Directors and the Supervisory Board and not the task of the shareholder to guide the operations of the company in this area of potentially conflicting interests.

12. The attitude of institutional investors is often crucial if a company becomes the object of a contested takeover. The decisions that ABP makes in such circumstances are the result of its own financial interests in the long term. This may conflict with the goals of other stakeholders. The decisive factor will be whether the bidder or targeted company should be deemed in a position to realize a sustainable maximum return on the capital made available by ABP.

13. ABP's policy with regard to corporate governance is further elaborated in the Code Corporate Governance

VI. Amendment of this Code

The issues handled in this Code are subject to continuous discussion, both inside and outside the ABP organization. ABP will therefore periodically revise this Code.[36] New insights will be included in this Code.

The Hague, December 21, 2000

Chairman,	Secretary,	First Vice-Chairman
B. de Vries	B.H.J.J.M. Volkers	P.M. Altenburg

40

Annex 1.B: Index of Governance Framework Document— Australian Prudential Regulation Authority (APRA)

1. Foundations

1.1 APRA's history
1.2 APRA's legal structure
1.3 APRA's business

2. Key Roles and Relationships

2.1 Role of the APRA board, chair, and CEO
2.2 Subcommittees of the board: RMAC
2.3 APRA's relationship with government

3. Internal Accountability Framework

3.1 Management reporting to the board
3.2 Monitoring the exercise of delegations
3.3 Risk assessment and internal audit
3.4 Board self-assessment

4. External Accountability Framework

4.1 Overview of external accountability framework
4.2 General duties of board members under the CAC Act
4.3 Managing conflicts of interest
4.4 Reporting and compliance
4.5 Requirements to consult
4.6 Secrecy provisions
4.7 Additional considerations and legislated responsibilities

1

5. Consequences of Failure to Meet Responsibilities

5.1 Indemnity under the APRA Act
5.2 Consequences of breaching the CAC Act

Appendix A—Statutory Responsibilities of Board Members

Commonwealth Authorities and Companies Act 1997
Australian Prudential Regulation Authority Act 1998

Appendix B—Matrix of Delegations

Treasurer's delegations
Board's delegations

Notes

1. Possibly the best known of the publicly managed mandatory schemes are those operated by Asian countries such as Singapore and Malaysia. Australia, in contrast, runs an unfunded public pension scheme that is not linked to wages during employment, alongside a privately managed mandatory contributory scheme.
2. The Korean scheme began to operate only in 1988.
3. It should be noted that three quarters of total global assets are those in the partially funded plans of Japan and the United States.
4. See, for example, the definitions given by the OECD (1999 p. 2 and 2001 p. 1).
5. The IMF practices are set out in detail in the *Code of Good Practices on Fiscal Transparency* and the *Code of Good Practices on Transparency in Monetary and Financial Policies*. Both are available on the IMF's website at http://www.imf.org/external/standards/index.htm
6. For example, in Croatia parametric changes involving the indexation of pensions in progress were rejected by the courts, resulting in a large liability related to retroactive pension payments (Anusic et al. 2003).
7. Although the taxpayers forced to fund deficiencies may well be the taxpayers of future generations.
8. For more information about the CPP, see the Government of Canada's website at: www.cppib.ca.
9. Most countries use representative boards; only three are known to use purely professional boards (Palacios 2002). See the paper by Hess and Impavido for this conference for additional detail regarding board size and composition and other governance practices in a sample of developing country public pension funds.
10. Among other things, candidates are required to have: sound judgment; analytical, problem-solving and decision-making skills; the capacity to quickly become familiar with specific concepts relevant to pension fund management; adaptability; high motivation; ethical character and a commitment to serving the public; experience in a senior capacity in the financial industry; broad investment knowledge; experience as a chief financial officer or treasurer of a large corporation or government entity or consulting experience

in the pension area; and a generally recognized accreditation as an investment professional.

11. For more information about the New Zealand public pension scheme see McCulloch and Frances' (2003) paper prepared for this conference and the New Zealand Government website: www.treasury.govt.nz/release/super/#15October.

12. Even in this case however, parallel regulations defining the level of partial funding could be applied.

13. See Anne Maher's (2003) paper prepared for this conference. The full text of the National Pensions Reserve Fund Act is available on the online at: www.ntma.ie/Publications/Pen_Res_Fund_Act_2000.pdf.

14. Since writing this paper the authors have become aware of a governance questionnaire prepared by the Canadian Association of Pension Supervisory Authorities (CAPSA) for private pension fund managers. This questionnaire, which covers much of the issues raised in our suggested question lists was sent to Canadian pension fund managers for finalization in July 2003. Information about the questionnaire can be found at the website of the Association at www.capsa-acor.org.

15. See Australian Government (2003). In this review, the Australian government found that the combined impact of these factors was minimal for around 15 years, after which it generated a growing fiscal gap that reached 2 percent of GDP by 25 years and 4 percent by 35 years.

16. Annex 1.A provides one example of a general investment policy statement by one of the largest public pension funds in the world, the ABP in the Netherlands.

17. The one area in which prohibitions or restrictions may play a positive role is with respect to investing in the government's own securities. See, for example, Maher (2003) for details of the Irish public pension fund's prohibition of investment in Irish Government securities.

18. Canada, Ireland, and New Zealand are among the few countries that state clearly that the purpose of the scheme's investments is solely to benefit members.

19. See Iglesias and Palacios (2000) and Hess and Impavido (2003).

20. For example, as noted earlier (Maher 2003), the Irish Public Pension Scheme imposes such a prohibition.

21. Singapore, for example, has instituted such a policy.

22. This raises the additional issue of administrative costs associated with the loan program, which may be charged to the fund, thereby negatively affecting the accumulation.

23. See the chapter by John Ilkiw (2003) prepared for this conference with regard to strategic decisions on asset class allocation.

24. For example, the Canadian Pension Plan Investment Board (CPPIB) states its funding ratio target explicitly and its target real rate of return is consistent with this objective.

25. Investment process: The entire body of rules which ABP describes as "the investment process" consists of the following: a) Provisions in the Dutch Pension and Savings Fund Act; b) Provisions in the articles of organization of the foundation 'Stitching Pensioenfonds ABP'; c) Regulation on Investment Procedures, which stipulates the tasks and responsibilities of the Governing Board, Board of Directors and Investment Committee in the decision-making process regarding investments; d) The Investment Committee Regulation, which stipulates the composition, tasks and working methods of the investment Committee; e) Rules relating to the internal power of decision and the external power of representation, i.e.: The Regulations for the division of responsibilities of the Board of Directors, the Regulations for the Board of Directors, the competence rules for ABP Investments, and the powers of attorney as registered in the Commercial Register; f) The risk parameters established by the Governing Board; g) The Manual on Market Risk Management and the Credit Risk Manual; and h) The Code of Conduct, which contains rules of conduct to combat conflicts of interests.

26. Article 15, section five, of ABP's articles stipulates that, with a view to making investments, the Governing Board of ABP should establish a Regulation on Investment Procedures. The Regulation on Investment Procedures deals with the duties and responsibilities of the Governing Board, Board of Directors and Investment Committee in the decision-making with regard to investments.

27. The desired strategic asset allocation, the return target per asset class and the currency policy .

---

* The foundation 'Stitching Pensioenfonds ABP' is registered in the Commercial Register of the Chamber of Commerce and Industry for South Limburg under registration number: 41074000.

28. Investment Instruments and investment techniques: This passage describes the use of derivatives within the investment policy. Whether a transaction in a derivative instrument is prudent is answered in the same way as an investment in underlying assets, namely in the light of the investment in underlying assets, namely in the light of the investment process described and the terms and restrictions contained in it. On this basis it can be assessed whether the transaction contributes to the achievement of the investment goals. This agrees with the view of the Pension-en verzeke- ringskamer (pensions and insurance supervisory authority of The Netherlands) as described in its circular of April 24, 1996. In this document it states that the use of datives by a pension fund or insurer is assessed according to guidelines "analogous to the requirements which apply to the general investment policy". One of the guidelines is:

> The role and use of derivatives in the general investment policy should be clearly elaborated and formulated and meet the requirements of solidity and prudence. There should be unambiguous internal guidelines for, amongst others, the kinds of permissible derivatives and the permitted use, including for example position limits and permitted counterparties.

29. In the Manual on Market Risk Management the following subjects are dealt with: a) Aims; b) Investment process; c) Organization of Risk Management; d) Control of market risks (definition, quantification (ratios), control); e) Performance measurement and attribution; f) Systems; and g) Procedures.

30. *Socially initiated investments:* ABP considers this to be a practice whereby investments are made or not made primarily with a view to achieve a social objectives. A socially initiated investment may take two forms: (i)certain investments are refrained from in order to put pressure on the party seeking capital, or (ii)certain investments are made with the intention to influence (for example, by exercising shareholders' rights- socially undesirable behavior).

Economically targeted investments: This is understood by ABP to be investments primarily made with a view on securing concomitant economic results that are considered desirable by interested parties. For example, maintaining employment in a certain economic activity (venture capital), maintaining a certain industry in a region or a country.

31. Human rights are laid down in treaties concluded by treaty-concluding parties. These treaties sometimes include obligations involving effort: the nations are obliged to strive for a certain aim, for example, by introducing legislation. The so-called 'basic social rights', in particular, require an effort on the part of the treaty-concluding nations. The nations need to create the preconditions within which these basic rights may fully come into effect. Examples of basic social rights are, for instance, to be found in international labor law.

    Absolute human rights and fundamental freedoms, on the other hand, may be called upon without further (national) legislation. No one may be subjected to torture; everyone has the right to privacy; everyone has the right to freedom of speech.

    The nature of these rights and freedoms imply an immediate applicability; they are always in effect.

32. The organization for Economic Co-operation and Development (OECD), the International Corporate Governance Network (ICGN) and the Council of Institutional Investors have drawn up such principles.

33. Examples of correction mechanisms might be: a powerful Supervisory Board independent of the Board of Directors; a system of proxy voting also accessible to institutional investors and proxy solicitation; a very liquid share whereby the investor has an option to 'implied voting' (the Wall Street rule) without risking adverse effects on his investment; a company which might become the object of a take-over-bid due to the absence of anti take-over devices. In ABP's opinion, it is difficult to align the application of the Dutch so-called structure regime, an accumulation of oligarchic regulations and anti take-over devices with the aim of creating correction mechanisms.

34. Examples of correction mechanisms might be: a powerful Supervisory Board independent of the Board of Directors; a system of proxy voting also accessible to institutional investors and proxy solicitation; a very liquid share whereby the investor has an option to 'implied voting' (the Wall Street rule) without risking adverse effects on his investment; a company which might become the object of a take-over-bid due to the absence of anti take-over devices. In ABP's opinion, it is difficult to align the application of the Dutch so-called structure regime, an accu-

1

mulation of oligarchic regulations and anti take-over devices with the aim of creating correction mechanisms.

35. This refers to a practice of disclosing such information to persons such as analysts, brokers, bankers or investors outside the scope of the company and its advisors.

36. This refers to a practice of disclosing such information to persons such as analysts, brokers, bankers or investors outside the scope of the company and its advisors.

Governance of Public Pension Funds: Lessons from Corporate Governance and International Evidence

David Hess and Gregorio Impavido

Governments are paying increasing attention to the management of their public pension fund reserves. Rather than cutting benefits or increasing contributions to enlarge these reserves, they are focusing on the more politically appealing alternative of improving their investment performance (Palacios 2002). They are, however, facing growing pressure to use these funds to improve the local economy or achieve other social goals, and such use obviously can have a significant negative impact on investment performance. There consequently is a strong need for public pension reform to focus on the governance structures and practices of these funds.

There is extensive research on the governance of corporations. The field of corporate governance generally is concerned with the basic issue of instilling investors with the confidence that will permit them to hand over their money to managers. As noted by Davis and Useem (2000), corporate governance deals with the basic issue of "the ways in which suppliers of finance to corporations assure themselves of getting a return on their investment" (Shleifer and Vishny 1997: 737), as well as the broader cultural and institutional arrangements affecting the governance of firms. Over the past two decades, corporate governance has become a leading topic of discussion for researchers in finance, management, and law. Their goal is to find the optimal organizational arrangements to both protect shareholders' rights and at the same time increase economic efficiency.

A leading theory used to analyze corporate governance and provide prescriptions on governance structures and incentives is the agency theory. This paper examines the applicability of this theory to the governance of public pension funds. The first section discusses the application of agency theory to corporations. Included in this discussion is the problem of the separation of ownership and control, where certain inefficiencies result when those making the decisions for the organization do not fully bear the risks of those decisions. Corporations use various mechanisms to attempt to control these problems. The following section discusses the agency problems that may exist in public pensions. The next section provides an analysis of the control of agency problems that impact the management of pension funds, and demonstrates the need for a strong, well-functioning board of trustees. The section after that discusses the implications of using behavioral controls (as opposed to outcome controls) to solve agency problems associated with the structure and functioning of the board of trustees. This section also provides the results of a survey of 26 pension funds from various countries.[1] Conclusions follow in the final section.

Agency Theory and Corporate Governance

Agency Problems: Separation of Ownership and Control and Moral Hazard Problems

Agency theory deals with the problems that can arise when one person (an agent) acts on behalf of another (the principal). Specifically, the delegation of authority to the agent may result in the agent taking actions that are not in the principal's best interests (i.e., that are acts of self-interest on the part of the agent) but which are unknown to the principal. The goals of agency theory are to constrain agents from acting improperly and to provide them with incentives to act appropriately.

In the context of the corporation, agency theorists view the firm as a "nexus of contracts" between shareholders, managers, and other stakeholders. These parties each may have conflicts of interests with the other contracting parties. For example, if a manager owned 100 percent of a firm's equity there would be no conflict of interest, as the manager would receive all the benefits of his or her efforts and would bear all the costs of any shirking or opportunistic behavior (Jensen and Meckling 1976). As the manager's fraction of the equity declines, the manager is more likely to "appropriate perquisites out of the firm's resources," and the manager's "incentive to devote significant effort to creative activities such as searching out new profitable ventures falls" (Jensen and Meckling 1976). When the manager's ownership moves toward zero percent of the corporation's equity, significant agency problems can result. This is the basic problem of separating ownership from control that dominates discussions of U.S. corporate law and finance—those making the decisions do not bear the full wealth consequences of their actions.

It should be noted that the problem of separation of ownership (the shareholders) from control (management) is rare outside of the United States and the United Kingdom. In other countries, corporations typically are owned by majority shareholders (Davis and Useem 2000). While such shareholders may take actions for their own benefit and to the detriment of minority shareholders, the presumption is that large shareholders work toward the increase of share value, and this is to the benefit of all shareholders. When control is exercised by small minority shareholders (management) the same presumption cannot safely be defended, for the reason that minority shareholders may receive more value from actions that provide a personal benefit at the expense of share value.

In addition to the issue of the separation of ownership from control, there are other problems that can afflict any type of agency relationship. These can result from uncertainty and goal conflict or from an inability to write a contract that fully specifies the behavior of the agent in all situations (Levinthal 1988). With respect to uncertainty, agency theorists have identified two categories of problem. First, there is the moral hazard problem, which involves an agent failing to exert the necessary effort to satisfactorily perform his or her job (shirking) or taking actions that benefit himself or herself at the expense of the principal (opportunism). These problems result from a lack of monitoring or ineffective incentives. Second, there is the adverse selection problem, arising when an agent lacks the competence to perform the job. This results from an inability or failure of the principal to verify the claimed skills of the agent.

The goal conflict problem results when the principal and the agent have different goals and it is difficult (and/or expensive) for the principal to monitor the agent's behavior (to ensure appropriate behavior) (Eisenhardt 1989). The source of the conflict can be the self-interest of the agent or simply different attitudes toward risk. Where the goals of the agent and principal do not conflict, uncertainty is not an issue as the principal can rely on the agent to act in furtherance of their shared goals.

A fundamental assumption of agency theory is that individuals are self-interested and will act on that self-interest; that is, they are opportunistic. Whenever there is a conflict between the interests of the agent and the principal, the agent thus can be expected to act in his or her own self-interest. For example, in publicly held corporations, managers (the agents) are contractually bound to work in the shareholders' (the principal's) best interests, but if they know that they will not be monitored nor therefore potentially punished they may exert less effort than is appropriate (shirking) or take advantage of company resources for their own personal benefit. In such situations an agency problem will occur whenever management has an incentive to pursue its own interests to the detriment of shareholder interests. This is not to say that all managers are opportunistic, but the threat of opportunism is significant enough that preventative measures must be taken.

Resolving Problems

Behavioral versus Outcome Controls

The goal of agency theory is to find the most cost-effective governance mechanisms to solve any existing or potential agency problems. Governance mechanisms are generally either behavior-oriented or outcome-oriented (Eisenhardt 1989). Behavior-oriented mechanisms focus on the specific actions of the agent, and include, for example, information systems that allow the principal to monitor the agent's behavior. Outcome-oriented mechanisms focus less on the specific actions of the agent and more on the results the agent achieves. Such mechanisms include stock options for managers, thus rewarding them for achieving the goals of the shareholders (increased share value).

Choosing the appropriate category of governance mechanism to use depends on several factors, including the amount of goal conflict, the task performed, the degree of outcome uncertainty, and the measurability of the outcome (Eisenhardt 1989). The application of these factors is summarized in Table 2.1.

Corporate Governance Control Mechanisms

Because there are significant benefits to having a specialized managerial group running a corporation, certain agency costs can be tolerated. To mitigate these costs, the corporate governance system has various behavioral

Table 2.1: Agency Relationship Characteristics

Risk aversion	The less risk-averse the agent (compared to the principal), the better it is to use outcome-based mechanisms, as such mechanisms pass risk on to the agent
Outcome uncertainty	Where various factors beyond the control of the agent can create significant variations in outcomes (such as government policies or changes in the general economic climate), using outcome-based control mechanisms becomes less attractive, as there is no clear link between job performance and organizational performance.
Goal conflict	The less goal conflict there is between the principal and agent, the less need there is to monitor the agent's behavior (as both principal and agent are working towards the same goal). The choice of mechanisms depends on risk sharing.
Task programmability	Task programmability is the extent to which the specific behaviors of the agent can be established in advance. With highly programmed tasks, the behavior of the agent can be easily monitored and behavior-based mechanisms therefore efficiently used.
Measureability of outcome	Where it is difficult to measure the outcome or, the contribution of each team member to an outcome, or where the outcome cannot be meaningfully measured except over a long period of time, then behavior-based mechanisms may be best.
Length of time of the principal-agent relationship	With longer-term relationships, the principal is better able to collect information about the behavior of the agent and can effectively use behavior-based controls. With short-term relationships and less time to learn about the abilities of the agent, outcome-based controls may be more attractive.

and outcome-based control mechanisms. Some of these controls are external to the firm and some are internal.

External Controls

The first external control of managerial behavior is the market for corporate control. If a corporation is underperforming due to poor management, another organization will recognize the lost value and purchase the corporation from its shareholders. If management does not act in the best interests of shareholders it will thus lose control of the firm. For this market to work, however, the firm's share price must accurately reflect the behavior of management.

A second external control is the product (or service) market. If management is not appropriately doing its job (or is incompetent), the corporation will fail and go into bankruptcy. Competition in the product market thus disciplines management, especially where there is also a functioning labor market for top management; that is, managing a corporation into bankruptcy will have a negative effect on a manager's career prospects.

A final external control involves monitoring by large shareholders. A shareholder with a significant interest in the firm has an incentive to expend the resources necessary to monitor management and also to intervene when necessary. Rather than simply sell their shares if they disagree with how the firm is being managed, large shareholders have an interest in improving the firm.

The first two of these mechanisms are outcome-based controls. Shareholder monitoring, although shareholders may push for some outcome-based controls, is behavioral.

Internal Controls

The board of directors can serve as an information collection system for the monitoring of management behavior (Eisenhardt 1989), and as such has become broadly regarded by corporate governance activists, scholars, and practitioners as the best continuous, cost-effective monitoring device (Singh and Harianto 1989). For it to fulfill this role, however, directors must have the proper incentives—just as managers may have a conflict of interest with shareholders, so may directors.

2

In the corporate governance literature it is common to distinguish between inside and outside (or independent) directors. Inside directors are managers of the firm, while outside directors have no employment relationship with the firm. Inside directors bring to the board extensive knowledge of the firm, but they are expected to have a conflict of interest with shareholders and through siding with the CEO to provide no protection against problems of moral hazard. They typically will support the CEO's interests over those of the shareholders because the CEO controls the trajectory of their careers within the firm (Lin 1996). Outside directors are generally considered to be sufficiently independent of the CEO to be capable of protecting the rights of those shareholders who may be harmed by the CEO's behavior.

Boards that include directors that represent all stakeholder groups are uncommon. While some corporations in Germany, for example, are required by law to have employee representatives on the board (typically on a two-tiered board), the ability of these representatives to protect the rights of their constituents or to influence corporate policy is not clear. Studies have even suggested that shareholder representatives may act to specifically limit the impact of such employee directors; shareholder directors, for example, have been known to exclude employee directors from meetings at which sensitive information is discussed (Becht et al. 2002).

Concerns about the ability of inside directors to perform their role has led corporate governance reformers to push strongly for a more independent board. The National Association of Corporate Directors and the Business Roundtable both recommend that a board consist of a "substantial majority" of outside directors (Bhagat and Black 1999). The California Public Employees' Retirement System (CalPERS), a pension fund active in corporate governance reforms, even recommends that the only inside director on the board should be the CEO (Bhagat and Black 1999).

The empirical evidence of the effectiveness of an independent board in reducing agency problems nonetheless is ambiguous. Some commentators argue that it is difficult to establish a statistical relationship because the board is a poor monitor of management regardless of its ratio of inside to outside directors. The independence of outside directors furthermore has been challenged by those who claim that CEOs have significant control over the selection of board members and will only choose those who are sympathetic to their view (see Shivdasani and Yermack 1999; Zajac and Westphal 1996; Westphal and Zajac 1995; Wade et al. 1990). Other critics argue that any outside directors appointed with the support of the CEO are unlikely to challenge the CEO's actions (see Lin 1996; Main et al. 1995; Lorsch and MacIver 1989). Mechanisms to mitigate against CEO control of a board include legal and financial incentives to encourage directors to exercise their own judgment in protecting shareholder interests. The labor market can provide a similar incentive.

While the board serves as a behavioral control on management, the board's incentives are outcome-based controls. First, corporation laws create fiduciary obligations, including the duties of loyalty and care, for directors. The duty of loyalty involves conflicts of interests and the avoidance of actions that would benefit the director at the expense of shareholders. The duty of care requires a director to act with good faith and "with the care that an ordinarily prudent person would reasonably be expected to exercise in a like position and under similar circumstances" (American Law Institute [ALI] Principles, section 4.01). This requires that a director be well informed on the subject at hand and that he or she act in the best interests of the corporation. If directors breach their duties they may be personally liable for any loses resulting to the corporation. In the United States, the incentive effects of liability for directors are limited to only the most egregious abuses, as courts are reluctant to second-guess the business decisions of directors even if they have turned out to be disastrous for the firm.

A second form of incentives for directors is reputation capital. Several scholars have argued that directors are motivated to fulfill their monitoring role by a concern to protect their reputation in the labor market (Fama 1980; Fama and Jensen 1983b). Directors develop and maintain their reputations as "experts in decision control" (Fama and Jensen 1983b: 315). During a director's tenure on a board, the company's performance will determine the director's reputation. If the company performs poorly, the director's reputation will be tarnished. This can lead to the director being offered fewer, or less prestigious, board seats in the future (Lin 1996).

Third, directors are motivated to perform their duties based on their own equity stakes in the firm. This theory is based on the notion of a "convergence of interests" (Lin 1996: 918): that a director who holds equity in a firm and who acts on his or her own financial interests necessarily also is acting in the interests of other shareholders.

The corporate governance literature in law and financial economics is dominated by researchers who have used an agency perspective. Management literature researchers additionally have considered factors such as team dynamics and organizational cultures. For example, one of the few consistent findings from empirical research on boards is that the greater the number of board members, the worse the organizational performance. In general, any board with more than 15 or 20 members will likely have a negative impact on performance. This finding has held for studies both in the United States and elsewhere (Davis and Useem 2000). With an increasing number of members, the ability of the board to work together as a team diminishes and the willingness of a director to be actively engaged in board activities decreases (Davis and Useem 2000).

In recognition of the need for smaller workgroups, it is common to find corporations using separate committees for matters such as investments, audits, governance, and compensation of management. The investment committee is usually responsible for defining the investment policy of the fund. The audit committee is usually responsible for oversight of the external auditor, including its qualifications and independence; the performance of the corporation's internal audit function and external auditors; and the responsibilities of senior management to ensure that an appropriate system of controls exists to (a) safeguard of the assets and income of the corporation; (b) ensure the integrity of the corporation's financial statements; and (c) maintain compliance with the corporation's ethical standards, policies, plans, and procedures and with laws and regulations. The governance committee usually exercises general oversight with respect to the governance of the board of directors: it would review the qualifications of and recommend proposed nominees to the board and would be responsible for (a) evaluating and recommending to the board corporate governance practices applicable to the corporation and (b) leading the board in its annual review of the board's performance. The compensation and management committee usually reviews and approves the corporation's compensation and benefit programs, ensures the competitiveness of these programs, and advises the board on the development of and succession for key executives.

Agency Problems in Public Pension Plans

This section takes a closer look at public pension funds to determine potential agency problems. By taking a "nexus of contracts" approach to public pensions we can examine what the various stakeholders expect from public pensions and where there are potential conflicts. This discussion will also provide insight into who the principals (or "owners") of the pension plan are.

Who Are Public Pension Fund Stakeholders?

To develop an understanding of the appropriate governance structure of public pension plans it is necessary first to identify the stakeholder groups and their interests. The three key stakeholder groups relevant to this analysis are the plan participants, the government, and the taxpayers. The plan participants group includes active members (the current contributors), retired members (those currently receiving benefits), and survivors and dependents of plan participants. The membership of this group can be broad or limited, depending on whether the pension plan is a national scheme or a specific civil service group. This stakeholder group clearly has the most direct interest in the pension system's performance (Mitchell 2002). In the United States and the United Kingdom, the law governing private pension plans requires that the plans be managed solely in the best interests of participants and beneficiaries. This stakeholder group has an interest in the amount of their benefits, in the assurance that they will receive those benefits at a future date, and in the size of their contributions to the plan.

A second stakeholder group is the government, which has an interest in the administrative costs of running the plan and in the performance of the plan's assets, as these factors influence the amount of the government's contribution for DB plans. As an employer (in the case of civil service plans), the government is interested in the financial health of the plan for its impact on the ability to recruit new employees and retain existing employees (Mitchell 2002). In addition, the financial health of the plan can have an impact on pay and benefit negotiations with employee representatives. The government, however, may desire to use the plan's assets to further other government objectives, such as making investments to help the local economy.

Finally, taxpayers are natural stakeholders of any defined benefit (DB) public pension fund and any defined contribution (DC) scheme with minimum return guarantees. In a DB plan, the beneficiary is given set retirement benefits based on a formula that considers years of employment, salary, cost of living adjustments, and other factors. The pension fund sponsor must make sure that the assets of the fund are sufficient to provide for current and potential liabilities (i.e., the payment of benefits to retirees). In this situation, the taxpayer bears the ultimate obligation to maintain adequate funding levels. If a pension fund obtains sufficient market returns through investment, the government may lower its contributions to the fund, which means it may directly lower taxes or use those funds for other projects. If market performance is poor and liabilities exceed assets, the government will have to use taxpayer money to increase the plan's assets. This will result in either an increase in taxes or fewer available funds for other government services. Funding problems in civil service plans can have other effects for taxpayers: for example, significantly underfunded pension plans can reduce property values, due to the expectation of future tax increases, or reduce the bond or credit ratings of local government (Mitchell 2002).

Potential Agency Problems

In the same way that they can create problems for corporations, goal conflict and uncertainty can create agency problems for public pension funds. It is useful to consider two potentially separate problems: traditional problems based on the direct self-interest of trustees, such as self-dealing and corruption, or simply shirking; and problems based on the political goals of the trustees, such as the use of pension fund assets to further the social goals of the governing party. The latter occurs, for example, when the trustees, without considering the risk-return characteristics of the investment, direct the pension's assets toward investments that support local businesses and employment.

In the United States, unresolved agency problems based on self-interest often involve politically motivated actions, commonly when politically appointed or ex officio trustees make decisions not to further the beneficiaries' interests but to improve their own situation. For example, during her campaign for public office a former ex officio trustee of the New York City pension fund publicized the corporate governance activism in which she had participated as a trustee of the city pension fund (Romano 2001 and 1993). Critics argued that she had spent the fund's assets on corporate governance activism not because she believed it would improve the fund's performance but because it would bolster her reputation as a populist politician who would stand up against big business.

This category of agency problems also includes the exercise of direct financial self-interest, such as the use of pension fund assets to benefit friends and family of the board. In the United States, the trustees of a

Maryland state pension fund were criticized for investing funds through a money manager that was a significant campaign donor to the state governor. Despite having consistently low performance, the money manager received fees that were significantly higher than those paid to other managers.

A further example of a politically based agency problem is the funding of local initiatives for their social benefit without appropriate weight being given to the risk-return characteristics of the investment. For example, a pension fund may choose to invest in a financially troubled local business to save the jobs that the company provides, but at a risk to the fund's assets, or government bonds may be purchased at lower than market interest rates to further the borrowing ability of the government. The trustees in such cases may be acting on their own initiative, perhaps in their role as a publicly elected official, or they may be acting under pressure from outside political parties. Other examples from the U.S. experience include decisions to select investment advisors based not on their performance but on a preference for in-state managers or to further affirmative action goals (Romano 1993). Such investment managers are likely to be small and unable to take advantage of economies of scale on transactions, which will reduce fund performance.

It is important to remember that the party in power chooses the goals served by politically motivated actions, and that other parties may oppose these goals. These actions thus may be a way for the ruling party to further its social goals without following the regular political decision-making procedure for resource allocation. For example, some commentators in the United States have raised concerns that the California Public Employees' Retirement System (CalPERS) is dominated by Democrats and that they are using the system's assets to attempt to bring about social change without regard to the direct financial health of the system (Walsh 2002). Such actions nonetheless may be widely supported by the public.

Romano (1993 and 1995) has argued that public pension funds with trustees who are susceptible to political pressure will perform significantly worse than those boards with politically independent trustees. United States Federal Reserve Chairman Alan Greenspan likewise has argued against the investment of social security funds in equities: "In sum, because I do not believe that it is politically feasible to insulate such huge funds from governmental influence, investing social security trust fund assets in equities compromises the efficient allocation of our capital."

Given that politically motivated decisions may have broad popular support, as is arguable in the case of CalPERS, there remains much debate concerning the significance of agency problems founded in political motivations. Recognition of the need to control self-interest-based agency problems in contrast may be assumed to be universal. In a survey conducted for this paper of pension funds in various countries, two of the 26 respondents answered "yes" to the following question: "Has there been any serious case of fraud or other scandal that resulted in formal investigation in the last five years?" Their responses indicate that this is a problem that deserves serious consideration when structuring the governance of public pension plans. The next section considers the extent of the second type of agency problem.

Political Involvement:
Government Restrictions and Social Mandates

That there is political involvement in the investment choices of public pension funds is well known. This involvement can come in the form of legislation passed on the initiative of trustees or can involve mandates to make certain investments or prohibitions on other investments.

In the United States, the use of economically targeted investments (ETIs) was in the 1990s one of the most controversial issues facing public and private pension fund management. ETIs are investments in which the fund managers take into consideration not only the investment return but also the economic benefits to the local community (GAO 1995; Watson 1994). Examples of ETIs include California's investment of US$ 375 million in single-family homes to help increase affordable housing and create jobs, Connecticut's investment of US$ 25 million in a local company to save 1,000 jobs, and Pennsylvania's decision to provide favorable interest rates for home mortgages (Stevenson 1992). Another common ETI practice involves using pension funds to provide venture capital to in-state companies that may not be able to attract the attention of other venture capitalists (GAO 1995). Until recently, the National Pension Fund (NPF) of the Republic of Korea met a requirement to contribute to economic and social development by lending to the government at nonmarket rates and purchasing nontradable government bonds.

The Singaporean Central Provident Fund (CPF) similarly has many objectives in addition to its core objective of ensuring sufficient retirement benefits. It administers schemes covering housing, medical savings accounts, and education; it also permits extensive pre-retirement withdrawals for investment in real estate, financial assets, and even gold and commodities. The CPF has different accounts to which individual contributions are credited. The ordinary account can be utilized for financing housing purchases, for investments in approved shares and stocks, and to finance children's tertiary education. The special account is a true pension retirement account. The medical account is used to pay for hospital services, certain outpatient services, and catastrophic health insurance premiums. Contribution rates to the different accounts vary by age and for workers up to 35 years of age the contribution rates to the three different accounts are 26 percent, 4 percent and 6 percent, respectively (Chia and Tsui 2003).

Advocates of ETIs claim that such investments can be structured to obtain a market rate of return, but they face significant opposition. Proponents of ETIs further argue that gaps in the capital market leave certain socially desirable projects underfunded; opponents claim that the true motivation for these pension fund investments is political. In 1992, a lobbyist for CalPERS referred to ETIs as "politicizing" pension investments rather than "maximizing" them (Vise 1992). Nofsinger (1998: 89) argued: "[ETIs] are often highly visible projects that attempt to generate a public good in a concentrated, geographical region. The claimable political benefits of an ETI policy can be large and the costs of claiming them small. The agency cost that taxpayers bear is not visible at the initial investment because the costs are not realized until some distant time when an increase in funding is needed for the underfunded pension plan."

ETIs may be able to achieve an acceptable rate of return and taxpayers may be willing to take on the extra risk in exchange for social benefits, but few pension funds have established criteria for selecting ETI projects (Iglesias and Palacios 2000). They are thus entirely under the purview of the board or of the ruling political party.

In addition to the mandating of certain investments, political interference may also see restrictions placed on the types of investments a fund may make. For example, a pension fund may be restricted from investing in foreign markets or in anything other than government bonds. The difficulties presented by such restrictions are compounded where there are limited investment opportunities in the home country (Iglesias and Palacios 2000). Even where explicit developmental and social mandates do not exist, prohibitions on certain types of investments may be sufficient in themselves to ensure that funds are invested in social projects. The five public pension

Figure 2.1: Investment Restrictions (percentage of funds surveyed)

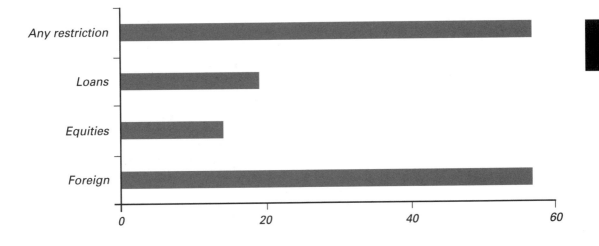

2

funds in Honduras that were surveyed for this paper do not have any explicit developmental mandate, but they are restricted from investing abroad. Attempts to diversify the fund's portfolio within the context of the limited domestic opportunities have seen approximately 30 percent of fund assets invested in housing loans to participants, often at a subsidized rate.

In Ghana, the Social Security and National Insurance Trust (SSNIT) is required to be invested in assets with adequate yield and liquidity and an acceptable risk level. Managers must follow basic portfolio theory rules for asset diversification as they seek to maintain an optimal funding ratio and to secure long-term rates of return for the fund (Dei 2001). However, the SSNIT investment policy includes social and developmental mandates in the following areas: housing finance, student loans, and industrial estates. Although returns on these assets were not reported, Dei comments that the student loan scheme has become a burden for the SSNIT. These loans are provided to students (including university students) at a subsidized interest rate. While the number of students has increased considerably, postgraduate unemployment also has increased, creating a further burden on the system. The loans furthermore are indexed to inflation, and as they increase in size,

Figure 2.2: Investment Mandates (percentage of funds surveyed)

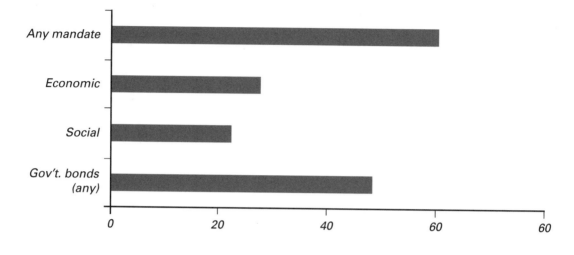

government delays in the payment of interest subsidies to the SSNIT again increase the overall burden on the fund.

This paper's survey of public pension funds around the world revealed that the use of restrictions and mandates is widespread. The most common restriction is on foreign investments, with 57 percent of the surveyed funds facing prohibition on investment abroad. Other restrictions include prohibitions on equities (14 percent) and loans (19 percent) (see Figure 2.1).

Explicit investment mandates also are common, with 60 percent of the funds operating under at least one type of mandate. These mandates include requirements to invest in government bonds (including national, state, provincial, and municipal bonds) (48 percent), in social projects such as housing (24 percent), and in general economic development obligations (32 percent). The use of restrictions and mandates furthermore may be more widespread than these figures indicate, as trustees may self-impose these investment practices on the fund in the absence of explicit requirements.

The Effects on Fund Performance

One result of policies that seek to fulfill social objectives beyond fund value maximization is poor asset allocation, which in turn may lead to low investment returns. Recent studies show that asset allocation can explain up to 90 percent of the variability in the return on assets over time (Brinson et al. 1986; Brinson et al. 1991). Where asset allocation decisions are based on politics rather than on sound portfolio theory, investment performance is sure to suffer—to the extent that in some countries public pension fund returns are consistently lower than the interest rate paid by banks to individual savings accounts in those same countries (Iglesias and Palacios 2000).

Table 2.2 illustrates the portfolio allocations of the funds surveyed for this paper. The average fund has 35 percent of its assets allocated to government bonds, 25 percent to bank deposits, and 15 percent to equities. More than 20 percent of the funds have at least 80 percent of their assets allocated to government bonds or bank deposit, with the average fund having 60 percent of its assets in either government bonds or bank deposits. Almost one-quarter of the sample have no investments in equities, and approximately two-thirds have less than 10 percent of their assets in equities. By contrast, analysis of 111 U.S. state and local pension funds from 2000 revealed the average fund to have 59 percent of its assets allocated to equities.[2]

The funds in our international sample used a wide range of asset allocations. Examination of the minimum and maximum portfolio allocations demonstrates this variety: while some funds face restrictions on investments in loans, one fund has invested 39 percent of its assets in loans. Another fund has more than half of its assets in real estate.

Table 2.2: Allocation of Assets for 26 Pension Funds (% of Portfolio)

Investment type	Average	Median	Minimum	Maximum
Government bonds	35	20	0	98
Bank deposits	25	23	0	93
Equities	15	7	0	63
Loans	6	2	0	39
Corporate bonds	4	2	0	22
Real estate	8	2	0	52
Other	4	1	0	23

Solving Agency Problems

Separation of Ownership and Control

A fundamental problem with public pension funds is how to achieve a workable separation of ownership and control. For example, if the plan participants are taken to be the owners of the fund, problems may result where another group (of, for example, government officials) controls the pension fund. This section considers the implications of the separation of ownership and control on pension plan governance. It considers first the situation of private pension plans and then the more complex problem of public pension plans.

Ownership and Control in Private Pensions

Recent work by Besley and Prat (2002) applies agency theory to private pension fund governance. Their goal was to find the optimal governance structure of defined contribution (DC) and defined benefit (DB) pension plans with respect to three potential sources of agency problems: the responsibility for monitoring the asset manager ("vigilance"), asset allocation decisions, and the plan's level of funding. Governance structure matters because, due to the inability to exactly specify the obligations of all parties, the plan's beneficiaries and sponsor do not have complete contracting ability. Thus, the incentives are important that encourage the parties to monitor or make appropriate asset allocation decisions. The optimal governance structure is one in which the risk-bearer is also the decision-maker (that is, there is no separation of ownership from control).

Determination of the optimal governance structure requires that the owner of the plan (which may also be termed the risk-bearer or residual claimant) be identified and if possible granted decision control responsibility. The residual claimant is the group with the greatest incentive to act with vigilance because it is this group that is best positioned to enjoy the benefits of such actions. For DC plans, the residual claimant is the beneficiary, as benefits suffer from poor financial performance but increase with better financial performance. For DB plans, because the benefits such plans do not change with the performance of their assets the residual claimants are the sponsors, as it is the sponsors that bear the risks of poor financial performance. If the beneficiaries have a comparative cost advantage in acting with vigilance, the plan therefore should be structured as a DC plan. If the sponsors have a comparative advantage, the plan should be structured as a DB plan.

This model considers only a single sponsor and a single beneficiary. With joint residual claimants, such as multiple beneficiaries, potential free-rider problems may reduce the incentive to monitor. That is, while the costs to monitor the asset manager would be borne by a single beneficiary, all beneficiaries would enjoy the benefits equally. This is similar to the problem of shareholders that have small ownership stakes in a corporation. For DC plans in which the residual claimants include numerous beneficiaries, we would argue that there is a strong need for a third-party monitor, such as a board of trustees. These trustees could be either insiders or outsiders. (Insiders are plan beneficiaries, hereafter referred to as "member trustees" to avoid confusion with insider directors of corporations.) Member trustees have an incentive to monitor as they have a financial interest in the plan as well as a bond with the other beneficiaries (for example, coworkers and friends), but they typically have little financial expertise. Outsiders, in contrast, are trustees with professional skills related to monitoring but with no financial interest in the plan (hereafter referred to as "professional trustees"). As an incentive for the professional trustees, their role should have a strong reputational effect. For such an incentive to exist there must be present an efficient career market for the trustee and a direct link between monitoring and the rate of return on assets. Defined benefit plans ideally should rely more on professional trustees, while DC plans should use self-motivated member trustees (as they are part of the residual claimant group).

With respect to asset allocation decisions, the implications of residual status on choice of governance are similar. The residual claimant is the efficient asset allocator. For example, the sponsor in a DC plan is not an efficient asset allocator because it does not fully bear the costs of its decisions and may have an incentive to invest in its own interests (for example, to overinvest in the sponsor company's stock). In DB plans the sponsor again may not be an efficient asset allocator if, for example, it has limited liability for the insolvency of the plan: with limited liability, the sponsor may be willing to take on excessive risk.

Consistent with agency theory, Besley and Prat (2002) argue that if decision-makers do not bear the full cost of their decisions inefficiencies can result (Fama and Jensen 1983a). These inefficiencies can have a significant impact on the residual claimant. With respect to private pension plans, the identification of the residual claimant is necessary to determine the most effective governance structure. Besley and Prat argue that for DC plans the beneficiary is the residual claimant, but for DB plans it is the sponsor. However, the sponsor in a DB plan is a qualified residual claimant to the extent it has limited liability for insolvency of the plan.

Ownership and Control in Public Pension Funds

The identification of the residual claimant is less straightforward in public pension plans. In the context of civil service public DB plans that are not pay-as-you-go, Murphy and Van Nuys (1994) argue that the residual claimants are the taxpayers. Because benefits are defined, funding problems with the pension plan may fall not on the beneficiaries but on the taxpayers, who must put up funds to cover unfunded liabilities. This argument holds to the extent that benefits paid to plan participants cannot be reduced. If benefits can be reduced, the plan participants (especially those retired members currently receiving benefits) are also residual claimants. In addition, where poor management of the pension plan's assets leads to an increased contribution rate for the plan participants, current plan members also have a status similar to that of residual claimants. One potential difference between beneficiaries and taxpayers, however, is the ability of beneficiaries to more completely protect their interests through contractual relationships with the pension plan sponsor.

For DC plans, the residual claimants are the beneficiaries. This stakeholder group bears the cost of poor asset management in the form of lower retirement benefits, although it may be the case that there is a guaranteed minimum rate of return on the assets. It also may be that government practices create an implicit guarantee that if market returns become so low as to render such pension instruments ineffective, the government will finance the retirement benefits of those with less than a politically acceptable cash balance in their retirement accounts. In such a case, the taxpayers again are the residual claimant.

Overall, there may be multiple different groups claiming residual claimant status and that therefore have the incentive to monitor the performance of the pension plan. To the extent that both taxpayers and beneficiaries are residual claimants, a basic application of agency theory would dictate that both should have decision control rights, including asset allocation decisions, the monitoring of asset managers (including hiring, firing, and establishing compensation agreements), and other management decisions. Of course, these groups may have significant conflicts with respect to how the plan should be managed. For example, a pension fund's increased performance can either be distributed to the plan members through higher cost-of-living adjustments and lower employee contributions, or it can be distributed to the taxpayers through a lowered government contribution. The exact allocation of decision control rights will depend on the structure of the pension plan. For example, in a DC plan without minimum guarantees the taxpayers are not residual claimants and the decision control rights should go to the plan participants, who bear the wealth consequences of their choices (see Murphy and Van Nuys 1994).

For national and civil service pension schemes (in which the beneficiaries are a more clearly defined group of individuals), the widely dispersed nature of the beneficiaries means that they must exercise their control through trustee representatives. These representatives, however, may not bear sufficient wealth consequences of their decisions for there to exist for them the incentive to avoid moral hazard problems or to maximize pension value. They may in this sense be similar to Besley's and Prat's (2002) professional trustees of private pensions and require external incentives such as the external labor market. Likewise, for corporate boards directors have an incentive to perform well to develop their reputations as "experts in decision control" (Fama and Jensen 1983a: 315). In both cases, the trustees/directors have incentives to do their job appropriately and with vigilance, because their actions will be rewarded or punished in their future career paths.

A similar analysis should be conducted for public pensions. That is, we should ask if there is an external labor market for trustees that will take into consideration a trustee's performance on the board. In many ways, the external labor market works as an outcome control, but there are problems with using outcome controls for public pensions. Namely, will the external market make a direct link between the trustee's monitoring performance and the fund's performance? It is quite possible that the market would only punish poor performance and would fail to reward solid performance. For example, many trustees in the United States fear negative publicity should their fund perform poorly but expect no reward (financially or from the media) for a strong performance. There is an incentive as such to concentrate on the avoidance of negative publicity rather on maximizing the fund's value. Additionally, the labor market for some trustees is the political market, engendering a motivation that can worsen agency problems rather than serve as a control mechanism, as trustees may use the fund's assets to win the favor of certain constituency groups. In such situations the use of self-motivated member trustees may be needed. This solution will work better for civil service pension plans than for national schemes, because the member trustee will have a closer bond to the plan (as argued in Besley and Prat [2002]).

Implications for Governance

The above analysis demonstrates the importance of involving the residual claimant in monitoring and control, and its value in reducing the inefficiency caused by the separation of decision-making from risk-bearing. For example, consider the decision of whether or not to allocate assets to economically targeted investments, which may or may not have similar risk-return characteristics to other investment options: In the case of a DB plan, where there is no chance of raising participant contribution rates or lowering benefits, the taxpayers are the sole residual claimants and their representatives on the board (government officials) bear the risk. In such a situation, the decision-making would be efficient if there were sufficient incentives for the board to perform its job appropriately.

The challenge facing public pension fund managers is how to create the appropriate controls and incentives for trustees. To determine which governance mechanisms are appropriate, it is necessary to identify for which behaviors the trustees would be rewarded or punished. Recalling some of the agency relationship characteristics identified by Eisenhardt (1989), we see that there are problems with using outcome controls. Most indicators point toward the use of behavioral controls. A key governance characteristic is outcome uncertainty. Many factors beyond the control of trustees can affect the performance of a fund; for example, limited local investments or short-term economic downturns can greatly affect performance. Likewise, there is a problem with the measurability of the outcome. Should the trustees be judged against a standard of short-term returns or consistent long-term performance? It is as difficult to make an interim judgment of performance toward a long-term goal as it is to accurately assess the worth of an investment decision based on the achievement of short-term goals. Furthermore, it is difficult to determine the contribution of any single trustee toward the accomplishment of a goal, and this creates the potential for a free-rider problem.

To the extent that there is goal conflict between the agent and principal (for example, whether to invest the fund's assets for value maximization or invest them to achieve other social goals), there also is a need for behavioral controls. This is especially true for public pensions, as decisions to invest in ETIs may not significantly affect investment performance until years in the future, and possibly after the trustees supporting the initiative are no longer on the board. Likewise, decisions on actuarial assumptions or benefits may produce little change in the short run while creating significant long-term costs.

All of these factors support the use of behavioral rather than outcome controls for trustees. These potential controls are discussed in the next section. First, however, there is a discussion of the limitations of external controls. The corporate governance system relies heavily on external controls, but no such controls are available for the governance of public pensions. This further demonstrates the importance of a governing board to public pensions.

External Controls

There are three types of external controls for corporations: the product market, the market for corporate control, and large shareholders. Should managerial agency problems reach the point where they significantly harm performance, a corporation may go bankrupt (fail in the product market) or be taken over by another organization (fail in the market for corporate control).

These external controls are available neither for national public pension plans nor for civil service plans. In a centralized system, participants are unable either to shift their assets from one plan to another or to withdraw their assets from the plan. There is thus no equivalent of a product market. For civil service plans, the quality of those plans may have an effect on employee recruitment and retention, and failure to recruit employees may arguably be seen as equivalent to failure in the product market. However, in matters of finance, money is provided for a future payment and it is difficult for an outsider—in the case of a public pension plan, the plan participants—to determine if there is a problem with the use of those funds. This is in contrast to a consumer product purchase, where the consumer can typically and readily ascertain if there is a problem (Caprio and Levine 2002). This problem increases where there is inadequate disclosure, because in such cases the portfolio composition of pension funds can easily be altered without the knowledge of the fund's stakeholders. There thus are significant limits on the capability of the participant labor market to discipline management of the pension fund.

Nor is there a market for corporate control, as the plan participants do not have an ownership interest that can be traded on a secondary market. In addition, the fact that ownership interests are nontransferable means that other mechanisms of the corporate world, such as managerial ownership and equity incentives, are also not available (Mayers et al. 1997). Finally, because everyone's ownership interests are essentially equal, there is no possibility of a single shareholder emerging with an incentive to monitor the organization's performance. A group may serve this role—for example, a labor union may represent the interests of its membership with respect to the pension fund—but different unions within the general taxpayer population may have disagreements on how the fund should be managed. This is in contrast to the corporate situation in which shareholders can be assumed to have the same interest (increased share value).

In situations where external controls are not available, agency theory predicts a greater emphasis on the board as monitor. In other words, the various control technologies can substitute for one another. For corporations, this means that where a market for corporate control is not available greater emphasis will fall on the outside directors on the board. Mayers et al. (1997) supported this substitution hypothesis in a study of mutual and stock insurance companies. In mutuals, ownership rights are connected with customer insurance policies and therefore are nontransferable. In stock companies, ownership rights are not connected with policies and are freely transferable. Compared to stock insurance companies, mutuals are significantly more likely to have either a majority of outside directors on the board or a majority of outsiders on standing committees. The presence of outsiders also reduces management's consumption of perquisites, such as salary, while other costs that do not involve a conflict between management and owners are not significantly different.

Implications for the Governing Body of Public Pension Plans

Public pension funds thus clearly need a strong governing body. Compared to corporations, for which there are available a variety of external and internal control mechanisms, for public pensions the board is essentially the only available control. The following sections provide an initial analysis of the issues that should be addressed when creating a board that has the appropriate incentives to be an effective monitor and manager of a fund. Using Eisenhardt's terminology, these are mostly behavioral rather than outcome controls.

Board Composition

The trustees of U.S. civil service plans generally fall into one of three categories: they are elected by plan participants, appointed by the government, or serve as ex officio members. Trustees may be elected by either active employees or retired plan members, and they themselves may be active or retired members. Appointments are typically made by a chief elected official such as the governor or mayor or by a governing body such as a legislative committee, and often are made to provide representation for stakeholder groups in cases where beneficiary groups are not allowed to directly elect their own representatives. Ex officio trustees will serve on the board by virtue of their holding a particular public office, such as that of state treasurer or controller.

As discussed earlier, corporations have both inside directors and outside directors. Inside directors are also managers of the corporation in question, and can be either the source of moral hazard or lack the incentives to control moral hazard problems originating with the CEO. For public pensions, moral hazard problems (or goal conflicts with plan participants) typically are rooted with those trustees that also are government officials or that are appointed by government officials. A government may be able to bypass the board to use a fund's assets for other social or political goals (Iglesias and Palacios 2000), but it also may be able to achieve the same result if the board is dominated by trustees sympathetic or otherwise allied to it. Government-affiliated trustees are effectively the equivalent of corporate insider trustees.

Member trustees that are elected by plan members are not subject to the same political pressures as ex officio and appointed trustees. In this sense, their political independence makes them analogous to independent, outside directors on corporate boards. Just as outside directors theoretically are able to focus on shareholder interests without undue influence from corporate insiders, so too are member-elected trustees able to focus on beneficiary interests without undue political interference. They may also serve to monitor politically affiliated trustees. Trustees appointed by the government to represent specific stakeholder groups also may fall into this category, depending on how they came to be selected for appointment.

The composition of the board for a national pension plan is likely to differ from that of a board for a civil service plan. In the United States, for example, there are hundreds of state and local pension plans for civil servants, including those for teachers, judges, police, and firefighters. In such cases, plan members may be able to usefully elect their own representative. For national schemes, however, the election of trustees may not be feasible and may actually undermine the pension fund's goals (Palacios 2002). Instead, national schemes often have a tripartite board, with board members nominated to represent unions, employers, and government.

Analysis of a data set of more than 200 state and local U.S. civil service plans in the 1990s showed the composition of trustees on the average board to be approximately two-thirds with political affiliations and one-third elected by plan members. On average, almost one-half of the trustees were appointed by government official or committee and one-third were not members of that pension plan. The size of the board averaged 8.5 trustees, with a range of 3 to 32 trustees.

For our sample of 26 public pension funds, the number of trustees on the board averaged 12, with a range of 3 to 29 (see Table 2.3). The average proportion of ex officio trustees on the board was just less than 20 percent, and 70 percent of trustees were appointed. In 10 of the 26 plans, the entire board consisted of government-appointed members. Only eight of the 26 respondent funds had at least one trustee that was elected to the board. Instead of elected members, it was not uncommon for government-appointed trustees to represent trade unions or other employee associations: approximately 25 percent of board members represented trade unions or other employee associations and less than 15 percent represented employers. Approximately 40 percent of the board therefore could be classified as "outside" directors under the corporation analogy, as they are potentially independent of the government. This is approximately the same percentage as for U.S. state and local pension plans. However, while these trustees are appointed to represent different stakeholder groups, government influence may impact their ability to act as an independent monitor.

A final issue with respect to trustees that act as representatives of different groups is the expertise of those trustees. Only 62 percent of the

Table 2.3: Board Composition (fraction of board)

	N	Minimum	Maximum	Mean	Median
How selected to board:					
Ex officio	26	0.00	0.85	0.1850	0.0000
Appointed	26	0.09	1.00	0.7044	0.8167
Elected	26	0.00	0.91	0.1407	0.0000
Trustees representing specific groups:					
Trade unions	25	0.00	0.62	0.1844	0.2000
Employers' association	25	0.00	0.38	0.1291	0.0000
Other employees' association	25	0.00	0.38	0.0885	0.0000
Government as plan sponsor	25	0.00	1.00	0.3104	0.2500

funds surveyed indicated that they had at least one expert or professional member on the board, but among these funds on average 47 percent of trustees were identified as experts. One fund indicated that all of its four trustees were experts.

Nomination and Termination

An independent and vigilant board requires trustees that are not subject to political influence and that are free to exercise their independent judgment. These are the reasons behind the strong push toward corporate governance for boards dominated by outside directors. It is feasible for the participants of smaller civil service pension plans to directly elect some outside trustees, but for national schemes this may not be possible. Instead, the government may appoint trustees to represent stakeholder groups or to bring independent expertise to the board. The government's involvement in such appointments inevitably raises the concern that the trustees selected will be biased toward the government's policy goals and therefore will not be truly independent, however.

The equivalent situation on a corporate board would be that of the CEO selecting outside directors; should this occur, these directors at a minimum could be expected to be sympathetic to the CEO's views and therefore to be incapable of providing independent monitoring (Zajac and Westphal 1996;

Main et al. 1995). The corporate governance solution to this problem has been to establish a nominating committee comprised entirely of independent directors. While the CEO will still have some influence in selecting new directors, it will be minimized. It is also recommended that the committee have fixed criteria for the selection of new directors, to ensure that the directors are qualified and to provide another control against favoritism in the selection process. Some public pension funds are experimenting with similar mechanisms.

The Canadian Pension Plan Investment Board (CPPIB) provides one example of how a pension fund is attempting to depoliticize the nomination of public pension plan governors (MacNaughton 2001). For the CPPIB, the federal finance minister and the finance ministers of the nine participating provinces appointed a nominating committee. Each government nominated one committee member, and the federal finance minister chose a private sector CEO as chair. For trustees, the committee identifies a set of qualified (as previously defined) prospective candidates from across Canada, referring this set to the federal finance minister. The federal finance minister then consults with his provincial counterparts on the proposed names before making final selection from the list recommended by the committee.

In New Zealand, the Minister of Finance appoints a committee to nominate potential trustees of the New Zealand Superannuation Fund. At least four members of the nominating committee must have work experience qualifying them as investment professionals. The Minister of Finance must then consult with parliament before recommending the nominees to the Governor General for appointment (Palacios 2002). The board is only responsible for investments, however: should this model be applied to a board that has control also over such matters as benefits, there are additional concerns that first should be taken into consideration.

It is also important that there be set procedures for the removal of trustees, to permit the fair removal of those that abuse their position while preventing the arbitrary removal of those who are performing their job. Trustees that are not subject to arbitrary termination are more likely to exercise independent judgment and less likely to bow to outside pressures (Carmichael 2002). The termination of a trustee should be fully disclosed to all interested stakeholders and should be made in accordance with predetermined processes and conditions of termination. The CPPIB appoints trustees on the basis of three-year terms, renewable three times, and no director may be removed from the board during his or her term in office for any reason other than illegal or immoral conduct. In New Zealand, by contrast, the Minister of Finance may remove any board member for any reason that the minister deems appropriate (Palacios 2002). In our sample of pension funds, only one-third of the funds surveyed had written criteria establishing acceptable causes for dismissal.

Accountability

The governing body should have a clear understanding of to whom they are accountable. In corporations, it is clearly understood that the board is accountable to the shareholders. For public pension funds, in contrast, there can be ambiguity on the issue of accountability. There are two possible groups of residual claimants, taxpayers and plan participants, and trustees may view themselves as being accountable to one or both of these stakeholder groups. They also may see themselves as being accountable to the political administration in power. In the United States, law mandates that private pension plans be managed solely in the best interests of the plan participants, and the trustees thus are accountable only to those participants. In some countries the same applies to public pension funds. For example, the Canada Pension Plan Investment Board Act directs the board "to manage any amounts that are transferred to it…in the best interests of the contributors and beneficiaries under that Act; and to invest its assets with a view to achieving a maximum rate of return, without undue risk of loss, having regard to the factors that may affect the funding of the Canada Pension Plan and the ability of the Canada Pension Plan to meet its financial obligations" (Palacios 2002).

Establishing a clear understanding of to whom the board is accountable is important for several reasons. A recent empirical study on the application of agency theory to nonprofit boards of directors in the United States reveals some of these reasons (Miller 2002). First, for nonprofit organizations, there are no clear owners. Certain parties make donations to the organization, and some suggest that those parties may serve as monitors of the board (Fama and Jensen 1983b), but they are not generally considered to "own" the organization. In addition, there is no residual claimant: instead, the board has a more general accountability to society. In her study, Miller found that some boards were able to articulate an "ownership" group—typically arising through the organization's perceived accountability to the community—while other boards only stated a general accountability to the board itself, founded in a responsibility to maintain the organization as a going concern.

For those boards that could articulate an ownership-like group, the trustees were able to meaningfully discuss the interests and expectations of that group. These board members recognized a clear mission for the organization and were able to keep their focus on that mission. By contrast, those boards that viewed themselves as only accountable to themselves were seen as less capable of fulfilling their oversight roles. While the board members recognized a fiduciary responsibility to the organization and the management of its finances, they did not know how to work toward these goals. Miller stated that for such boards, their "objectives for monitoring lack specificity." In addition, she found that board members would use the rhetoric of fulfilling fiduciary duties, but they usually uncritically accepted all of the information that was provided to them by management staff. These boards did not believe that they could change the organization's behavior and were less vigilant than the boards with an identified ownership group.

Boards thus need to have a clear and specific statement citing to whom they are accountable. Many pension funds have already identified this group as the plan participants, or have had this group identified for them by statute or regulation. If this "ownership" group is to be expanded, those other stakeholder groups that are to be included must be specified. Without a clear understanding of to whom it is accountable, the board is likely to be ineffective in monitoring or managing the fund.

Performance Measures

Related to accountability is the issue of how a board measures its performance. For corporations, performance can easily be measured by share value or return on investment. For public pension funds, however, the board could base its performance on funding levels, the size of investment return, achieving a set investment return target, reducing administrative costs, or some other measure (or any combination of these measures). Similar to the issue of identifying an ownership group, failure to specify a performance goal can lead to a less vigilant board of trustees. Miller's study of nonprofit organizations is again instructive on this issue.

For nonprofits, there is no widely accepted clear measure of performance. In her study, Miller found that some boards had developed a consensus on clear performance goals in such areas as budgetary issues, recruitment of donors, and the success of community service programs. Other boards, however, could not articulate a set of performance goals. For the boards with performance goals, the members had a better understanding of the information they needed to perform their oversight role and of how to use that information. For the boards that were unable to articulate performance goals, the members typically monitored them based on their personal skills. For example, board members who were lawyers in their professional lives considered the legal issues and accountant members considered the financial issues. These members gathered information they needed to fulfill these limited roles but had little knowledge of the performance of the organization outside these areas. In some cases, and even though they believed that they were fully informed, the trustees were not even aware of the programs operated by the organization. They were unaware of these programs because they did not involve issues related to their particular expertise. These members clearly lacked the necessary information to meaningfully monitor the organization, and their actions in addition did not focus on achieving any specific goal. As Miller stated, the focus of the board's actions were "primarily on form, not on substance." For the boards with criteria for measuring performance, however, a comprehensive strategic plan aimed at achieving those goals was easily developed.

Roles of the Board

The board may have control over a wide variety of decisions with respect to the fund, including the setting of actuarial assumptions, investment of fund assets, setting of benefits, and other decisions that relate to the management of the fund. In this sense, the governing board of a pension fund is more involved in the running of the organization than is a corporate board of directors. Where a corporate board may assist in the general setting of strategy, it serves mostly to provide advice to management and to monitor management's behavior on behalf of shareholders. In public pension funds, the board typically takes on an active management role, including delegation to professional managers, in addition to monitoring the pension fund staff.

In the United States, the board typically has authority over investment decisions. For example, a sample of state and local pension funds in 1998 showed 88 percent of funds to have investment authority. For the remaining 12 percent, investment decisions were most likely made by a state investment board that is separate from the board of trustees. The board also usu-ally had control over actuarial assumptions and benefits decisions (89 and 68 percent, respectively). The funds in our international survey showed a similar use of authority. The responses indicated that for 92 percent of the funds the board has authority over investments and for 77 percent it has authority over actuarial assumptions. In addition, 73 percent of the boards have authority over the selection of managers of fund activities.

One of the key roles of the board is to develop an investment strategy that maximizes returns at a risk level tolerable to the fund's stakeholders and that provides sufficient liquidity to meet benefit payment requirements (Mitchell 2002). To establish a strategy that is right for the fund, the board must decide how to allocate its assets and who will manage the funds: should it outsource to a private firm or employ the fund's own staff to conduct investments? The asset allocation decision involves many different factors, including the division between equities and fixed income investments, the level of diversification, the sectors of the economy in which to invest, whether or not to invest outside the borders of the country, and so on.

With respect to the use of investment managers, approximately 75 per-cent of U.S. state and local plans used external managers for all fund assets. From the international sample, only one fund of the 25 funds that responded to the question reported using external managers for all assets. The average fund used external managers for just 13 percent of its portfolio, but more than 50 percent of funds did not outsource any assets at all. Of those funds using external asset managers, less than 40 percent had explicit, written criteria for selecting managers. This creates the possibility of trustees grant-ing asset manager awards based on political or personal preference, rather than on criteria that would identify managers most likely to act in the best interests of the plan participants. Overall, this evidence suggests that boards are keeping significant control over their fund's assets.

Some pension funds seek independence from political interference through the structure of their pension system and the assignment of differ-ent roles to different trustees. In Canada there are two separate entities, the Canada Pension Plan (CPP) and the CPP Investment Board (CPPIB), and two separate governing bodies. The CPP is the exclusive responsibility of the federal and provincial governments. These governments design, admin-ister, and set policies for the plan for tasks such as the paying of benefits and the collection of contributions. The CPPIB is a separate organization that serves only to invest the funds of the CPP. Additionally, the CPPIB is governed independently of government by professional managers and its own board of directors.

The boards of corporations often divide their work and assign primary responsibility for that work to separate committees, according to the different roles of each. Due to concerns over agency problems, it is recommended that key oversight committees, such as the compensation committee and the audit committee, be staffed by independent directors. For example, a compensation committee staffed by insiders may establish a CEO compensation and incentive plan that is overly generous; outside directors are more likely to exercise independent judgment and reduce such abuses. The boards of pension funds also use committees, but these are not as widespread as in the corporate world. For example, while all corporations are required to have an audit committee, less than half of the funds (45 percent) in our international sample used an audit committee. Sixty-four percent had an investment committee and 21 percent a governance committee. Governance committees are fairly new in corporate governance. While boards have typically had a nominating committee to assist the nomination of directors, more firms are switching to governance committees to which they can defer additional responsibilities, such as the establishment of board meeting agendas, adoption of guidelines for governance practices, selection of directors to serve on committees, and so on. In spite of the fact that only a few pension plans in our sample had governance committees, it is encouraging that pension managers are recognizing the importance of boards and are establishing proper board practices.

Standards of Behavior

Corporate boards of directors are subject to fiduciary duties, and failure to comply with those duties can result in legal liability. In the United States, private pension plans are subject to the strict fiduciary requirements of the Employee Retirement Income Security Act (ERISA) statute. ERISA's "exclusive benefit" (duty of loyalty) and "prudent person" (duty of care) rules require trustees to make sound, well-planned investment choices for the sole benefit of plan participants. For example, some have argued that it would be a breach of fiduciary duty for a private plan trustee to take into consideration certain social or community benefits when making investment decisions, because as a consequence such a decision could not be for the "exclusive benefit" of plan participants.

Even though U.S. public pension plan trustees are not subject to ERISA, some commentators have argued that the common law of trusts establishes a fiduciary duty that is not significantly different from the ERISA standard (Romano 1993). In addition, many public pension plans are required by state law or internal policy to operate under the "prudent person" rule, which is a duty of care to act as a reasonably prudent person who is familiar with these matters in managing the investments of the fund. In the U.S. state and local sample, more than 90 percent of the funds operated under such a rule.

A key incentive to follow these standards is the existence of legal liability for actions that do not meet the standards. For example, the prudent person standard would likely not be met if a trustee made a significant investment decision without making the effort to first become reasonably informed about the decision. The trustee in such a situation could be legally liable for damages resulting from that breach of duty. More likely, however, is that pension fund trustees, like corporate directors, will be indemnified by the organization for any liability resulting from acts taken in good faith. In our international sample, the responses indicated that one-third of the funds did not maintain personal liability for trustees. For the other two-thirds of the funds, there is no legal liability. The consequence is that there is less incentive for the trustees to be vigilant in the performance of their duties.

Another tool with which to control the behavior of boards is a code of ethics (or conduct). During the 1980s and 1990s the maintenance of a code of ethics became standard practice for corporations, and more than 90 percent of large corporations now have such codes (Adams et al. 2001). Codes of ethics similarly have become increasingly common among public pension funds. Among the sample of U.S. state and local pension plans, the number of plans that used a code of ethics increased from 50 percent to 70 percent in the period 1992 to 1998.

Codes of ethics are expected to improve the performance of public pension funds. For trustees, the code cover such issues as conflicts of interest and the acceptance of gratuities. It should provide guidance to trustees and instruct them to avoid practices, such as the hiring of money managers based on favoritism, that may adversely affect plan members. Through such provisions it should guide trustees toward decisions based on prudence rather than personal gain, and this in turn should lead to better overall performance for the pension fund. Similar to the prudent person standard, a code of ethics should act as a control on agency problems. From the international sample, 52 percent of the funds have a code of conduct, 48 percent have conflict-of-interest rules, and 65 percent have one or the other. In New Zealand, trustees follow a code of conduct and are required to disclose any conflicts of interest they may have (Palacios 2002).

Information and Transparency

Information is an important and necessary part of behavioral controls. The trustees need information to perform their job with vigilance and the key stakeholder groups need information to hold the trustees accountable. As Eisenhardt (1989) stated, an agency perspective allows us to see that information is a commodity that can be purchased. Information should be provided up to the point where the marginal benefit of the information disclosure exceeds or equals the marginal cost of producing the information. As administrative costs can be significant in public pension plans, this is important. The information disclosed also should include explicit statements on the issues surrounding performance measures and accountability.

Information can come from many sources and pertain to many different items. Two key pieces of information are audits and annual reports. Audits provide the board with the information they need to perform their job appropriately and provide the public with the information they need to evaluate the financial health of the plan. Seventy percent of the funds in our sample produce an independent external audit on a regular basis. Likewise, annual reports provide the public with information on the actions of the board and the performance of the fund. All but one of the funds included in the sample indicated that they produce an annual report, and approximately half of the funds produce quarterly reports. In addition, 61 percent use an investment performance assessment.

To be useful, this information must of course be complete and accurate. In the United States, corporate securities laws dictate that management disclose all "material" information to shareholders and hold management liable for producing false information. In the context of corporate law, material information is that which a reasonable investor would consider important when making an investment decision. By law or policy, the board should specify what information is "material" for the stakeholders of the public pension fund. This should ensure that the disclosures provided by most pension funds do not omit any information that stakeholders would find useful.

Other relevant information includes the investment policies of the pension fund (63 percent of the funds in the international sample produce a written investment policy). Such policies provide the board both with guidance and possibly with performance goals. In our sample, the following items were included in the investment policy: short-term target rates of return (32 percent); long-term target rates of return (59 percent); quantified asset allocation guidelines (57 percent); and target measures of risk or volatility of returns (80 percent).

Included in the investment policy should also be a statement on the use of fund assets for social goals. As noted by Iglesias and Palacios (2002), most funds do not have established criteria for social investments. In some cases, the fund is prevented by law from investing in any way other than that which maximizes profit. For funds without such restrictions, there should be established criteria for when goals other than those pertaining to the maximizing of value can be taken into consideration. For example, many have pointed out the potential distortion that large pension funds could cause to smaller capital markets. Funds could include in their policy the explicit identification of situations where such social and local economic issues should be taken into consideration.

Conclusion

Agency theory has been useful for understanding and improving the governance of corporations. Likewise, it should be useful for improving the governance of public pension funds. However, just as there is not a one-size-fits-all governance structure for corporations throughout the world, or even within a single country, there is no single governance structure that can be universally applied to public pension funds. Different goals, restrictions, political environments, and local market conditions; the availability of competent asset managers; and many other factors will affect the appropriate governance structure for any pension fund, but it is important that the board recognize potential agency problems—whether they are based on uncertainty or on potential goal conflicts—and then utilize the appropriate governance control mechanisms.

Different asset allocations will require different governance practices, for example. Using our survey results, we compared those funds that allocate more than 10 percent of their assets to equities with the funds that do not. The funds with more 10 percent of their portfolio in equities were more likely to provide their trustees with written conflict-of-interest rules. In addition, these funds operated more transparently: they were more likely to have written disclosure rules and more likely to regularly produce independent external audits and actuarial reports.

These differences suggest that funds recognize the potential for agency problems when investing in equities and the need for governance mechanisms to prevent these problems. For example, with equity investments there is a greater chance that trustees may purchase securities from individuals or businesses with which they have financial or political ties. In response, pension funds may adopt conflict-of-interest rules to mitigate this problem. Such rules would be not as necessary if the funds could be invested more heavily in government bonds. Interestingly, the funds with more equity investments had significantly fewer elected trustees. One possible explanation for this finding is that such funds favor the appointment of trustees as a means of ensuring that the board has the expertise necessary to invest in equities.

Overall, developing an understanding of agency theory and the various mechanisms that can control the agency problems that potentially exist in public pensions would enable pension fund sponsors to adopt the optimal governance tools at the lowest administrative cost.

References

Adams, Janet S., Armen Tashchian, and Ted H. Stone. 2001. "Codes of Ethics as Signals of Ethical Behavior." *Journal of Business Ethics* 29(3):199–211.

American Law Institute. 1995. *Principles of Corporate Governance*. St. Paul, Minnesota: American Law Institute Publishers.

Becht, Marco, Patrick Bolton, and Alisa Röell. 2002. "Corporate Governance and Control." NBER (National Bureau of Economic Research) Working Paper 9371. Cambridge, Massachusetts: NBER.

Besley, Timothy, and Andrea Prat. 2002. "Pension Fund Governance and the Choice Between Defined Benefit and Defined Contribution Plans." London School of Economics. Processed.

Bhagat, Sanjai, and Bernard Black. 1999. "The Uncertain Relationship between Board Composition and Firm Performance." *Business Lawyer* 54:921–963.

2

Brinson, Gary P., L. Randolph Hood, and Gilbert L. Beebower. 1986. "Determinants of Portfolio Performance." *Financial Analysts Journal* 42:39–44.

Brinson, Gary P., Brian D. Singer, and Gilbert L. Beebower. 1991. "Determinants of Portfolio Performance II: An Update." *Financial Analysts Journal* 47:40–48.

Caprio, Jr., Gerard, and Ross Levine. 2002. "Corporate Governance in Finance: Concepts and International Observations." Paper presented at the 2002 World Bank, IMF, and Brookings Institution Conference, Building the Pillars of Financial Sector Governance: The Roles of Public and Private Sectors.

Carmichael, Jeffrey. 2002. "Building the Pillars of Financial Sector Governance: The Roles of the Public and Private Sectors." Paper presented at the 2002 World Bank, IMF, and Brookings Institution Conference, Building the Pillars of Financial Sector Governance: The Roles of Public and Private Sectors.

Chia, Ngee Choon, and Albert K. C. Tsui. 2003. "Life Annuities of Compulsory Savings and Income Adequacy of the Elderly in Singapore." *Journal of Pension Economic and Finance* 2(1): 41-65.

Davis, Gerald F., and Michael Useem. 2000. "Top Management, Company Directors, and Corporate Control." In Andrew Pettigrew, Howard Thomas, and Richard Whittington (eds.): *Handbook of Strategy and Management*. London: Sage.

Dei, Henry. 2001. "Public Pension Fund Management in Ghana." Paper presented at the 2001 World Bank Public Pension Fund Management Conference. Available online at www.worldbank.org/finance.

Eisenhardt, Kathleen M. 1989. "Agency Theory: An Assessment and Review." *Academy of Management Review* 14(1):57–74

Fama, Eugene F. 1980. "Agency Problems and the Theory of the Firm." *Journal of Public Economics* 88(2):288–307.

Fama, Eugene F., and Michael C. Jensen. 1983a. "Agency Problems and Residual Claims." *Journal of Law and Economics* 26(2):327–49.

———. 1983b. "Separation of Ownership and Control." *Journal of Law and Economics* 26(2):301–25.

GAO (United States Government Accounting Office). 1995. "Public Pension Plans: Evaluation of Economically Targeted Investment Programs." GAO/PEMD 95–13.

2

Iglesias, Augusto, and Robert J. Palacios. 2000. "Managing Public Pension Reserves. Part I: Evidence from the International Experience." Social Protection Discussion Paper 3. Washington, D.C.: World Bank.

Jensen, Michael C., and William H. Meckling. 1976. "Theory of the Firm: Managerial Behavior, Agency Costs, and Ownership Structure." *Journal of Financial Economics* 3:305–60.

Levinthal, Daniel. 1988. "A Survey of Agency Models of Organization." *Journal of Economic Behavior and Organization* 9:153–185.

Lin, Laura. 1996. "The Effectiveness of Outside Directors as a Corporate Governance Mechanism: Theories and Evidence." *Northwestern Law Review* 90:898–976.

Lorsch, Jay W., and Elizabeth MacIver. 1989. *Pawns or Potentates: The Reality of America's Corporate Boards*. Boston, Massachusetts: Harvard Business School Press.

MacNaughton, John. 2001. "Principles and Practices of Governance for Public Pension Funds." Paper presented at the 2001 World Bank Public Pension Fund Management conference. Available online at www.world-bank.org/finance.

Main, Brian G. M., Charles A. O'Reilly III, and James Wade. 1995. "The CEO, the Board of Directors, and Executive Compensation: Economic and Psychological Perspectives." *Industrial and Corporate Change* 4:293–332.

Mayers, David, Anil Shivdasani, and Clifford W. Smith, Jr. 1997. "Board Composition and Corporate Control: Evidence from the Insurance Industry." *Journal of Business* 70(1):33–62.

Miller, Judith L. 2002. "The Board as a Monitor of Organizational Activity: The Applicability of Agency Theory to Nonprofit Boards." *Nonprofit Management and Leadership* 12(4): 429–450.

Mitchell, Olivia S. 2002. Redesigning Public Sector Pensions in Developing Countries." Pension Research Council Working Paper 2002–9. University of Pennsylvania.

Murphy, Kevin J., and Karen Van Nuys. 1994. "Governance, Behavior, and Performance of State and Corporate Pension Funds." Working Paper: Harvard University.

Nofsinger, John R. 1998. "Why Targeted Investing Does Not Make Sense!" *Financial Management* 27(3):87–96.

Palacios, Robert J. 2002. "Managing Public Pension Reserves Part II: Lessons from Five Recent OECD Initiatives." Social Protection Discussion Paper 219. Washington, D.C.: World Bank.

Romano, Roberta. 1993. "Public Pension Fund Activism in Corporate Governance Reconsidered." *Columbia Law Review* 93:795–853.

———. 1995. "The Politics of Public Pension Funds." *The Public Interest* 119: 42–53.

———. 2001. "Less is More: Making Institutional Investor Activism a Valuable Mechanism of Corporate Governance." *Yale Journal on Regulation* 18: 174–251.

Shivdasani, Anil, and David Yermack. 1999. "CEO Involvement in the Selection of New Board Members: An Empirical Analysis." *Journal of Financial Economics* 54:1,829–1,853.

Shleifer, Andrei, and Robert W. Vishny. 1997. "A Survey of Corporate Governance." *Journal of Finance* 52(2):737–783.

Singh, H., and F. Harianto. 1989. "Management-Board Relationships, Takeover Risk, and the Adoption of Golden Parachutes." *Academy of Management Journal* 32:7–24.

Stevenson, Richard W. 1992. "Pension Funds Becoming a Tool for Growth." *New York Times*, March 17, 1992, at D1.

Vise, David A. 1992. "A Billion-Dollar Battle over Pension Plans' Purpose." *The Washington Post*, December 6, 1992, at H1.

Wade, James, Charles A. O'Reilly, III, and Ike Chandratat. 1990. "Golden Parachutes: CEOs, and the Exercise of Social Influence." *Administrative Science Quarterly* 35:587–603.

Walsh, Mary Williams. 2002. "CalPERS Wears a Party, or Union, Label." *New York Times*, October 13, 2002.

Watson, Ronald D. 1994. "Does Targeted Investing Make Sense?" *Financial Management* 23:69–74.

Westphal, James D., and Edward J. Zajac. 1995. "Who Shall Govern? CEO/Board Power, Demographic Similarity, and New Director Selection." *Administrative Science Quarterly* 40:60–83.

Zajac, Edward J., and James D. Westphal. 1996. "Director Reputation, CEO–Board Power, and the Dynamics of Board Interlocks." *Administrative Science Quarterly* 41:507–529.

Notes

1. The questionnaire used for this survey can be found in the working paper version of this paper at econ.worldbank.org.
2. This analysis—and later discussions of U.S. state and local pension plans—uses survey-based data collected by the Government Finance Officers Association from 1990 to 2000. This data set is commonly referred to as "Pendat."

2

Chapter 3

Transparency and Accountability of Public Pension Funds

Anne Maher

The collapse last year of Enron, WorldCom, and Andersens appalled investors all over the world. Millions of people saw their savings and pensions vanish. While these highest-profile failures were all located in the United States, many other countries had their share of similar, if smaller, collapses. Structures, standards, and regulations can never be a complete defense against individuals determined to do wrong, nor can they wholly protect against a culture of corporate greed and loose ethics. They are nonetheless our best assurance that savers, investors, and employees are protected from problems of this kind.

Several countries consequently have introduced new legislation and regulation affecting accounting and corporate disclosure and governance. For example, in July 2002, U.S. President George W. Bush signed in to law the Sarbanes-Oxley Act, which has the stated purpose of protecting U.S. investors by improving the accuracy and reliability of corporate disclosures made pursuant to U.S. federal securities laws. In the United Kingdom reforms have been proposed following reports by Derek Higgs and Sir Robert Smith and following a review of the regulatory regime of the accountancy profession. The reforms are intended to raise standards of corporate governance, to strengthen the accountancy and audit professions, and to provide for a more effective system of regulation of the accountancy profession.

Also in July 2002, the Organization for Economic Cooperation and Development (OECD) published its Guidelines for Pension Fund Governance. The guidelines were developed as part of an OECD project on financial governance and draw inspiration from the existing OECD Principles of Corporate Governance. The adoption of an EU Pensions Directive to harmonize the activities of institutions for occupational retirement provision additionally is imminent. A primary aim of the first EU Pensions Directive is to ensure the security of pensions, and one of its main requirements is the provision of comprehensive information to pension fund members and beneficiaries. National pension regulators and supervisors also all have some level of focus on accountability and disclosure in their requirements for private pension funds.

In the United Kingdom, the Myners Review on Improving Institutional Investing included recommendations on benchmarking and transparency. The author of the review, Myners (The Myners Review), recommended that the trustees of pensions schemes should regularly inform stakeholders about the investment principles and strategic plans of pension schemes and of performance relative to the plan—specifically to include explanation of any departure from the principles and the plan. He also recommends the requirement for an internal information system that would relate investment results to the accountabilities for those results, including the contributions the trustees themselves are making.

This increased focus on compliance—and in particular on accountability and transparency—in relation to corporate entities and private pension funds must also have an impact for public pension funds. Many of the issues are similar, as is the potential for problems.

Relevance

Accountability is an essential part of good governance: without accountability, governance cannot be monitored or improved. Good governance in effect is a function of the responsibilities and accountabilities of key players in relation to the entity.

The need for transparency and accountability in the management of public funds is self-evident. If public funds do not have the confidence and support of those for whom they are established they are unlikely to succeed. Public awareness of and interest in the fund is probably the best discipline for such funds, and where there is transparency and accountability, this will in itself create a demand for good overall governance.

Research has been done to examine possible links between different aspects of public pension fund governance on public pension performance. Whilst there are some differences in the results these would seem to suggest that governance has a significant impact on public pension performance and that inconsistent performance is associated with indicators of poor governance.[1] As accountability is an essential of good governance it would therefore appear to have a clear link with performance.

An examination of the drivers of organizational performance furthermore found that in private pension funds organizational performance is strongly correlated with certain governance indicators, of which one is the presence of mechanisms to communicate with plan stakeholders.[1]

Key Components

The Key Components

The first requirement for accountability is that there must be a focus of liability on a governing body or person that is in turn accountable to someone else. If responsibility is not clearly imposed there is no scope for clear accountability, and the result is likely to be confused decision-making.

The governing body or person must comply with good governance requirements in the running of its own entity as well as in its running of the public pension fund. For instance, if the governing body is a corporate entity it must comply with the accounting and other requirements that apply to a corporate entity of its kind.

Effective accounting and audit requirements serve two purposes: they monitor and confirm the financial dealings of the fund, and they serve as a channel of communication to the public of important financial information. The question of auditor independence in this area has become a key concern, and the United States, United Kingdom, and other countries consequently are bringing in new requirements in this area.

Effective custody is another important requirement for accountability. Fund assets must at all times be held in safe, independent custody as otherwise all of the other requirements will be worthless at the end of the day.

The requirements for public transparency and reporting to all stakeholders should be at the heart of any public pension fund. A public pension fund is made up of the public's money: it came directly or indirectly from the public and is intended to provide retirement income for them. The public need to know and understand what is happening to their money and what they can reasonably expect in the future. Public pension funds additionally can have a variety of other stakeholders and a high level of transparency and accountability also applies to these.

Finally, it is desirable that there should be independent oversight of a public pension fund. As well as providing a safeguard, this oversight helps to create and maintain public confidence in the management of the fund.

Each of these key components is discussed in more detail below.

Focus of Liability

It is easy to identify the focus of liability for a private pension fund, and this is almost always confirmed by the national legislation under which the fund operates. It is less easy to establish a clear focus of liability for a public pension fund, because of the large number and sometimes high diversity of stakeholders involved. The most important stakeholders should be the current and prospective beneficiaries, although the interests of each of these groups of beneficiaries can differ. The government is also an important stakeholder in any public pension fund, because provision of retirement income systems is always either a direct or indirect government concern. The relationship between the various stakeholders should be clear—and in particular, the relationships between the governing body, the government, and the public.

It is important that the governing body or person have a clear focus of responsibility. Lack of such clarity will cause confusion, resulting in poor decision-making and consequent poor performance. Whether or not the responsibility should be personal is a matter of debate. It has been suggested that personal liability of truly independent governors should be established.[2] Others suggest that it may be sufficient to focus the liability on a corporate entity. However, most would agree that even if personal liability is not a feature there should at least be some form of personal accountability to an independent body.

A further difference between public and private funds is that public pension funds do not usually come within the scope of national pension supervisory authorities. The governing body however cannot be left in a vacuum, accountable to no one. As it is a public fund the ideal body to which it should be accountable is the public's representative body: parliament.

Good Governance of the Governing Body

The governing body must itself practice good governance as appropriate to its legal status. Ideally, it should also be independent, particularly from the political pressure that both directly and indirectly is one of the biggest threats to any public pension fund. Clear statutory independence, while not an absolute guarantee, is probably the best guarantee that the governing body can have. Sound appointment and removal procedures for governors or directors of the governing body are important. These should be transparent and open so that they inspire public confidence.

Conflict identification and management is also necessary: not only must there be no conflict in decision-making or influence but there also must be clearly seen to be no conflict. It is impossible to assure against conflict arising in relation to the assets, investment, or beneficiaries of the fund, and the important thing therefore is to have an open and transparent method of identifying conflicts and dealing with them when they arise. The objective of conflict identification and management is to prevent any actions being taken that are not in the interests of the beneficiaries.

The responsibilities and requirements for members of the governing body must be clear. They must understand what they are there to do in order that they be in a position to deal with their responsibilities in an efficient and effective way.

Clear mandates and objectives are also very important, in that it is hard to discharge accountability requirements or to measure their effectiveness if the original mandate and objective are not clear to all involved.

Effective Accounts and Audit

Accounts should be required at regular intervals, clearly defined to enable clear measurement and comparison. They should be prepared to the highest national accounting standards. It is a problem in many areas of global trade and markets that there is not yet widespread use of international accounting standards. This makes it difficult to get the best value from accounts and to make valid comparisons. Work is being done in this area and we are likely to

3

3

see some progress in the coming years. For the moment, probably the highest aspiration for public pension fund accounts is that they comply with best national accounting standards.

The accounts should have prescribed contents, ideally as a statutory requirement. This is particularly necessary in relation to the disclosure of specific fees and expenses that may have been incurred.

An internal auditing function is desirable but not essential. What is essential is that there must be an external audit provided by auditors who are truly independent. There should be a time frame for completion of this audit, which should be made at regular intervals to coincide with the timing of the accounts preparation and publication dates. The audit should adhere to highest national auditing standards. The audit should include an actuarial valuation of assets and liabilities, as appropriate, and this should again be done independently and to the highest national professional standards for actuaries.

At present, there are still differences of opinion between countries on the most appropriate auditing standards and the supervision and regulation of auditors. This means that there is no appropriate standard at this time other than the national standard in the relevant country.

I have heard some discussion on development of an international standard for accounting and auditing of public funds. This would be a useful development and I hope that it will be pursued by interested parties.

Effective Custody

Secure custody of fund assets is essential. The custodian must be external and should be independent of all parties connected with the fund. It should be independent and reputable and should be clearly seen to be so. There are a number of effective global custodians now operating and whether one global custodian or a number of separate custodians are used it is important that all relevant areas are covered for custody purposes.

Public Transparency and Reporting

Reports should be published at regular intervals, prescribed to enable presentation of a clear, comparable picture. The contents of the report should also be prescribed to ensure that all relevant information is included.

The publication of a regular report can be the basis of a formal reporting mechanism to whomever the governing body is accountable—preferably parliament. Presentation of the report to parliament should be made formally and should be supported by the requirement that parliament give it some level of consideration.

Such reports should be publicly promulgated; ideally, there should also be wide public awareness of the report and of its availability. There should be a clear mechanism for the public to seek and obtain the report and any other relevant information in relation to the Fund. This can be most appropriately done through the media and through the use of a website.

Where the fund has actual or potential beneficiaries there should be a requirement that these beneficiaries be given specific information on their entitlements, including statements of benefits expressed in clear, unambiguous terms.

Independent Oversight

External examination and verification of fund management and status is essential because of the public interest issue involved. At the minimum, this should take the form of an external audit, external actuarial valuations of assets and liabilities, and external verification of investment returns.

It furthermore is desirable that the government (or other party to whom the governing body is accountable) have the right to commission independent examinations of any area or aspect that is a cause of concern to the government or to the public. It is probably best that the scope for such an examination not be clearly defined, as this would introduce the danger of excluding an area that had not originally been envisaged as being of concern. The scope of the examination could perhaps be left instead to some form of "public interest" test.

Good Models: What They Do

Good Models

Levels of transparency and accountability vary greatly amongst public pension funds. This is, of course, influenced by the culture within which they operate. Three public funds that stand out as good models for transparency and accountability are the Canada Pension Plan, the Norwegian Government Petroleum Fund and the California Public Employees' Retirement System (CalPERS). It is not perhaps a coincidence that these three funds are also considered to be successful and good examples of public pension fund performance. This section looks at some of the key features of these plans.

Canada Pension Plan

An underlying principle of the Canada Pension Plan (CPP) is that good governance, by defining responsibilities and accountabilities, leads to positive outcomes. A key principle of the plan's governance is disclosure. This commitment is underpinned by the Canada Pension Plan Investment Board Act, which contains detailed provisions dealing with matters such as financial disclosure, auditing, public meetings, and availability of information.

Roles within the CPP are clearly defined. The CPP Investment Board (CPPIB) is responsible for investing funds in capital markets, and independence from political interference is achieved by having two separate juridical persons for the CPP and CPPIB. The objects of the CPPIB are clearly defined in the legislation as being to manage amounts transferred to it in the best interests of the contributors and beneficiaries and to invest its assets with a view to achieving a maximum rate of return, without undue risk of loss.

The appointment of CPPIB directors is subject to a process that is designed to ensure independent appointments and minimize the risk of political interference. The CPPIB codes of conduct are public documents, and contain a number of interesting features, including tight controls on the personal investing of directors and employees. Directors and employees are required to clear trades before executing them for their personal accounts and are required to report on their investment activity on a regular basis. Another key requirement is that all directors and board employees must disclose in writing or request to have entered in the minutes of a meeting of the board of directors or one of its committees any interests that would constitute a conflict. Such disclosures must be made in a timely fashion and lead to restrictions on the director's right to vote or participate in discussions on any relevant transaction. Failure to comply with the conflict disclosure requirements gives the courts the right to set aside the transaction.

The CPPIB is required to establish an audit committee. The duties of the audit committee include:

- requiring the board to implement internal control procedures and reviewing, evaluating, and approving these procedures;
- reviewing and approving the board's annual financial statements and reporting to the board on these;
- meeting with the board's auditors to discuss the annual financial statements and the auditor's report;
- reviewing all investments and transactions that could adversely affect the return on the board's investments that are brought to the committee's attention by the board's auditor or officers.

The CPPIB is required to appoint an independent auditor and for this purpose independence is a matter of fact: the external auditor has strong and clearly defined rights to information for the purpose of carrying out its work. The CPPIB is required to adhere to a procurement policy in relation to its selection of all outside providers of services. It also must appoint an external custodian, and there is a detailed process of due diligence for the selection of this custodian. To protect cash and portfolio assets, there additionally are procedures for determining signing authorities and limits.

Another provision contained in statute is that the relevant government minister may appoint an auditor to conduct a special audit of the CPPIB or any of its subsidiaries. The minister must cause a special examination to be carried out at least once every six years in respect of the CPPIB or any of its subsidiaries to determine if the systems and practices relating to financial and management control are maintained in a manner that provides reasonable assurance that they meet the statutory requirements.

The actual reporting requirements for the CPPIB are clear and prescriptive. A quarterly financial statement must be prepared and sent to the relevant minister and appropriate provincial ministers within 45 days after the end of the three-month period to which it relates. There also is a requirement for an annual report that must be provided to the relevant minister and appropriate provincial ministers within 90 days of the end of each financial year. Copies of this report must be made available to the public. After receiving the annual report the minister must cause it to be laid before each House of Parliament on any of the next 15 days during which that house is sitting. The report is made widely available through stakeholder groups and public libraries and is posted on the CPPIB website.

The CPPIB annual report contains:

- the financial statements for the previous year
- the auditor's report for that year
- a certificate, signed by a director on behalf of the board of directors, stating that the investments held during that year were in accordance with the legislation and with CPPIB investment policies, standards, and procedures
- a statement of the objectives of that year and a statement on the extent to which the objectives were met
- a statement of the objectives for the next year and for the foreseeable future
- a statement of the investment policies, standards, and procedures.
- a statement of corporate governance
- information on board committees
- decisions requiring board approval
- information on the compensation of the five principal officers of the CPPIB

The CPPIB transparency and reporting includes:

- rates of return
- market value of assets
- conference calls
- public meetings
- effectively conducting a broad dialogue and reporting campaign with Canadians from coast to coast.

The CPPIB has stated that its aim is "disclose, disclose, disclose." Its legislation and reporting clearly appear to support this stated aim.

Norwegian Government Petroleum Fund

The Norwegian Government Petroleum Fund is established in a way that enforces very clear accountability. The Ministry of Finance is the "owner" of the fund and decides the investment strategy and benchmark. Major changes are debated in parliament. The central bank, Norges Bank, is the operations manager and is responsible for "value-added" against the benchmark. The ministry also uses independent consultants for a second opinion on performance.

Norges Bank reports results, risk, and costs every quarter. Its reports are released at press conferences and on the Internet.

The fund itself also produces a detailed annual report, containing:

- a statement of the mandate for the fund
- the annual return on the fund
- fixed-income management
- equity management
- risk exposure
- organization of management
- management costs
- reporting of the accounts
- the auditor's report
- the management mandate
- the organization chart of Norges Bank
- holdings of equities at year-end
- fixed-income investments at year-end

A particularly useful feature of the annual report is a summary of key data (see Annex 3.A); another is a cost comparison with other funds. The latter involves submission of data to Canadian consulting firm Cost Effectiveness Measurement Inc. (CEM), which has a database containing the cost figures for capital management of more than 150 pension funds. From this database CEM selects a peer group of funds that have similar total assets to the Petroleum Fund. The costs of this group are used as a basis for assessing the costs of managing the Petroleum Fund.

The Petroleum Fund Annual Report is a model of transparency. Further information is available on Norges Bank's website, at: www.norges-bank.no.

California Public Employees' Retirement System (CalPERS)

CalPERS is the largest public pension fund in the United States and is one of the highest profile and largest pension funds in the world. Its core values are quality, respect, integrity, openness, and accountability, and its guiding principles include the provision of meaningful information and education to all constituents in a timely manner. An interesting feature of CalPERS is the blending of its values and its business practices. In this context its business philosophy includes "demonstrating accountability by taking responsibility for our actions" and "supporting open communication." Its strategic goals also prioritize this issue, and include fostering an environment that values openness and accountability.

CalPERS meets the first component necessary for transparency and accountability in that it lays out clear fiduciary duties for those responsible for management, investment, and administration. The CalPERS governance structure includes a high level of accountability to beneficiaries and the fund has also adopted a policy of full disclosure to beneficiaries that extends beyond its regulatory requirements. This commitment to transparency and accountability has enabled it to pursue corporate governance activism in the market, which it is believed has led to improvements in performance. For instance, in March 2003 CalPERS "named and shamed" those companies on which it will be focusing its corporate governance activism in the coming proxy season. Out of the 1,800 U.S. corporations in which CalPERS invests, six have been criticized for their poor corporate governance. A feature of this criticism has been failure to communicate.

CalPERS additionally is working to improve its own disclosure. In March 2003, it announced that it is aiming to improve the disclosure of its private equity investments to provide a higher level of transparency. Following a vote by the board of administration the fund will publish internal rates of return for its fund and fund of funds, and will disclose the amounts of cash invested and the profits realized from that cash investment. The disclosure will be made on a quarterly basis. This information had been available in the past, but was withdrawn in 2001. The reversal of the decision to withdraw was based on the aim expressed by the president of the board to "provide the highest level of transparency that will not conflict with our fiduciary duty to our members to maximize investment returns."

Central to the effort of CalPERS to improve its transparency and accountability is its website, which includes:

- information on corporate governance
- names and occupations of trustees
- a board meeting calendar and agenda
- laws and board decisions

- the fund approach to corporate governance
- a "guest" section where questions can be asked and comments made
- the fund investment policy

Irish National Pensions Reserve Fund

I would also like to suggest the Irish National Pensions Reserve Fund as a good model which scores well on the key components for transparency and accountability. However, as I am presenting "Public Pension Funds Accountability: The Case for Ireland" later in this conference I will describe the transparency and accountability of the Irish Fund at that time.

Models with More to Do

Southeast Asia Region

Public fund management in Southeast Asia has had mixed results. This is for a variety of reasons, but typical problems are a lack of transparency and accountability. Defined contribution schemes, which are by definition funded, are widespread in the region. This is consistent with emerging international trends in financing retirement. It has been suggested that to obtain maximum economic benefits from these schemes the region needs to improve pension fund governance, including transparency and accountability, and that this may require the setting up of provident and pension funds authorities.[3]

Central Provident Fund in Singapore

In Singapore, the process of investment of Central Provident Fund (CPF) balances has raised transparency, adequacy, and fiduciary responsibility issues.[4] Suggested reforms include that the CPF board give higher priority to fiduciary responsibility and that it improve transparency of the investment process and outcome. It has also been suggested that the nontransparency and nonaccountability of CPF balances, along with an administered rate of interest, has turned the CPF from a nominally defined contribution, fully funded scheme to a notional defined benefit scheme financed on a pay-as-you-go basis.

Japan

The Japanese Government Pension Investment Fund (GPIF) reports to the Minister of Health, Law, and Welfare. This minister has political rather than economic responsibility, which may present a weakness in the reporting responsibilities of the GPIF. One area where there may be room for improvement is in the disclosure of information.[5]

Conclusion

Transparency and accountability are essential ingredients for good governance. All principles of governance, such as the OECD Principles of Corporate Governance, recognize this.

There is increasing global focus on transparency and accountability as a response to recent corporate and accounting problems. The issues which needed to be addressed for corporates also apply, and, in fact, could be said to be even more relevant to public pension funds.

While it is not always possible to establish a clear linkage between the success of a fund and the standards of transparency and accountability exercised in the management of that fund, there is enough empirical evidence to suggest this linkage exists. Some of the examples quoted in this presentation would appear to support this view.

Public pension funds with high standards of transparency and accountability are useful as models. However, there is no ideal model as the transparency and accountability put in place needs to be country-specific: it should be based on the capacity of that country to regulate; on its standards of accounting; on trust law, where this applies; and on the general governance quality operating within the country. This applies to all global or cross-border standards because what is effective in one country may not work in another.

Finally, while good transparency and accountability requirements must be enshrined in legislation and regulation, this alone is not enough. The legislation and regulation must be made to work, and be seen to work, in practice.

Annex 3.A: The Norwegian Government Petroleum Fund—Key Figures, 2002

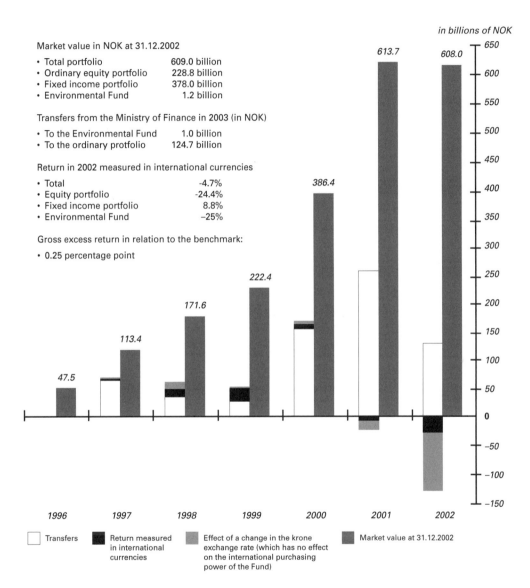

Market value in NOK at 31.12.2002

- Total portfolio   609.0 billion
- Ordinary equity portfolio   228.8 billion
- Fixed income portfolio   378.0 billion
- Environmental Fund   1.2 billion

Transfers from the Ministry of Finance in 2003 (in NOK)

- To the Environmental Fund   1.0 billion
- To the ordinary protfolio   124.7 billion

Return in 2002 measured in international currencies

- Total   -4.7%
- Equity portfolio   -24.4%
- Fixed income portfolio   8.8%
- Environmental Fund   −25%

Gross excess return in relation to the benchmark:

- 0.25 percentage point

in billions of NOK

Transfers | Return measured in international currencies | Effect of a change in the krone exchange rate (which has no effect on the international purchasing power of the Fund) | Market value at 31.12.2002

105

References

Ambachtseer, K. 2001. "A Framework for Public Pension Fund Management." Paper presented at the First World Bank Conference on Managing Public Pension Reserves, September 20–22, 2001, Washington, D.C.

Asher, M. G.,2001. "Investment of State Pension Funds in Singapore and Malaysia." Presentation presented at the First Public Pension Fund Management Conference, Washington, D.C., September 20–22, 2001.

Hess, D. and Impavido, G. 2003. "The Governance of Public Pension Fund Management: Lessons from Corporate Governance and International Evidence." Paper presented at the Second World Bank Conference on Managing Public Pension Reserves, May 5–7, 2003, Washington, D.C. Published in this volume.

Usuki, M. 2001. "Public Pension Fund Management in Japan." Presentation presented at the First Public Pension Fund Management Conference, Washington, D.C., September 20–22, 2001.

Notes

1. Ambachtseer (2001).
2. Hess and Impavido (2003).
3. Asher (2001).
4. Asher (2001).
5. Usuki (2001).

Chapter 4

The Canadian Experience on Governance, Accountability and Investment

John A. MacNaughton

Good morning, ladies and gentlemen. It is a pleasure to be back at this second global conference on public pension fund management and to share with you some information from a Canadian vantage point.

It was obvious yesterday, from some of the questions and some of the comments, that all of our nations are at different stages of development and reflection on these issues. I hope that my comments will be helpful to you in identifying areas that might be worth considering as your own plans evolve, and I look forward to hearing other presentations, as I did yesterday, because I think we all take away something of value when we participate in sessions such as this.

It is through information exchanges of this nature that we can learn from each other how to better care financially for our aging populations. In many respects the world is facing a ticking demographic time bomb: working populations are in decline in Europe and Japan and we will be called upon to support a swelling pensioner population. This demographic shift to a growing population of retirees has profound ramifications for global economic growth, the financial markets, political expression, and government fiscal stability. At the same time and in stark contrast, in many developing countries the young population is expanding rapidly, creating a different set of political and economic challenges.

We share many common challenges, however. Specifically, how can we keep the most financially vulnerable in society out of poverty in their retirement years? How can we ensure that money set aside to pay pensions is not used for political purposes? And how should pension funds be invested to avoid higher contributions by tomorrow's workers. I shall address each of these questions from the Canadian perspective, and I propose to do so by isolating four factors that drive the investment aspects of our public pension reform.

The first factor is our governance model, and the way in which it protects against the risks of political intrusion. The second is the integrity of the organization; that is, who decides what is right or wrong and how we benchmark what are essentially moral judgments. The third is what I will describe as our unencumbered investment mandate: Canada's national pension fund has few investment constraints. The fourth factor that characterizes the Canadian experience is our leadership on transparency. We have a strong commitment to robust public reporting and accountability, and it is this that underpins the credibility of our governance model. My review of these four factors will explain also our investment philosophy and practices, and will detail the progress and performance made by the Canada Pension Plan (CPP) Investment Board since it became operational in October 1998.

Background

First, some brief background information on Canada's public pension system. I apologize to those of you who first heard this two years ago, but it is important to your understanding of our reform thinking that you can place it in its proper context.

Canada is a federal state. We have a central government, 10 provincial governments, and three territorial governments. The provinces have considerable powers and responsibilities. Some of these, including stewardship of the national public pension plan, they share with the federal government.

Canada has existed as a sovereign state for nearly 136 years, and for 75 of those years we have provided financial relief for the elderly. In 1927 Canada introduced an old age security program as the first step toward reducing poverty among seniors. The next major milestone in the creation of Canada's income retirement system was the establishment in 1966 of the

Canada Pension Plan, a mandatory plan for working Canadians to which all employees and their employers must contribute. The plan, a pay-as-you-go scheme indexed to inflation, was created by the federal government and nine of the provincial governments. The tenth province, Quebec, opted out but maintains its own plan that parallels the CPP.

The Canada Pension Plan is not a state-sponsored plan: the federal and provincial governments have no financial liability for the plan, other than to match the contributions of their own employees. The federal government does, however, have two social security programs for the elderly, the general income supplement and old age security, that it funds out of general revenues. These programs are available to everyone based on need.

There is some confusion in the literature about the ownership of the pension assets. The Center for Strategic and International Studies highlighted this key issue: "The success of [its] reforms will depend on whether Canada … [is] better at building firewalls between public pension reserves and general government revenues than other countries have been."

To clear up this point: Pension reserves in Canada are totally segregated from federal government assets and are accounted for separately. The equity assets of the Canada Pension Plan are carried on our balance sheet at the CPP Investment Board and the securities are held by a private sector custodian in a segregated fund. The government can ask for the return of funds only to pay pensions, and for no other purpose. The remaining CPP assets—bonds and the cash reserve—are administered by the federal government but over the next three years also will be transferred to our balance sheet. Legislation to this effect was approved by Parliament in April 2003. Once this transaction is completed all CPP assets will be protected by the firewall that is already in place.

The stewards of the Canada Pension Plan, the federal and provincial governments, are responsible for the plan's design, for plan administration, and for funding policy. They set contribution rates and they determine benefits. The federal government additionally collects contributions, pays entitlements, and administers the plan.

The CPP was in the beginning designed not to be fully funded. The thinking was that each generation would pay the pensions of the previous generation. This made sense back in the 1960s, when the number of Canadians over the retirement age of 70 was small relative to the working population, and over the next 30 years the plan worked fairly well. Substantially more money flowed in than flowed out, assuring all working

4

4

Canadians of retirement income and all families of financial support should the breadwinner die or become disabled. Along the way the eligibility age for the full pension was lowered to 65 and for a reduced pension to 60.

By 1996, however, more money was going out than was coming in. In that year alone, C$17 billion was paid out in benefits and only C$11 billion collected in contributions, producing a one-year deficit of C$6 billion. Clearly, the plan was heading for serious trouble.

Particularly worrisome is the changing ratio of seniors to workers. In 1966 there were seven workers for every pensioner. Today that ratio is five contributors for every beneficiary, by 2030 there will be only three workers to support every pensioner, and by 2050, 1.6 contributors per retiree. This is a dramatic demographic shift with huge economic repercussions, and yet pales alongside the problem facing other industrial countries. According to United Nations data, Canada's working population, driven by immigration, is expected to increase 14 percent by 2050. (That of the United States is forecast to increase at twice even this high rate.) The working population of other Organisation for Economic Co-operation and Development (OECD) countries in contrast is projected to shrink, by 8 percent in France, for example, and by as much as 42 percent in Italy.

This impending pension crisis sparked an extensive review by the Canadian federal and provincial governments, leading to the institution in 1997 of some important changes. One key change was an increase in contribution rates, which have since risen by more than 60 percent, from 6 percent in 1997 to 9.9 percent in January 2002. The current contribution rate applies to earnings of up to C$39,900.

Other key changes were improvements in plan administration and the creation of an independent organization, separate from the plan itself, to manage the reserve assets. The CPP as a result is moving from being an exclusively pay-as-you-go scheme to being partially funded, a model that is increasingly popular worldwide.

In Canada's case, the goal is to build up assets from the 1996 level of 8 percent of liabilities to more than 20 percent of liabilities by 2015. We are making good progress. Since 1996, CPP assets have grown by C$11 billion, to more than C$55 billion. This growth has come equally from two sources: higher contributions from workers and their employers during a period of rapid job creation; and income earned from the investment of CPP assets, as managed by the CPP Investment Board. (The investment board was established following the 1996 decision of the federal and provincial governments to invest excess funds, until such time as they are needed to pay benefits, in capital markets. The board is under professional management and is independent of government.)

The federal and provincial governments believe that the contribution rate of 9.9 percent, when combined with investment income, will keep the CPP in a steady funding status indefinitely. Under these conditions incomings are expected to exceed outgoings—that is, the money that is needed to pay pensions—for at least another 18 years.

Governance

Let me now turn to the factors that drive the Canadian Public Pension reform on the investment front, beginning with how the CPP Investment Board was set up to immunize it politically. As Robert Palacios stated in a recent paper for the World Bank[1], "In the past, most public pension funds have not been invested effectively largely because of political interference."

That interference falls broadly into two categories: interference with directors or trustees in the fulfillment of their fiduciary duty, and interference in the decision-making of the investment professionals. Canada's position on both of these issues is exemplary thanks to the foresight of its federal and provincial politicians, who opted for a governance model that balances independence from political and government influence with rigorous public reporting and accountability.

Despite this, in the minds of Canadians the threat of political interference in the management of the CPP is real. According to public opinion research, nearly 70 percent of Canadians worry that government will at some point meddle in our investment decisions.

The directors and management of the CPP Investment Board are confident that it will not. Legislation requires that the board of directors include "a sufficient number of directors with proven financial ability or relevant work experience." In other words, it mandates that we have a knowledgeable board. The system governing appointments to the board, which is a departure from the traditional practice of government-owned corporations and of most public pension funds that are governed by nominees or representatives of governments, unions, and employers, further serves to ensure that this mandate is met.

In the case of the CPP Investment Board, the federal and provincial finance ministers appoint a special nominating committee of public and private sector people, chaired by an individual from the private sector. The committee identifies suitable board candidates and submits a list of nominees to the federal finance minister. The minister must choose exclusively from the list, and must make all appointments in consultation with the provincial finance ministers. This consultation is an effective check on partisanship and cronyism because the federal and provincial governments in Canada are at any given time led by different political parties.

Once appointed, directors serve for terms of up to three years. They can serve three consecutive terms, with reappointment possible only on the recommendation of the nominating committee. No director may be removed from the board, other than for just cause, during his or her three-year term. The chair of the board is appointed by the federal finance minister in consultation with his or her provincial counterparts and the directors already on the board.

As a result of this process the board consists of professionals with accounting, actuarial, economic, and investment credentials. They are experienced in the private and public sectors and they have informed opinions on public and private sector governance. And they are not only independent: I can tell you from regular experience, they are also independently minded.

The board, as an aside, has its own rigorous process for evaluating its performance and that of its committees. This is an important component of good governance in any organization. The self-evaluation process keeps the directors focused on their fiduciary duties of representing the best interests of Canadians—the people who contribute to the plan and who benefit from it.

Legislation gives the board broad powers that further enforce the buffer zone between government and those who oversee the fund's investments. For example:

- The board appoints the chief executive officer who reports to the board. For most crown corporations in Canada, the CEO is appointed by the Prime Minister and reports to a minister.
- The board approves the policies that frame management's discretion in decision-making and in the formation of our annual business plans and budgets. For most crown corporations these approvals are given by a cabinet minister.

- The board has the responsibility and full authority to appoint the external and internal auditors who report to the board's audit committee. Most crown corporations in Canada are audited by the Auditor General, an independent audit officer serving Parliament.
- In providing oversight of management, the board sets the compensation for management. This compensation is linked to performance. The compensation at most crown corporations is determined by the government.
- The board reviews and approves management's recommendation of external investment managers and other major suppliers. For most crown corporations this process is controlled by government.

Speaking as chief executive officer, there is much to commend being required to report to a knowledgeable board of directors. The fact that the directors ask their questions based on experience is greatly reassuring to the management team, as it gives us the comfort of knowing that every aspect of our investment practices is being queried and probed by exceptional people whom we respect.

There is an additional important dynamic that is introduced by an independent board. The board sets my compensation and performance objectives. At year-end it reviews what the organization has accomplished and what incentive payments, if any, I and the members of senior management deserve. It then approves our objectives for the next year. I, in turn, put the senior executives through a similar process, consistent with the best practices of private sector corporate governance.

I do not want to leave the impression that we could operate as some rogue government agency, doing whatever we want with other people's money, because this is not the case. The government can at any time check on what is being done with Canada Pension Plan money, and is in fact required to do so: the federal finance minister must every six years authorize a special examination of the CPP Investment Board's books, records, systems, and practices. This will occur in consultation with the provinces within the next two years. The federal finance minister also has the authority to appoint, at his or her discretion, a firm of auditors to conduct a special audit if there is an area of particular concern. The federal and provincial ministers additionally must review our legislation and regulations every three years as part of their mandatory review of the Canada Pension Plan.

Integrity

Let me now turn to the second factor that drives our reform: the integrity of the organization. The legislation empowers the board of directors to approve a code of conduct, policies for procedures, and policies that address potential conflicts of interest. In other words, the directors are required to determine the ethical standards of the organization.

The CPP Investment Board faces an interesting challenge in setting its ethical foundation because we have one foot in the private sector and the other in the public sector. We are a federal crown corporation operating (at arm's length from government) in the public sector, and we are an investment management company competing in the private sector. How should we balance the standards on conflict of interest for the public and private sectors?

Those who view the CPP Investment Board as an instrument of public policy, the primary responsibility of which is to help secure the financial future of the Canada Pension Plan, will be inclined to apply public sector expectations. Those who see the CPP Investment Board as an investment management company competing in capital markets will be inclined to apply private sector expectations. In most cases the standards and expectations are the same, but in some instances they are not. For example, in the public sector the use of blind trusts is a standard means of separating private investment interests and public duties. In the private sector this notion is alien. From the point of view of the CPP Investment Board, we frankly were concerned that we would have difficulty recruiting qualified employees and directors if they were obliged to put their personal investments in a blind trust.

Our legislation accepts that conflicts of interest are inevitable for directors and executives. It accordingly requires that the board develop procedures to resolve these conflicts—not necessarily to eliminate them, but to resolve them.

One obvious goal is to ensure that directors and employees do not profit or otherwise benefit from a transaction made by or with the CPP Investment Board. All directors and employees must disclose any related interests and directors must disclose any personal relationships that might be seen to compromise their independence or their ability to provide impartial or objective advice. Directors also must disclose any business activity that directly or indirectly affects the activities of the CPP Investment Board or that could be construed as a conflict. The process by which such issues are discussed is clearly laid out, and culminates with the board's governance committee recommending a resolution to the full board.

The conflict-of-interest procedures have worked well. In the more than 40 board meetings held since the CPP Investment Board was established four directors have excused themselves, on six occasions, from discussions involving transactions in which they had a real, perceived, or potential conflict. These transactions mostly concerned the board's consideration of suppliers to provide investment or operating services. In each case the conflicted director did not participate in the discussion of or vote on these matters. The conflict-of-interest procedures and code of conduct for employees are much the same.

We also enforce tough personal trading procedures. We maintain lists of securities in which directors and employees are not permitted to trade, and for other securities they must preclear with our general counsel any proposed purchases or sales. Directors must provide written confirmation semiannually that they are in compliance with the board's trading procedures, and employees must have their broker or financial advisor file monthly or quarterly statements with our external auditor disclosing all securities transactions.

The CPP Investment Board is a major presence in the Canadian capital markets. We have C$18 billion already invested, and by 2014 we expect to have more than C$160 billion in assets under management. The fact that we are a large shareholder in hundreds of Canadian companies is in itself sufficient to attract a great deal of public interest, and undoubtedly other conflicts, real or perceived, could arise. The question thus becomes how we should benchmark acceptable behavior.

One way is to ask the experts what they think. In May 2002, we asked three specialists in private and public sector ethical conduct to review our policies and procedures, and specifically to assess whether or not our policies and procedures were robust enough to guide us through a period of rapid growth and change. The three specialists rated highly our established standards and procedures, but they did also suggest several enhancements.

One of these suggestions was that we define a potential or perceived conflict of interest, to clearly differentiate it from a real conflict of interest. We have since made this change, guided by a former supreme court judge who specializes in ethical matters. We defined what is meant by a private economic interest, to help our directors and managers gain a better understanding of how to deal with any potential conflict with the public interest, and we introduced a self-administered loyalty test to identify any potential problems that might arise through our directors serving on the boards of other companies in which the CPP Investment Board owns shares. Our directors are expected to support the achievement of the objectives of the CPP Investment Board without reference to any other association they may have.

Another suggestion by our outside advisors was that we consider appointing a part-time external advisor on conflicts and ethical conduct. The CPP board accepted this suggestion and will appoint an external part-time conduct review advisor later this year. This advisor will be accessible to directors, employees, and even to concerned stakeholders to advise on the often complex and difficult issues that arise in an environment of changing expectations.

Our governance model and our commitment to high ethical standards shape the culture in which we manage and make investment decisions, and I am confident in saying that many of our policies on conduct, conflicts, and related issues are leading-edge.

Investment Policy

We are fortunate also to have an investment mandate that is unencumbered by non-investment considerations. This is the third factor that drives the Canadian experience.

We currently have two investment objectives. First, we must manage the CPP assets in the best interests of planned contributors and beneficiaries. That means in the best interests of 16 million people, or approximately 50 percent of the population of Canada. Second, we must maximize investment returns without incurring undue risk with regard to the CPP's financial requirements and future obligations. We are not allowed to conduct any business that is inconsistent with these two objectives.

This year, as a result of legislation recently approved in Parliament, we will have an additional third objective: to provide cash liquidity to the CPP so that it can meet its monthly pension obligations.

Our investment mandate differs from that of many national public pension funds. We are not a captive source of credit for government. We do not have to buy government debt unless we decide to build a bond portfolio, and even then we will do so only if the terms are attractive and in keeping with our legislated and fiduciary duties. And we are not required to make loans to state-owned firms, nor do we have social investment requirements (in short, we do not invest according to any public policy objectives other than the very important one of keeping the public pension promise. This alone is a worthy social objective that deserves a focused investment mandate undiluted or distracted by other public policy goals and social causes, however worthy they may be).

Our investment strategy has been evolving over the last few years, and the asset mix profile that is emerging is similar in many respects to that of other large public sector pension funds in Canada and the United States. When we began investing in October 1998, the CPP assets were solely 20-year government bonds and liquid short-term government securities. I referred earlier to the steady state funding policy of our federal and provincial finance ministers; with the contribution rate set at 9.9 percent, that funding policy assumes that CPP assets will earn a real return of 4 percent; that is, 4 percent above the rate of inflation. Government bonds, in our view, will not achieve this level over the long term, so we must assume some additional risk to earn those higher returns. Because we have 18 years before we are expected to pay income into the CPP, we can assume greater risk in the fund than could a mature fund that needs income to pay pension benefits today.

From the beginning, we decided for two reasons to invest excess funds in equities. First, to diversify the asset base; and second, because, compared to bonds, history tells us that equities pay a premium over the long term for the extra risk assumed. Investing in equities thus makes sense in its own right, although earning that extra risk-adjusted premium can require riding out a lot of short-term market volatility.

For most of the last four-and-a-half years we have been investing passively in public equities, through externally managed funds that replicate stock indexes in Canada, the United States, and globally. While our investment mandate is unencumbered, we do face one significant constraint: we must invest 70 percent of assets at cost in Canada, and thus no more than 30 percent outside Canada.

This requirement, known as the foreign property rule, applies to all Canadian pension plans, as well as to registered individual retirement savings plans. We are in strict compliance with this constraint, although like many investors we would prefer to have no constraints. As a rule, any investment constraint has a cost.

4

We invest outside Canada to the maximum extent permitted by law. There are many reasons for this, primary among which is our desire to diversify our portfolio by geographic market. The world's economies do not move in lockstep, and although Canada has in recent years been one of the strongest industrial economies there are faster-paced opportunities in other markets. Another reason relates to the size of the Canadian economy. Canada's equity markets represent less than 3 percent of the global market capitalization, and the requirement to invest 70 percent of our assets in this relatively small market has risks in and of itself. The only major index for Canadian equities furthermore is a thin representation of the Canadian economy as a whole: some productive sectors are represented by just two or three companies, and others are not represented at all. The corollary is that other sectors are overrepresented.

We are also in the early stages of moving away from traditional index fund investing toward a strategy of investing passively on an economic sector basis, from the global perspective. Depending on which sector analysis one uses, there are 10 to 12 key economic sectors internationally. The Canadian economy is underrepresented in such areas as healthcare and technology and is overrepresented in sectors such as financial services and energy. Our goal is to build a more efficient global portfolio than one constructed using geographic-capitalization-weighted indexes.

Bonds and publicly traded equities are the cornerstones of a diversified portfolio, but in the last two years we have begun to diversify beyond these two asset classes. Almost two years ago we moved into private equities, including venture capital, investing through private equity specialists in Canada, the United States, and Western Europe. Our goal is to invest as much of 10 percent of CPP assets in private equities, on a global basis. While private equity assets can take eight to 12 years to realize full value, we believe the wait is worth it and that the higher risk-adjusted returns (compared to public equities and bonds) will justify the wait.

We are also committed to investing a portion of our total portfolio in real-return assets—such things as real estate, infrastructure, natural resources, and real return bonds. We have the support of our board to invest as much as 5 percent of CPP assets in real estate and infrastructure. In January, we acquired our first direct ownership in Canadian shopping centers.

We also have committed funds to real estate investment firms—ultimately we will own office buildings, industrial, retail, and multi-residential properties—and we are considering investments in infrastructure. These assets fit within our mandate as a long-term investor. They require large amounts of capital and patience to produce the level of returns that we need.

Finally, we are considering investing in natural resource assets and real-return bonds. Real-return bonds are a good match for index pension funds as they guarantee rates of return above inflation, but the supply has dried up and current returns are below the minimum required to sustain the CPP's steady contribution rate.

The future security of the Canada Pension Plan ultimately will rest on a diversified asset base. As of 31 December 2002, bonds represented 58 percent (C$32 billion) of the CPP's assets, equities 32 percent (C$18 billion), and cash 9 percent (C$5 billion). We are moving toward a heavier equity weighting and will decide the long-term asset mix policy later this year, after further discussions with our board of directors.

Overall, CPP assets have earned an annualized nominal rate of return averaging 3.8 percent since 2000. Those returns have been volatile, ranging from a high of 7 percent in 2001 to a low of 0.8 percent so far this year. We expect a negative return of slightly more than 1 percent for fiscal 2003. These results compare favorably with those of other Canadian public sector pension funds, which, like the CPP, have suffered for three years because of the declining equity markets. Our losses in these markets have been offset to a considerable extent by fixed income gains.

We have a rapidly growing asset base and we are Canada's largest pension fund investor, but the CPP Investment Board is actually quite a small organization: our operating budget is only C$14 million this year, and we have a staff of fewer than 35 people. Despite our size, however, we believe that we employ the best talents in the marketplace anywhere in the world. The CPP has to date retained more than 45 firms with different areas of expertise, and our staff monitors and reviews their progress against performance expectations. These external fund managers report to management, not to our board of directors, and as a consequence we are accountable for their performance and their behavior.

The CPP is a shareholder in approximately 2,000 companies worldwide. Our shareholdings give us ownership rights in these companies and we have a responsibility on behalf of our stakeholders to exercise those rights. We do not, of course, seek to manage the companies in which we own shares; rather, we aim to focus corporate management on serving our best interests—after all, management works for the shareholders, not the other way around. We therefore support resolutions that empower boards of directors

4

on behalf of the shareholders and that reaffirm management accountability. We also support performance-based incentive programs that require executives to put their own capital at risk in the same way that shareholder capital is at risk, by requiring that while they are with the company they own a minimum value of shares. For us, this goal is better achieved through stock grants made at market value than through the granting of stock options.

Most of all, however, we want boards and managements to take a long-term view of their company's best interests and those of its shareholders. We are a long-term investor consistent with the long-term needs of our plan. With billions of dollars committed to equity ownership we cannot (nor would we choose to) walk away from companies by selling our shares every time we feel that they are not acting in our best interests. We will support boards and management teams through difficult periods as long as their long-term visions and strategies are clear, compelling, and focused on the enhancement of long-term shareholder value. We oppose resolutions that are likely to diminish long-term shareholder value even though they may produce short-term gains. It is profit growth over the long term that ultimately drives returns on equities, and from CPP's perspective the priority of management accordingly should be to enhance the sustainable long-term profitability of the company.

Many Canadians believe that there is more to share ownership than supporting profit-making to improve share price, and we agree. Employees, customers, suppliers, governments, and the communities in which our investing communities operate have a vested interest in the exercise of the good corporate conduct that can influence future value. We therefore support reasonable shareholder resolutions that ask companies to make full disclosure on the issues that relate to our social investing responsibilities: ethical behavior, sustainable development, and good corporate citizenship. There is ample scope for companies to demonstrate leadership on disclosure and to build and sustain investor and public confidence in the free market system.

Accountability

This brings me to the fourth factor that drives the Canadian experience: our decision to demonstrate leadership on pension fund disclosure and in the process to assuage public anxiety about our ability to operate at arm's length from government.

Full and timely disclosure is one of the most important governance principles. To paraphrase a well-known maxim that we heard yesterday: daylight is the best policeman; sunlight is the best disinfectant. Our public accountability and reporting is extensive and goes beyond legislative and regulatory requirements.

We are accountable to Parliament through the federal minister of finance, who tables our annual report. We do not report to this minister; we just deliver to him a copy of our annual report, as indeed we send it to all members of Parliament; to provincial legislators; to shareholder groups, such as trade unions, pensioner associations, and business associations; to economic and social policy research institutes; to universities; and to every public library in the country. We also publish the report on our Web site.

We are required to disclose a good deal of information in the annual report, including audited financial statements; our corporate governance practices, including the duties, objectives, and the mandate of the board of directors and the board's committees, their compensation, mandates, and activities; the decisions of management that requiring the board's prior approval; the procedures for the board to assess its own performance; and the director's expectations in respect to management. We are required to disclose our objectives for the past year and how they were met, and our objectives for the forthcoming year. We also must disclose the individual compensation of the top five officers and the total compensation of the directors.

We are accountable to the federal and provincial finance ministers and we file with them our quarterly financial statements. As I noted earlier, the finance ministers review our legislated and regulatory requirements every three years as part of their mandatory review of the Canada Pension Plan. We also are accountable to individual Canadians, and we seek to provide this accountability through public meetings that we hold in each province that participates in the CPP. So far we have held two coast-to-coast series of meetings.

We have in fact adopted a more proactive approach to disclosure and reporting than the government envisaged or for which it legislated. The opening paragraph of our disclosure policy, crafted in May 2002, reads:

"Canadians have the right to know why, how, and where we invest their Canada Pension Plan money, who makes the investment decisions, what assets are owned on their behalf, and how the investments are performing."

In accordance with this policy we release to the news media our quarterly financial results as well as our annual results. I hold a media conference when we release them. We publicly announce all new investments and external investment partners, and we post on our Web site all of our results and our policies, including those dealing with governance, investment, codes of conduct, conflict-of-interest guidelines, and procurement and personal trading by directors and staff. The Web site also carries a full list of our holdings of public equities and their market values, updated on a quarterly basis, and a summary of the market value of fixed-income securities and private equity holdings, along with historic investment results. There is also a discussion of our investment strategies, details on the firms we retain to implement our investment and operating strategies, and biographies of all directors and professional employees.

No other Canadian pension fund and few internationally discloses as much as we do, let alone quarterly. This degree of transparency in reporting means that politicians and the public can keep a close eye on us; it also makes it even more difficult for government to interfere in our investment mandate.

There is perhaps a danger that by committing ourselves to such full disclosure we expose ourselves to embarrassment should things go wrong. Our view on this, and our experience, is that if you give people the bad news as well as the good, and if you paint the full picture and you have timely disclosure, the public will understand. Our policy has obliged us to report some miserable quarters, with equities in particular returning bad results. It is arguable that a pension fund that invests over decades should not have to worry about what happens over three months, but in our view the public has the right to know.

Full and timely disclosure is a discipline that keeps us focused on how the contributors to our pension plan feel about what we are doing with their money. It forces us to explain ourselves in terms that they understand and with a fullness that they expect. Our experience shows us that the effort that we make is fully justified by its success in building confidence in our mandate, in our team, and in our strategy.

Concluding Remarks

Finally, let me conclude by restating the four factors that drive our reform:

- A strong governance model, created by the federal and regional governments, that ensures that management is able to operate independently of government under the watchful attention of a knowledgeable board of directors.
- A commitment to creating and testing ethical standards that reflect our role as a government corporation in the public sector competing as an investment management company in the private sector.
- An investment mandate that is unencumbered by public policy priorities and social investment criteria, giving us the freedom to invest in the best interests of those workers who pay into the CPP and who expect it to deliver to them a pension when they retire.
- A commitment to full accountability to Parliament, to the provinces, and to the public, to ensure that they are informed on a regular basis about what we are doing with their money.

The full realization of these four factors inevitably depends in part on the particular mosaic of Canada's political, economic, judicial, and social circumstances. I hope, however, that there are aspects of our experience that can be adapted to your plans and your structure. After all, in the end we all have the same goal, which is to enable people to retire in dignity and with some financial comfort at the end of their working lives. Thank you very much and I look forward to your questions.

Notes

1. Palacios, R. 2002. "Managing Public Pension Reserves, Part II: Lessons from Five Recent OECD Initiatives." World Bank Pension Reform Primer Working Paper series. Washington, D.C.: World Bank. Available online at: www.worldbank.org/pensions.

5

Public Pension Funds Accountability: The Case of Ireland

Anne Maher

Background to the Irish Fund

Present Pension Arrangements

Ireland has:

- A first-pillar pension arrangement providing either an old age contributory pension for those who satisfy certain work-related contribution conditions or an old age noncontributory pension, subject to a means test, for those who do not qualify for a contributory pension. The contributory pension is 31 percent of average industrial earnings and the noncontributory pension slightly less.

  The first-pillar pension arrangement is funded on a pay-as-you-go basis. This does not have a sustainability problem, and if pensions are indexed to prices spending on first-pillar pensions will fall relative to GNP over the next 50 years If pensions are indexed to wages, spending will rise relative to GNP, from the present level of 4.8 percent to approximately 8 percent in 2056.

- A public service pension scheme that faces greatly increased cost. The existing level of gross benefit expenditure is expected to more than double over the next 15 years.
- A demographic situation that is expected to evolve more favorably than that of other countries during the early decades of this century. At present there are five people who are economically active to every one retired.
- An economy that saw double-digit GDP growth over the last decade but which has recently encountered a downturn. Forecast GDP growth this year is 3.5 percent and next year, 4.1 percent.
- Experience of domestic and international investment.
- A well-developed funded occupational pension and personal pension plan sector.

Recommendation for Fund

Ireland is fortunate in that for the first two decades of this century it is projected to have a relatively strong demographic position. While alerted to the problems of an ageing demographic, it thus has time to address them. The country also must address the serious issue of the rising cost of public service pensions—the consequence of a boom in social provision in the 1970s—which will begin to hit early in the century. Ireland also examined its total retirement provision position through a National Pensions Policy Initiative, the objective of which was to examine and debate the overall pension system and agree a pension reform package.

Following from this background, three separate reports recommended the establishment of an explicit mechanism to fund, at least partially, the substantial growth that is expected to occur in First Pillar and public service pensions. These reports were the following:

- the National Pensions Policy Initiative Report (1998) on overall pension reform, which recommended partial funding of First Pillar pensions;
- the Commission on Public Service Pensions Report (November 2000), which recommended partially funding future public service pension costs;

- the Department of Finance Report of the Budgetary Strategy for Ageing Group (July 1999), which recommended partial prefunding of pension liabilities as part of overall national economic planning.

Fund Establishment

In July 1999, the Minister for Finance announced that the government had decided to provide resources on a planned basis to secure the pensions in retirement of a progressively ageing population. The government decided that an annual provision of 1 percent of GNP should be set aside to pre-fund part of the prospective cost. It also decided to allocate a tranche of the proceeds of the recent Telecom Éireann flotation to supplement these annual allocations.

In December 1999, legislation was passed setting up a Temporary Holding Fund in order that 1999 monies could be set aside.

In June 2000, the Minister for Finance published legislation that provided for the establishment, financing, and management of a National Pensions Reserve Fund. In December 2000, the National Pensions Reserve Fund Act was passed to provide for the establishment of the National Pensions Reserve Fund and the National Pensions Reserve Fund Commission, which would control and manage the fund and dissolve the Temporary Holding Fund for superannuation liabilities.

The establishment date of the fund was 2 April 2001, a date that also saw the official appointment of the seven commissioners for the fund.

National Pensions Reserve Fund Act, 2000

The National Pensions Reserve Fund Act provided for the establishment, financing, investment, and management of a fund to meet part of the escalating exchequer cost of social welfare and public service pensions from 2025 onward. In 2025, according to demographic projections, the proportion of people aged over 65 in the population will start to rise significantly. The act provides for:

- The establishment of a National Pensions Reserve Fund, to provide toward the exchequer cost of social welfare and public service pensions from 2025 onward.

- A statutory obligation to pay a sum equivalent to 1 percent of GNP from the exchequer into the fund each year until at least 2055, with provision for the payment of additional sums into the fund by resolution of Dáil Éireann (Irish House of Parliament).
- The establishment of the independent National Pensions Reserve Fund Commission to control and manage the fund. The commission will have discretionary authority to determine and implement an investment strategy for the fund, based on commercial principles. It will comprise a chairperson and six other commissioners, appointed by the Minister for Finance and each member subject to a statutory requirement for substantive expertise at a senior level in specified areas.
- A strictly commercial investment mandate for the fund, with the objective of securing the optimal return over the long term, subject to prudent risk management. The fund will not be allowed to invest in Irish Government securities, to ensure that it may not be used at some future date to artificially support government borrowing. There are also restrictions to ensure that the fund does not acquire a controlling interest in any company.
- A prohibition on drawdowns from the fund prior to 2025, with drawdowns thereafter to be determined under ministerial rules by reference to projected increases in the number of persons over 65 in the population and with a view to avoiding undue fluctuations in the net exchequer balance from year to year.
- The appointment of the National Treasury Management Agency as manager of the fund, to act as agent of the commission and to carry out such functions as are delegated to it for this purpose by the commission. The appointment of this agency will be for a period of 10 years, following which there will be the option, at five-yearly intervals, to extend further or to appoint an alternative manager.
- The appointment by the commission of investment managers to invest and manage the various components of the fund and custodians to ensure the safekeeping and security of the assets of the fund.
- Accountability of the commission to the Minister for Finance and to the Dáil Éireann, including the provision for detailed annual reports and for the appearance of the commission chairperson and/or the chief executive officer of the fund manager before the Committee of Public Accounts.

- The annual audit of the fund by the Comptroller and Auditor General.
- The transfer of monies from the Temporary Holding Fund to the Reserve Fund and the winding up of the Temporary Holding Fund.

Progress of the Fund since Establishment

Objective and Mission Statement

The fund started with a clear objective, set out in the National Pensions Reserve Fund Act as follows:

> 19. (1) Moneys, standing to the credit of the Fund shall, from time to time, be held or invested for the benefit of the Fund by the Commission, in or outside of the State, so as to secure the optimal total financial return, as to both capital and income, having regard to:
>
> (a) the purpose of the Fund as set out in section 18(1), and
>
> (b) the payment requirements of the Fund as provided for under section 20, provided the level of risk to the moneys held or invested is acceptable to the Commission.

The mission statement of the fund is:

> ...to meet as much as possible, within prudent risk parameters to be agreed by the Commission, of the cost to the Exchequer of social welfare and public service pensions to be paid from the year 2025 until the year 2055 as provided for in the National Pensions Reserve Fund Act, 2000.

Decision on Investment Strategy and Portfolio Construction

The commission determined, with external consultancy guidance, that the appropriate long-term strategic asset allocation for the fund should be 80

Table 5.1: Benchmarks

Asset Class	Allocation	Benchmark
Bonds	20%	Merrill Lynch Eurozone Government Bond Index (excluding Ireland)
Equities	80%	40% FTSE Eurozone 26.4% FTSE North American 6.8 FTSE Europe ex Eurozone 5.2% FTSE Japan 1.6% FTSE Pacific Basin

5

percent equities and 20 percent bonds. This reflects (a) the fact that drawdown of the fund cannot commence until 2025 and that drawdown must take place over a term of at least 30 years; (b) the fund's strong cash flow; (c) the nature of the promises made with regard to the pensions to be partly prefunded by the fund; and (d) an assumed average equity risk premium of 3 percent per annum over the life of the fund. The commission further decided, as required under the legislation, that the benchmarks against which the fund's investment performance would be measured as seen in Table 5.1

The commission also decided that half of the non-Eurozone currency exposure should be hedged into the euro (see Annnex 5.A for details of the portfolio construction).

Notwithstanding recent poor performance and concerns over the equity market, the commission has remained resolute over its selected equity weightings.

Appointment of Service Providers

Global tenders were held for the appointment of institutional investment managers, a global custodian, and a transition manager. Almost 600 applications were received for the 15 separate mandates for investment manager; these applications were processed and the managers appointed. A global custodian also has been appointed for the safekeeping of assets and a transition manager has been appointed to ensure the fund's smooth and efficient entry into the international capital markets. All of these appointments were made through open competition according to the Restricted Procedure under

Public Services Directive 92/50/EEC. This procedure comprises two phases. The first phase a notice be published in the Official Journal of the EU, inviting service providers to submit requests to participate in the tendering process. Thirty-seven days are allowed for the submission of applications. The second phase involves the invitation of a limited number of applicants to reply to a request proposal (RFP) within 40 days. The fund manager subsequently made site visits and viewed presentations ("beauty parades") by a further short list of candidates. The award criterion was that the award be made to the most economically advantageous tender.

Decision on Market Entry Strategy

The commission considered whether arrangements should be made for the fund to gain interim market exposure in the period to end-2001, when the investment managers were expected to be appointed. In the circumstances and given the particular uncertainties attaching to short-term market prospects, the commission decided against adopting an interim strategy.

The assets of the fund accordingly were held in cash from establishment of the fund in April 2001 to end-December 2001. The commission delegated to the National Treasury Management Agency authority to manage the cash against a short-term benchmark of an equal mix of one-, three-, and six-month deposits at Euribor minus 5 basis points, with the provision that at least 75 percent of the investments matured before December 2001 and 100 percent matured before March 2002.

The commission then decided to commit funds on an "averaging-in" basis to the appointed institutional investment managers, commencing in January 2002. As a consequence of its averaging-in approach the fund held strong cash balances—on average, about 35 percent of the fund value—through 2002, enabling it to buy into equity markets at the lower levels (see Annex 5.B for details of the market entry strategy).

Performance

The fund generated a return of 3.27 percent from its inception in April 2001 to end-December 2001, compared to a return of –0.6 percent for the average Irish-managed fund and –3.5 percent for the fund's long-term strategic benchmark. (Audited figures for end-2002 were not available at the time of writing, but estimates of performance figures to that date are shown in Annex 5.C.) The size of the fund at end-2002 was €7.4 billion, with 25 percent of this in cash. It has a €1 billion cash flow and 90 percent of its cash flow is still to be received.

Accountability: Requirements and Practice

Responsible Party

The National Pensions Reserve Fund Commission has absolute discretion to control, manage, and invest the assets of the fund in accordance with fund investment policy.

The commission is a body corporate with perpetual succession and a common seal and power to sue and be sued in its corporate name and to acquire, hold, and dispose of land or any interest in land and to acquire, hold, and dispose of any other property.

The commission consists of a chairperson and six commissioners, appointed by the Minister for Finance. All members of the commission are required to have substantial expertise and experience at a senior level in any of the following areas:

- investment or international business management
- finance or economics
- law
- actuarial practice
- accountancy and auditing
- the Civil Service
- trade union representation
- the pensions industry
- consumer protection

The minister is not allowed to appoint a person who currently holds a position in the Civil Service. Periods of office are set out in the legislation and remuneration is determined by the minister. A commissioner is disqualified should he or she:

- be adjudged bankrupt

- make a composition or arrangement with creditors
- be convicted of an indictable offence in relation to a company
- be convicted of an offence involving fraud or dishonesty
- be disqualified or restricted from being a director of any company

Should a commissioner have a pecuniary interest or other beneficial interest in any matter that falls to be considered by the commission, he or she must disclose this interest in advance of any consideration of the matter. The commissioner must neither influence nor seek to influence a decision to be made in relation to the matter and must take no part in any consideration of it. The commissioner must absent himself or herself from the meeting or the part of the meeting where the matter is being discussed, and must not vote on any decision relating to the matter. Such a disclosure must be recorded in the minutes of the meeting and the commission may, at its discretion, refer to the disclosure in its report to the minister. The commission is required to issue guidelines as to what constitutes an interest for this purpose (see Annex 5.D for these guidelines).

The commission is accountable to the Oireachtas (Irish Parliament) and the accountability requirements are set out in the National Pensions Reserve Fund Act.

Accountability Requirements in the Legislation

The National Pensions Reserve Fund Act, 2000 provides for:

- The preparation of accounts and the audit of these accounts by the Comptroller and Auditor General. (The Comptroller and Auditor General is the senior auditor in the State.)
- The publication by the commission of an annual report of its activities and of the audited accounts of the fund.
- The appearance before the Committee of Public Accounts of the chairperson of the commission and the submission by the chairperson of evidence on the policies of the commission in relation to the fund.
- The submission by the chief executive officer of the fund manager to the Committee of Public Accounts of evidence on the regularity and propriety of all transactions on the fund, and on the economy and

efficiency of the commission and the fund manager in regard to the expenses of operation of the fund.

(See Annex 5.E for legislative provisions on accountability and reporting.)

Accounts and Audits

The commission must keep all proper and usual accounts of monies and other assets appropriate to the fund. The accounts shall include a separate account of the administration fees and expenses incurred by the commission in the operation of the fund.

The audited accounts must note a record of expenses incurred by the fund manager.

Accounts kept in pursuance of this requirement, signed by the chief executive officer of the fund manager and by a commissioner authorized for that purpose, must be formally adopted by the commission and must be submitted as soon as may be, but not later than four months after the end of the financial year to which they relate, by the commissioner to the Comptroller and Auditor General for audit.

A copy of the accounts as audited by the Comptroller and Auditor General must be presented to the Minister for Finance as soon as may be and the minister must cause a copy of the accounts as so audited to be laid before each House of the Oireachtas (Parliament).

Report and Information to the Minister

Not later than six months after the end of each financial year the commission must make a report to the Minister for Finance of its activities during that year. The Minister must cause copies of the report to be laid before each House of the Oireachtas.

Each report must include:

- information on the investment strategy followed;
- a report on the investment return achieved by the fund;
- a valuation of the net assets of the fund and a detailed list of the assets of the fund at year-end;
- information about the investment manager and custodianship arrangements in relation to the fund; and

- information on fees, commission, and other expenses incurred by the commission and by the fund manager in the operation of the fund.

The report must also include any information in such form and about such matters as the Minister for Finance may direct.

Appearance before the Committee of Public Accounts

The Committee of Public Accounts is a parliamentary committee responsible for examining and reporting on departmental expenditure. It holds public hearings and conducts examinations of those required to appear before it. These hearings are widely publicized and reported where they relate to matters of public interest.

The chairperson of the commission must appear before and give evidence to the Committee of Public Accounts at such times as the committee may reasonably request. Any evidence given must, subject to confidentiality requirements concerning commercially sensitive information, relate to the policies of the commission in relation to the fund.

The chief executive officer of the fund manager also must, whenever required by the Committee of Public Accounts, give evidence to the committee on a variety of topics, including:

- the regularity and propriety of transactions recorded in any record subject to audit;
- the economy and efficiency of the commission and fund manager;
- the systems, procedures, and practices employed by the commission to evaluate its effectiveness; and
- any matter affecting the commission referred to in any report of the Comptroller and Auditor General.

The chief executive officer must not question or express opinions on the policy of the commission.

Other Requirements for Accountability

The Minister for Finance may from time to time appoint a person to carry out an examination of any or all aspects of the operation of the fund and the commission. The fund manager is required to assist this examination in every respect and to afford the person appointed by the minister access to all records, books, and accounts for this purpose.

The commission is required to commission, from time to time, independent valuations of the assets of the fund. It is also required to commission, from time to time, independent assessments of the investment performance of the fund.

Public procurement procedures, including EU procedures under Public Services Directive 92/50/EEC, must be used for the appointment of all service providers. These are stringent procedures ensuring fairness and transparency in all appointments of service providers.

Another function of the commission is that of appointing custodians for the assets of the fund. The legislation sets out the requirements to which the commission must have regard when evaluating prospective custodians. These include:

- custodianship expertise
- risk management systems and other information systems and technology, as appropriate
- corporate structure
- reporting capabilities
- financial strength
- internal ethical and compliance guidelines
- external regulatory obligations
- management fee, commission, and other expenses

The National Pensions Reserve Fund Act sets out further requirements that the contracts for the appointment of custodians should ensure also are met. In appointing a custodian, the commission may include a provision in the relevant contract enabling it to engage auditors to carry out an audit of the books of the custodian. In such a case, the custodian would be required to give access to the auditors to all appropriate records relevant to the assets of the fund.

There is a commitment in the act generally to open and transparent reporting, subject to the preservation of confidentiality on commercially sensitive information.

Other Ways of Accounting to the Public

The fund manager has a website on which all information relevant to the fund is available (www.ntma.ie). This information includes fund reports, press releases, and public procurement notices.

The commission and the fund manager hold press briefings from time to time to announce their reports and results. These are usually widely reported in the media.

The fund manager also speaks at a variety of conferences and is available to make presentations to relevant bodies or organizations.

Meeting the Requirements in Practice

The National Pensions Reserve Fund Commission Report and Financial Statements for the period 2 April 2001 to 31 December 2001 were prepared and published as required.

Public procurement procedures have been strictly followed for appointment of the various service providers.

Neither the chairperson nor the chief executive officer of the fund manager have yet been called to appear before the Committee of Public Accounts.

As previously mentioned, fund information is available on the Fund Manager website. Also press briefings have been held, for example at the end of 2002 when there was public interest in the returns of the Fund during the current difficult economic climate. Presentations which have been made by the Fund Manager in relation to the Fund have been informative and open.

Public Reaction

Awareness of the existence of the fund appears to be limited, and there evidently is little public understanding of the importance and relevance of the fund on a personal or national basis.

There has been intermittent questioning by economists and politicians as regards the merits of payments to the fund during the recent economic downturn in Ireland; there also have been questions as to the merits of having such a fund at all. Most of the economic arguments have tended to look at the issue from a broad perspective rather than considering the specifics of what is an unavoidable national issue. The debate has not been a good one and to some extent may have resulted in the spreading of misinformation.

During Ireland's 2002 national election campaign some of the political parties took positions on the fund, including suggestions that contributions to the fund be suspended for a time The incumbent parties were in the end returned to government and they have continued their clear commitment to the fund.

To date there does not seem to be any strong sense of the National Pensions Reserve Fund having become the "People's Fund."

Conclusion

Accountability is a vital ingredient for public funds. It must not only exist but must be seen by the public to exist. Public awareness and involvement provide probably the strongest discipline for such a fund.

Ireland has good legislative requirements in relation to accountability and transparency. The National Pensions Reserve Fund would appear to meet the criteria for a successful public fund, and no additional requirements have as yet suggested themselves for inclusion in the legislation governing the fund. With good legislation in place, the only thing that we need do is work hard at making accountability and transparency achieve the objective of the fund with the public for whom it has been put in place.

Annex 5.A: Portfolio Construction

Asset Class	Investment Style	Alpha (%)	Tracking Error (%)
Eurozone Equity X2	Passive	0.00	0.10
Pan-European Equity X3	Active-Core	0.75	5.00
U.S. Equity	Passive	0.00	0.10
U.S. Equity	Enhanced	0.25	1.50
U.S. Equity X2 (Value & Growth)	Active	0.90	6.00
Japanese Equity X2	Active	1.00	6.00
Pacific Basin Equity	Active	1.00	6.00
Global Equity X2	Active-Core	0.90	6.00
Long Euro Bonds	Passive	0.00	0.05
Long Euro Bonds	Active	0.30	2.00

5

Annex 5.B: Market Entry Strategy—"Averaging In"

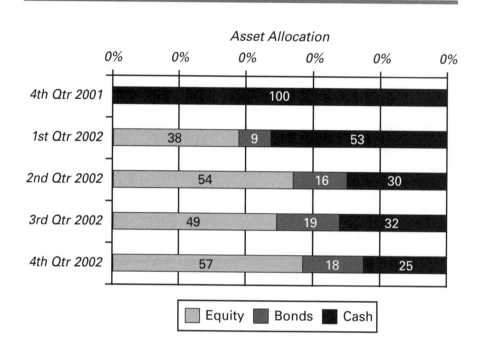

Asset Allocation

	4th Qtr 2001	1st Qtr 2002	2nd Qtr 2002	3rd Qtr 2002	4th Qtr 2002
Equity		38	54	49	57
Bonds		9	16	19	18
Cash	100	53	30	32	25

Equity   Bonds   Cash

Annex 5.C: Progress

	National Pensions Reserve Fund	Average Irish-Managed Pension Fund	Long-term Strategic Benchmark of the Fund
Apr to Dec 2001	3.27%	–0.6%	–3.52%
Year to 31 Dec 02 *(tentative estimates)*	–16.00%	–19.0%	–21.80%
Inception to 31 Dec 02 *(tentative estimates)*	–13.25%	–19.5%	–24.50%

5

Annex 5.D: The National Pensions Reserve Fund—Section 12 Guidelines

1. Introduction

The National Pensions Reserve Fund Commission (the "Commission") established under Section 5 of the National Pensions Reserve Fund Act, 2000 (the "NPRF Act", wishes to adopt Guidelines for the purposes of Section 12 of the NPRF Act and to ensure a high standard of corporate governance by the members of the Commission or any member of staff of the National Treasury Management Agency (the "Manager") and any member of a committee which may be established by the Commission pursuant to Section 14 of the NPRF Act (a "Committee") and to address the risk of actual or potential conflicts of interests and their disclosure.

For the purpose of these Guidelines the "Compliance Officer" means the officer appointed by the Manager to manage the compliance function on behalf of the Commission, any committee thereof and the Manager.

2. Duty to Disclose an Interest:

Section 12(1) of the NPRF Act, 2000 provide that

> "Where a commissioner or a member of the staff of the Manager or a member of a committee has a *pecuniary interest* or *other beneficial interest*, in *and material to*, any matter which falls to be considered by the Commission, the Manager or a committee, he or she shall-
>
> (a) disclose to the Commission or, as the case may be the Manager or the committee the nature of his or her interest in advance of any consideration of the matter.
> (b) neither influence nor seek to influence a decision to be made in relation to the matter,
> (c) take no part in any consideration of the matter, and where relevant—
> (d) absent himself or herself from the meeting or that part of the meeting during which the matter is discussed, and
> (e) not vote on a decision relating to the matter."

Subsection (7) of Section 12 provides that *"The Commission shall issue and publish guidelines as to that which constitutes **an interest**"* for the purpose of Section 12.

GUIDELINE 1

Definition of an "interest"

The Commission has determined that each of the interests on the list of registrable interests contained in the Second Schedule to the Ethics in Public Office Act, 1995 shall constitute an "**interest**" for the purposes of Section 12 of NPRF Act.

A copy of the Ethics in Public Office Act together with the Second Schedule list is attached to this note as a Appendix A.

That list should be construed as though references therein to a "designated directorship" were references to a member of the Commission or any Committee or any member of staff of the Manager.

GUIDELINE 2

Annual Disclosure Statements

The Commission has also determined that, in line with Section 17 of the Ethics in Public Office Act, 1995, there should be an annual disclosure statement (the "Annual Statement") prepared by each member of the Commission, any member of a Committee and any designated member of staff of the Manager.

A "**designated member of staff of the Manager**" means a person who has been designated by the Chief Executive of the Manager as a person who is engaged in the function to be performed under the NPRF Act.

Each such person shall in each year during any part of which he or she holds or held office as a member of the Commission, member of any committee or designated member of staff of the Manager prepare and furnish to the Compliance Officer a statement in writing of—

    (i)   the interests of the person, and

5

> (ii) the interests of which he or she has actual knowledge[1] of his or her spouse[1] or a child of the person or of his or her spouse[1]

which could materially influence the person in or in relation to the performance of the functions of the office by reason of the fact that such performance could so affect those interests as to confer on or without from the person or the spouse[1] or child a substantial benefit.[1]

The Annual Statement should be in the form of the statement attached to this note as Appendix B.

The first such Annual Statement should be supplied to the Compliance Officer at such time as the Chairperson of the Commission may determine.

All subsequent Annual Statements should be furnished to the Compliance Officer not later than 31 December in each year or at such other time or times as the Chairperson of the Commission may determine.

GUIDELINE 3

Disclosures to be made under Section (12(1) of the National Pensions Reserve Fund Act Guideline on pecuniary interest or beneficial interest.

The Commission has determined that for the purposes of Section 12(1) of the NPRF Act:

> (i) a person will be regarded as having a "**pecuniary interest**" if that person stands to gain money or money's worth or to avoid a loss of money or money's worth; and
>
> (ii) a "**beneficial interest**" includes—
>
>> (a) a right, privilege, office or dignity and any forbearance to demand money or money's worth or a valuable thing.
>> (b) any aid, vote, consent or influence,
>> (c) any promise or procurement of agreement or endeavour to procure, or the holding out of any expectation of, any gift, loan, fee, reward or other thing aforesaid, or other advantage and the avoidance of a loss, liability, penalty, forfeiture, punishment or other disadvantage; or other advantage and the avoidance of

a loss, liability, penalty, forfeiture, punishment or other disadvantage;

This definition of **beneficial interest** is the same as the definition of a "**benefit**" under Section 2 of the Ethics in Public Office Act. Note that a "**gift**" means money or other property.

When is an interest is "material"?

The Commission has determined that a person or a connected person[2] has a **material interest** in a matter falling to be considered by it **and therefore requiring disclosure pursuant to Section 12(1) of the NPRF Act, 2000** if the consequence or effect –

5

(a) of the performance by the person of a function of his or her office or
(b) of any decision made in relation to or in the course or as a result of the performance of of such a function by the person concerning that matter may be to confer on or withhold from the person or the connected person[2] a significant benefit without also conferring it on or withholding it from persons in general or a class of persons which is of significant size having regard to all the circumstances and of which the person or the connected person is a member.

This section is modelled on the definition of a material interest under Section 2(3) of the Ethics in Public Office Act, 1995.

A "connected person":

Any question whether a person is connected with another shall be determined in accordance with the following:

(i) person is connected with an individual if that person is a *relative*[3] of the individual,
(ii) a person, in his or her capacity as a trustee of a trust, is connected with an individual who or any of whose children or as respects whom any body corporate which he or she controls is a beneficiary of the trust,

(iii) a person is connected with any person with whom he or she is in partnership,

(iv) a company is connected with another person if that person has *control*[4] of it or if that person and persons connected with that person together have *control*[4] of it

(v) any two or more persons acting together to secure or exercise control of a company shall be treated in relation to that company as connected with one another and with any person acting on the directions of any of them to secure or exercise control of the company.

Appendix A: Ethics in Public Office Act, 1995,

Appendix B: Annual Statement

Appendix C: Sections 157 and 102 Corporation Tax Act, 1995.

Note: The contents of the above appendices are not reproduced here.

Annex 5.E: National Pensions Reserve Act, 2000; Part 4: Accountability and Reporting

25. (1) The chairperson of the Commission shall appear before, and give evidence to, the Committee of Public Accounts at such times as the Committee may reasonably request.

(2) Any evidence given under subsection (1) shall, subject to preserving confidentiality in relation to such commercially sensitive information, as determined by the Commission, relate to the policies of the Commission in relation to the Fund.

26. (1) The Commission shall keep in such form as may be approved of by the Minister all proper and usual accounts of all monies and other assets appropriate to the Fund. The accounts shall include a separate account of the administration fees and expenses incurred by the Commission in operation of the Fund.

(2) The audited accounts prepared under section 12 of the National Treasury Management Agency Act, 1990 shall note a record of expenses incurred by the Agency as the Manager.

(3) Accounts kept in pursuance of this section, signed by the chief executive officer of the Manager and by a commissioner authorized for that purpose, shall be formally adopted by the Commission and shall be submitted as soon as may be, but not later than four months after the end of the financial year to which they relate, by the Commission to the Comptroller and Auditor General for audit. A copy of the accounts as so audited shall be presented to the Minister as soon as may be and the Minister shall cause a copy of the accounts as so audited to be laid before each House of the Oireachtas.

(4) The chief executive officer of the Manager shall, whenever required by the Committee of Public Accounts, give evidence to that committee on:

a) the regularity and propriety of the transactions recorded or required to be recorded in any book or other record of account subject to audit by the Comptroller and Auditor General which the Commission is required by or under statute to prepare;

b) the economy and efficiency of the Commission and the Manager in the use of the resources made available to them under sections 17 and 23, respectively;

c) the systems, procedures, and practices employed by the Commission for the purposes of evaluating the effectiveness of its operations; and

d) any matter affecting the Commission referred to in a special report of the Comptroller and Auditor General under section 11(2) of the Comptroller and Auditor General (Amendment) Act, 1993 or in any other report of the Comptroller and Auditor General (in so far as it relates to a matter specified in paragraph (a), (b) or (c)) that is laid before Dáil Éireann.

(5) The chief executive officer of the Manager, if required under subsection (4) to give evidence, shall not question or express an opinion on the merits of any policy of the Commission or the objective of such a policy.

27. (1) As soon as may be, but not later than six months after the end of each financial year, the Commission shall make a report to the Minister of its activities during that year and the Minister shall cause copies of the report to be laid before each House of the Oireachtas.

(2) Each report under subsection (1) shall, having regard to the need for open and transparent reporting on the operation of the Fund but subject to preserving confidentiality in regard to commercially sensitive information, include the following for the year under review:

a) information on the investment strategy followed

b) a report on the investment return achieved by the Fund

c) a valuation of the net assets of the Fund and a detailed list of the assets of the Fund at the year end

d) information on fees, commission and other expenses incurred by the Commission and by the Manager in the operation of the Fund

(3) Each report under subsection (1) shall include information in such form and regarding such matters as the Minister may direct.

(4) The Minister may from time to time appoint a person to carry out an examination of any or all aspects of the operation of the Fund and the Commission and the Manager shall be required to assist this examination in

every respect and to afford the person appointed by the Minister access to
all records, books, and accounts for this purpose.

5

Notes

1. For the purpose of the Annual Statement the Commission will apply the same definitions as are used in the Ethics in Public Office Act, 1995. The words which are written in italics above have the meaning ascribed to them by the Ethics in Public Office Act.
2. See definition of a "connected person" above
3. Note that a "relative", in relation to a person, means a brother, sister, parent or spouse of the person or a child of the person or of the spouse.
4. In the definition of a "connected person" above the expression "control" has the meaning assigned to it by Section 157 Corporation Tax Act, 1976, a copy of which is attached as Appendix C. Please also see Section 102 of the 1976 Act which is cross-referenced in Section 157(8) of that Act.

Chapter 6

Key Differences in Public Pension Fund Management between Ireland and Poland

Krzysztof Pater

6

Good afternoon, ladies and gentlemen. I shall in this presentation briefly compare the social security schemes operated by Poland and Ireland. I will follow this with conclusions drawn of the experience specifically of the Polish fund. These are of a rather general character, and as such I think may be worthy of the consideration of some of the countries represented at this conference.

Background

The schemes that are in effect in Ireland and Poland are quite different. In Ireland, the statutory social security scheme is financed on a pay-as-you-go basis, and is in no need of reform. In Poland reform was needed, and this was initiated in 1999 to produce a new system that is financed partly on a pay-as-you-go basis and partly on a funded basis. The system that was used prior to reform also remains in place for those people who were aged more than 50 when the reform was implemented. For these people there was no change in the system.

Whenever we speak about reserve funds, we cannot avoid referring also to the demographic realities that increasingly inform our work. Since the early 1990s the number of pensioners living in the eastern European countries has grown dramatically, the result not only of demographic change but also of economic transformation in these countries. Over the same period the number of contributors to pension funds has fallen, producing for many countries in the region a significant increase in the system dependency ratio. This situation, as you know, is repeated all over the world. In some countries the problem will become critical within 10 years; in others, within 50 years.

In the case of Ireland, there currently are five people active for every pensioner. In Poland there are only 2.1 contributors for every retiree. It is this situation that provided the main impetus for the significant and deep reform of Poland's pension system, as clearly there was much work to do to ensure the long-term sustainability of the system. The reforms thus far have required an increase in public spending on the pension system to around 1.5 percent of GDP, to cover the transition costs. It will be a number of years before we can reduce this figure.

Funds' Main Objectives and Funding

Both countries have created reserve funds. The main purpose of Ireland's National Pension Reserve Fund, established by act in 2000 and made operational in 2001, is to meet part of the escalating cost of future pensions. In Poland the main purpose of the fund is to accumulate financial surplus in the system to support the pension part of the social security system through demographic change.

There was a significant delay in instituting Poland's fund. Despite being enshrined in law at the end of 1998 as part of the total legislation for reform, the fund started operation only in 2002. This delay was caused in part by political problems, but also by a failure to accurately anticipate the cost of the reform. Costing of the change was complicated by the fact that about 20 cohorts of the population had the option of remaining in the pay-as-you-go system, modified according to the concept of a defined contribution scheme, or of moving part of their contribution to the funded part of the system.

In the case of Ireland, every year 1 percent of GDP is transferred to the scheme. With the additional payments that also may be made to the fund, there is potential for the accumulation of a huge amount of money. In Poland, in contrast, the initial plan was to pay into the fund the equivalent of around 0.2 percent of GDP.[1] Because of the huge cost of the pension reform, however, in 2002 and 2003 the equivalent of just 0.02 percent of GDP was accumulated. We are aiming to increase this sum by 0.01 percent of GDP every year.

This raises the question of why we should be trying to save money in a reserve fund when we are at the same time transferring 1.5 percent of GDP into a social security scheme. There are a few reasons, I think, to do so. First, we are looking to the long term, with the goal of achieving at the minimum a pension component of the social security system that is fully financed and fully stable. Second, the reserve fund gives us the possibility to test the public management or combined private–public management of a public fund. And third, it serves as an example through which to demonstrate to politicians and citizens the importance of saving money for the long term, for the old age pension. By putting aside money for pensions the state provides a practical demonstration of its conviction that voluntary savings schemes, for example, are justified and necessary.

Ireland plans not to make any payments from its reserve fund until at the earliest 2025. In the case of Poland, which created its fund specifically to reduce the impact of demographic fluctuations on the social insurance system, all assets are likely to be withdrawn in 2009 and 2010. This estimate is based on calculations that take into account only demographic factors, and which show that, applying the current law, the need to cover spending on old age pensions will deplete the fund to zero by 2010. Accumulation to a new reserve fund will begin again a few years later.

Governance

The assets management practiced by the two countries is strikingly different. Where Ireland employs an external, independent commission to manage its reserve fund assets, Poland retains all management in-house. In Ireland, the independent commission determines the investment strategy and appoints investment managers; in Poland, responsibility for the investment strategy and basic asset allocation—along with diverse other responsibilities, ranging from the collection of contributions to the daily operation of the pay-as-you-go social insurance system—rests with the management board of the Social Security Institution. The rationale for these different practices lies with the

6

sizes of the funds managed: the Irish fund has accumulated assets of about US$8 billion, compared to the Polish assets of about US$100 million.

The President of the Social Security Institution is nominated by the Prime Minister on the joint application of the Minister of Finance and the Minister of Social Security. The presidency is not bound by time limits. Members of the Supervisory Board of the Social Security Institution are nominated by a supervisory council, such that employee unions, employer associations, and the government are equally represented on the board. The Supervisory Board in turn nominates members to the Management Board, on the application of the President of the Social Security Institution.

Investment Policy

The Social Security Institution has the right in law to decide the investment policy of the reserve fund, but only where that investment is to be made in treasury bills or securities issued by the State Treasury. (This in fact occurred in 2002 during the institution's first year of operation, when all assets were invested in treasury bills and state securities.) The institution is now considering converting some portion of the assets to mutual funds, which according to law may be handled by external managers. It is also tendering for the appointment of external managers for other fund's assets. Again, there are some limitations in law, most notably that no single external manager can be responsible for more than 15 percent of the assets.

The structure of the Irish fund portfolio is planned for the long term at a combination of 20 percent bonds and 80 percent equities (although it appears from recent announcements that additional classes of assets may also be permitted). The structure of the Polish portfolio also is constrained by law, but to a different degree. Poland does not have a tradition of fiduciary standards nor the concept of prudent manner, for example; rather, everything must be described by law. Other constraints arise in the reluctance of politicians to give too much freedom to the fund managers. At present, the proportion of fund assets invested in equities is limited at 30 percent, in company securities is limited at a cumulative total of 40 percent, and in securities as bonds guaranteed by the state treasury at 80 percent. There is no limit on the proportion of assets that is invested in treasury bills.

Public Awareness

Reaction to the reserve funds appears in Ireland and Poland to have been similar. In Poland, it seems few politicians understand our objectives for the fund. Many question why we have such a fund when the country is beset by budgetary problems. Payments to the fund are made out of public money and effectively are increasing the public deficit; one of the most popular schools of thought therefore is that we should cancel the fund and instead reduce the deficit. Economists—including those working as advisors to politicians—also on occasion fail to understand our objectives.

There evidently is much hard work that needs to be done to improve the level of public understanding. That said, I believe from my own observations that there is a growing need worldwide, in more and more countries, for the creation of reserve funds. These funds must be managed independently of the government, but not entirely without government involvement. For example, government should create the rules of operation or otherwise approve those rules, including those guiding the apportioning of assets to securities, equities, treasury bills, and so on. (It is essential that equities assume a significant share of the fund's portfolio, although defining the appropriate share is always problematic.) Government also has an important role to play in the nomination of the people who will be responsible for the fund.

Many politicians, as I have said, seem still not to understand the reason for regular payments to a reserve fund. The education process therefore is very important, and as such it is well to create the fund even if initially the value of its assets may be small, as in Poland's case. (A small fund carries small risk, and thus has the advantage of permitting its operators to create, implement, and test procedures without the fear of catastrophic failure should something go wrong.) A fund of any size assists in persuading politicians and society alike of the necessity of a long-term approach to social security, and specifically of the need for the state to set aside assets for long-term spending and of the need for people to save money themselves, for their future and to provide an income in old age.

The political climate in many countries means that it would be well to start the operation of such a fund step by step. By starting as Poland did with low-risk investments, in our case in the form of securities issued by the State Treasury, a country can keep at a minimum the negative sentiment directed against the fund while at the same time encouraging positive sup-

6

port. Starting in this manner also minimizes the risk that within the first two or three years of the fund the value of accumulated assets will fall below the total value of payments. Once the fund has been established for a few years it may then be appropriate to increase the investment risk, again step by step.

In many countries, including Poland, the issue of foreign investments also raises some problems. These tend to be of a psychological nature but they are important, and it is because of them that we have for the moment decided not to invest overseas. We may change our stance in the future, as Poland becomes a member of the European Union and a participant in the euro zone, but I think that during the early existence of the reserve fund it is better not to take the political risk of proposing foreign investments. For many countries, the prevailing social and political climate in fact simply would not permit outside investments.

Concluding Remarks

The step-by-step approach may in the long term be the best way to increase the value of assets collected in the fund. The evidence of the Polish case would seem to confirm this. I am sure that we would not have been able to maintain our fund if we had tried to keep to the initial decision to allocate 0.2 percent of GDP to the fund each year. In a situation in which the additional cost of our pension reform is around 1.5 percent of GDP, it is the decision to reduce investment in the fund to 0.02 percent of GDP, and to build gradually from there, that has kept the fund alive.

Thank you for your attention.

Notes

1. The basis for the calculation of this contribution is in practice the aggregate of salaries on which the social insurance contribution is assessed, but I have recalculated this to enable a direct comparison in terms of GDP.

Chapter 7

Governance of Public Pension Funds: New Zealand Superannuation Fund

Brian McCulloch and Jane Frances

Over the next 50 years or so, a permanently higher proportion of the population of New Zealand will become eligible to receive payments of New Zealand Superannuation. The New Zealand Superannuation Fund has been established to smooth the impact that this change will have on the Crown's finances.[1]

The objective of fund policy is to build up a portfolio of Crown-owned financial assets while the cost of New Zealand Superannuation is still relatively low. Those assets and their compound investment returns will be drawn on progressively to supplement the annual budget as the Crown's finances adjust to the rising level of expense of New Zealand Superannuation. The fund will in effect serve as a smoothing mechanism for what is fundamentally a pay-as-you-go universal benefit.

It is essential to the success of this policy that the financial assets that constitute the fund be efficiently managed. The projected large size of the fund means that even relatively small efficiency losses could have a significant negative effect on national welfare. The experience internationally has been that politically controlled public funds typically exhibit poor financial performance: a crucial element of the policy underlying the New Zealand fund was therefore the design of governance arrangements to ensure that the fund is managed as efficiently as possible. The objective was to establish a clearly defined portfolio of Crown financial resources, managed by an independent governing body with explicit commercial objectives and clear accountability.

After briefly reviewing the context within which the policy originated and the policy objective, this paper examines the key design elements of the governance framework for the fund that attend to each element of that objective: clearly defining the fund, assuring the governing body of an appropriate level of independence, providing explicit legislated commercial investment objectives, and establishing a robust accountability framework. Finally, the paper briefly reviews the experience of implementation to date and summarizes the arrangements surrounding the governance of other portfolios of financial assets owned by the Crown in New Zealand.

Context

New Zealand Superannuation Policy

New Zealand Superannuation (NZS) is a universal benefit paid to all individuals over the age of 65 who meet New Zealand residency criteria. The level of the pension ensures that a married person receives, after deduction of income tax, no less than 32.5 percent of the national average ordinary-time weekly earnings.[2] It is indexed annually. There are neither means tests nor income history requirements.

Indexation of the rate of NZS is based on inflation of the consumer price index, but is subject to the pension level not falling below the specified minimum relativity to average earnings. The pension level currently is above this minimum relativity, but the rise in real wage rates and earnings will within a few years mean that the minimum will be triggered and the pension will effectively become indexed to wage growth (see Figure 7.1).

The New Zealand Government has provided public pensions for more than 100 years (Preston 2001). These pensions have taken several forms, including means-tested schemes, social security taxes, and a compulsory contributory scheme. The forerunner of the current New Zealand Superannuation was introduced in 1977 in the form of a universal pension paid at age 60 and set at 80 percent of the average wage for a couple and 60 percent for an unmarried person. Between 1992 and 2001 the age of eligibil-

Figure 7.1: Bounds for Indexation of the NZS Rate

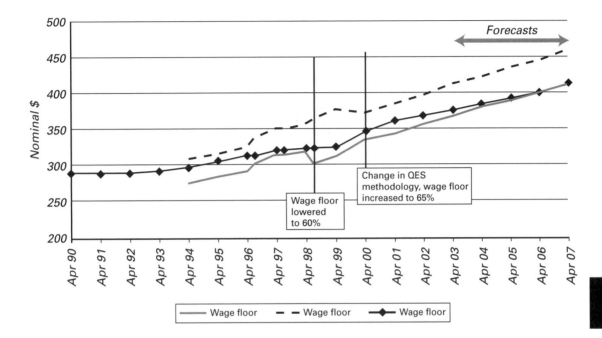

ity was progressively increased to age 65; indexation additionally was linked to price inflation instead of wage growth, with the result that the rate has progressively fallen toward a floor of 65 percent of average wages as the rate for a married couple (equating to 32.5 percent per married person).

The policy for New Zealand Superannuation entitlements is unchanged by the establishment of the New Zealand Superannuation Fund. The New Zealand Superannuation Act 2001 that established the fund reenacted the existing entitlement provisions with only minor drafting clarifications.[3]

Population Ageing

Populations around the world are ageing and the New Zealand population is no exception. While New Zealand is expected to experience slower overall population growth over the coming decades, the number of older people will increase and there will be a significant change in the age structure of the population.

Figure 7.2: New Zealand Population Age Structure

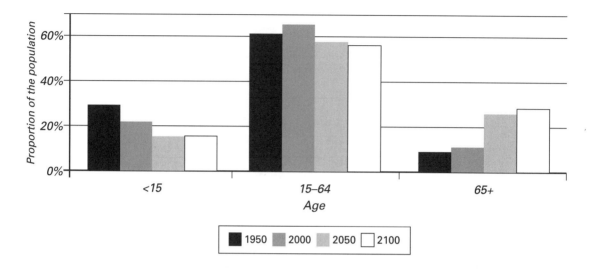

Figure 7.2 highlights the changing makeup of the New Zealand population.[4] The proportion of the population aged over 65 increased from 9 percent in 1951 to 12 percent in 2001 and is projected to increase to 26 percent in 2051 and 28 percent by 2100. In comparison, the working age population is projected to fall from 65 percent of the population now to 58 percent by 2051 and 56 percent by 2100. The youth population is projected to fall from 23 percent to 16 percent in 2051 and then remain at that level. This change in population structure is driven by lower expected fertility rates and higher life expectancy. The transition over the next 50 years to an older population therefore represents a permanent change. The post-Second World War "baby boom" accelerates the profile slightly but is not a major factor. Expected migration also has only a minor effect. The effects of declining fertility, increasing longevity, and migration are examined further in the following sections.

Declining Fertility

Figure 7.3 illustrates how the New Zealand fertility rate has moved over time.[5] Over the last 20 years the fertility rate has been below the replacement rate for the population of 2.1 births per woman. Forecasts assume that the rate will continue to fall to about 1.9 births per woman by 2010 and remain at that level. Women in New Zealand are having fewer children and are having them later in life.

Increasing Longevity

Life expectancy has increased steadily and is expected to continue increasing. A woman (man) born in 1956 is expected to live to 73 (68.2) years of age, while one born in 1996 is expected to live to 79.6 (74.3). By 2050, life expectancy for both men and women is expected to exceed 80 years of age. Increasing life expectancy generally has meant longer periods of eligibility for New Zealand Superannuation, but the changing policy on entitlement has at different times affected this overall length of eligibility. This is illustrated in Figure 7.4, which shows historical data to 1996 and forecast data from 2000. Prior to 1977, two benefits were in place: the Age Benefit, which was means tested and available from age 60, and Universal Superannuation,

7

Figure 7.3: Total Fertility Rate

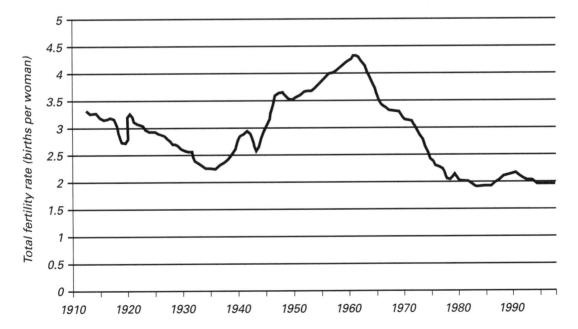

Figure 7.4: Years of Eligibility for New Zealand Superannuation

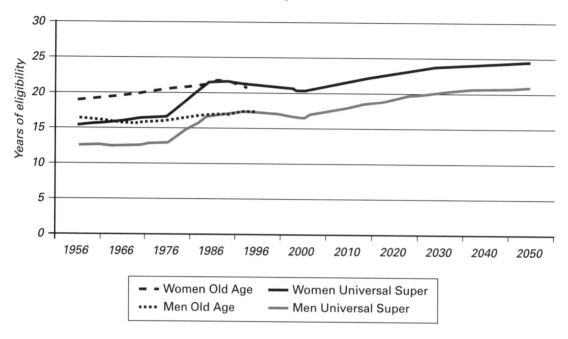

which was available to all from age 65. From 1977 to 1991, payments were available from age 60. Over the period 1992 to 2001 the age of eligibility was moved up to 65; the forecasts beyond 2000 assume that the eligibility age stays at age 65.

Migration

Migration trends will affect the population structure of New Zealand, but not to the same extent as fertility or life expectancy. Over the 50 years to 1998, positive net migration averaged 6,000 per annum. In comparison, natural increase (births less deaths) increased New Zealand's population by an average 33,000 per annum over the same period. Even if migration were to become a significant factor in the overall growth rate of the population, it is not clear what effect it would have on the age structure (current immigration policy tends to favor younger working-age applicants).

Implications for Crown Finances

Direct Cost of New Zealand Superannuation

New Zealand Superannuation is a universal payment, and the cost of NZS therefore is directly related to the number of people of eligible age. Since the rates of NZS are linked to wage levels, and since wage growth is strongly related to GDP growth, the cost to the Crown of NZS as a proportion of GDP under current policy can be reliably measured for several decades into the future.

Figure 7.5 illustrates the projected path of the net cost of NZS to the end of the century.[6] Several features are apparent. First, over the next few decades there will be a significant increase in the cost of NZS, with it expected to rise from about 4 percent of GDP to about 9 percent. Second, the higher cost will be a permanent shift, driven by the fundamental demographic changes discussed above. Third, the phenomenon of the baby boom generation will exacerbate the upward trend, as indicated by the hump in the slope between 2030 and 2040 when the bulk of baby boomers will be

7

Figure 7.5: New Zealand Superannuation as a Percentage of GDP

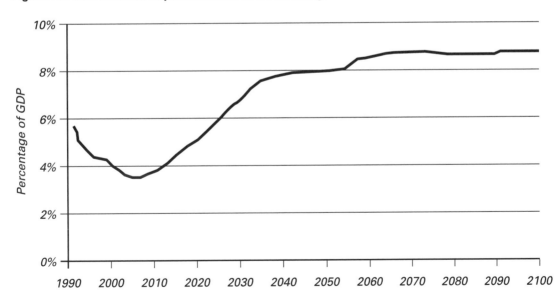

over 65 (there is another ripple in the slope, around 2070, as their children in turn will become eligible for NZS). Fourth, the decline in cost that has been experienced over the past decade is about to be reversed. The decline resulted not from demographic changes, but from a combination of policy changes: a rapid transition in eligibility age from 60 to 65, and a decline in the rates of NZS as a percentage of average wages.

Other Costs with an Ageing Population

New Zealand Superannuation is not the only cost to the Crown that will vary with the age structure of the population. In particular, there are likely to be significant increases in the cost of public healthcare as the population ages. Stephenson and Scobie (2002) survey the broader economic implications of population ageing in New Zealand.

While the older population will increase over the next few decades, the youth population is projected to decline (see Figure 7.2). The World Bank (1994) considered whether the cost to government associated with the increasing proportion of old people could be met through the diversion of resources away from the shrinking youth population. It concluded that it would not be possible to do so because (a) the cost to the government due to children is less than that due to older people; (b) the social resources needed by children (for example, schools) are different from those needed by older people (for example, pensions, hospitals, and custodial care); and (c) societies with few children have made a quantity–quality trade-off and would be more likely to invest more heavily in each child than reallocate resources to the elderly.

Policy Objective

Smoothing Crown Finances

Government policy is to preserve New Zealand Superannuation as a universal age-related benefit, retaining substantially the current provisions indefinitely. With tax revenue expected to stay in the region of 30 percent to 35 percent of GDP, a doubling in the cost of NZS from less than 4 percent of GDP to more than 8 percent (along with increases in other age-related costs) implies that there will be a significant change in the structure of the Crown's finances over the next few decades. The policy objective is to put in place arrangements to assist the Crown's finances to make this change. This will involve drawing resources off the budget for the next two to three decades and then progressively drawing on these resources as the annual cost of NZS continues to rise. The reserved funds ultimately will be exhausted but by such time that this happens it is planned that the budget will have adjusted to a new structure that incorporates the permanently higher cost of NZS.

This policy could be considered to be a form of tax smoothing. Davis and Fabling (2002) estimate that there is potential for significant welfare gains from a policy that uses tax smoothing to manage the fiscal implications of population ageing. They note also that this is dependent on having in place strong institutions to enable the gains to be captured: in particular, there need to be strong governance arrangements around the large pool of Crown financial assets implied by the tax smoothing fiscal strategy.

The smoothing objective for the New Zealand Superannuation Fund requires that the rate of total contribution from the budget to NZS (that is, the current year expense on NZS entitlements plus the capital contribu-tion to the fund) be set such that if that rate, as a percentage of GDP, were to be maintained over the next 40 years it would be just enough, with the accumulating fund and its investment returns, to meet the expected cost of NZS entitlements over that 40-year period.[7] Each year, the level of required contribution is recalculated based on the latest forecasts and a rolling 40-year time horizon.

The effect of this rolling time horizon calculation of the contributions to the fund is illustrated in Figure 7.6. Initially, an annual amount of 1 percent to 2 percent of GDP (being the positive gap between the two lines until the mid-2020s) is required to be set aside from the budget. This declines to zero by the mid-2020s, after which the reserve thus established and the compounding investment returns are progressively drawn on to smooth the continuing increase in the annual cost of NZS entitlements.[8]

Without the smoothing, the annual cost of NZS would more than double from 3.6 percent of GDP in 2003 to 8 percent by 2050. With smoothing, the effective charge against the annual budget (that is, the annual cost of payments to recipients, plus (minus) the capital amounts set aside (drawn on)) starts at 4.6 percent in 2003 and would reach only 6.5 percent by 2050. This represents an increase of less than one-half.

7

Figure 7.6: Smoothing the Cost of New Zealand Superannuation

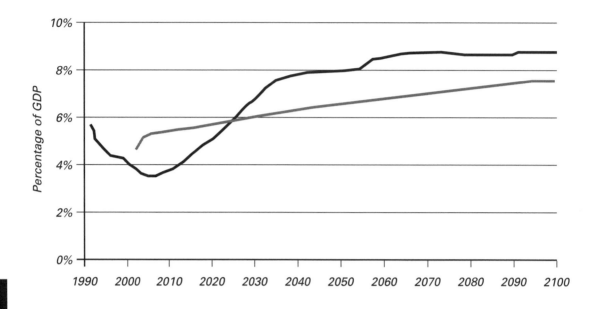

Instead of establishing the fund to hold and invest the capital contributions, the government conceivably could have decided to continue reducing
Crown debt by amounts equal to those contributions. This was not in the
end considered feasible because gross Crown debt is now down to relatively
comfortable levels after a decade over which debt repayment was seen as a
key fiscal priority.[9] Establishment of the fund was seen as a more credible
means of obtaining the stronger Crown financial position that in the long
term will be required to implement the smoothing policy.

The success of this policy depends crucially upon the fund being managed efficiently. With only a few recent exceptions, however, the experience
internationally is that the performance of public investment funds has been
nowhere near efficient (Iglesias and Palacios 2000). The fund is projected
to grow significantly over the next few decades, to the order of 50 percent
of GDP (McCulloch and Frances 2001a). As a result, even relatively small
efficiency losses could have a significant negative effect on national welfare
(Davis and Fabling 2002). Careful attention was therefore paid to placing

governance arrangements around the fund so that it is managed as efficiently as possible. These governance arrangements are discussed in detail in later sections of this paper.

New Zealand is not the only country to seek to implement governance arrangements to avoid the historical poor performance of public funds. The Canada Pension Plan Investment Board, the Irish National Pensions Reserve Fund, and the Norwegian Petroleum Fund provide notable examples of similar governance arrangements. This paper focuses on the arrangements implemented for the New Zealand Superannuation Fund, however; it does not present a detailed international comparison of governance arrangements.[10]

Other Issues

Retirement Income Policy

As described above, the policy for the New Zealand Superannuation Fund is essentially one of fiscal management. Establishment of the fund has not involved any significant changes to the parameters surrounding the payment of NZS. The focus has instead been on how to finance the existing policy.

Establishment of the fund nonetheless does not preclude changes to the entitlement parameters. For example, if the eligibility age were in the future to be increased, this would have the effect of reducing the forecasts of the annual cost of NZS (that is, would shift downward the line drawn in Figure 7.5 and the corresponding line in Figure 7.6). The capital contribution calculation, which takes into account the forecast of entitlement payments over the next 40 years, would as a result produce a lower ongoing required capital contribution. The policy objective of smoothing the impact on the rest of the budget would continue to be pursued.

On a broader scale, as it is primarily a mechanism for long-term fiscal management the fund cannot be considered a complete solution to issues of retirement income policy. It is simply a means to help the Crown meet the government's commitment to retain a universal old age pension—that is, the first pillar in the World Bank's multi-pillar framework (World Bank 1994). It does not preclude the introduction of other policies such as compulsory saving or incentives for voluntary saving.[11] Such policies would be considered on their own merits, regardless of the existence of the fund.

7

Contrast with an Archetypal Pension Fund in the Private Sector

Another implication of the fiscal management focus of the policy relates to the characterization of the fund. The New Zealand Superannuation Fund is not a pension fund in the normal sense of that term, it is an investment fund. The assets of the fund are simply a well-defined subset of the property of the Crown. Recipients of NZS, whether current or future, have no special claim over those assets; it is the Crown that is the legal and beneficial owner of the fund. While there are many issues of pension fund management generally that are relevant to the New Zealand Superannuation Fund, not all aspects of pension fund management apply. In particular, the scope of responsibility and the fiduciary duties of members of the fund's governing body are different from those of the trustees of a typical pension fund. The fund furthermore was not designed to ever fully finance the cost of NZS. It is simply a smoothing mechanism for what remains fundamentally a pay-as-you-go unrequited benefit.

Since the fund is not a superannuation scheme, it is not subject to the regulatory regime governing superannuation schemes in New Zealand.[12] However, as an investor the fund and the board are subject to the securities regulations of New Zealand and of other jurisdictions in which the fund invests. The fund has no exemption by virtue of being property of the Crown. Similarly, the financial statements of the fund are required to follow the same financial reporting standards that apply to other reporting entities, both public sector and private, in New Zealand.

Features of Policy Design

The key features of the design of the governance arrangements for the New Zealand Superannuation Fund are summarized in the following statement:[13]

> A clearly defined portfolio of Crown financial resources, … managed by an independent governing body … with explicit commercial objectives … and clear accountability.

Before proceeding to an explanation of these governance arrangements, three points should be noted. First, the arrangements have been implemented as a complete, unified package. They do not represent a menu that can be picked and chosen from. As the World Bank points out, there are strong interdependencies among the different parts of a fund's governance structure (Palacios 2002). While it may be important that a board have broad authority for investment management, this advantage could be undermined by partisan board appointments; equally, a strong board of independent investment experts may be of little benefit if the investment strategy is predetermined politically. Second, once the "big picture" has been sketched out (as in the statement above), the design of governance arrangements very quickly gets down to matters of relatively fine detail, any of which could turn out to be pivotal in the success of the overall policy. Third, these governance arrangements have been implemented in the context specifically of the New Zealand environment, which includes a well-developed legal system, open capital markets, a strong public sector management system, and a small, relatively affluent economy. Different arrangements may be appropriate in a different context.

"A clearly defined portfolio of Crown financial resources…"

The fund will consist almost entirely of financial instruments that are highly fungible and that could be a temptation for governments, which face continual pressures to allocate more resources than they have at hand. It is therefore important for the effectiveness of the policy that the assets that comprise the property of the fund be clearly defined, and that the capital contributions the government is required to make to the fund and the capital withdrawals it can take from the fund also be clearly defined. This is important from the point of view also of holding the board accountable for its administration of the fund. The credibility of the policy and the government's commitment to it also help define the portfolio in a forward-looking sense.

Property of the Fund

The New Zealand Superannuation Fund is not a separate legal entity[14] but is a part of the Crown. The property of the fund is defined in the legislation, and includes the capital contributions from the Crown, fund investments, and the returns from investment [section 38]. As explained below, the governing board of the fund, the "Guardians of New Zealand Superannuation," is a Crown entity that is separate from the fund.

Capital Contributions

One way that a future government could divert resources from the fund would be by limiting the capital contributions that are intended to be made to the fund over the next two decades or so. It was therefore important to be clear about what capital contributions are required to be made to the fund. The policy objective is to smooth the cost of NZS over time, based on a 40-year rolling horizon as described above. The algorithm for calculating the level of capital contribution required from year to year to achieve this objective is stated in the legislation [section 43].[15] Prior to the start of each financial year the Treasury must calculate the amount of required capital contribution implied by this algorithm and publish it in the Budget Economic and Fiscal Update, along with a statement of assumptions [section 42].[16]

While it is important that the government make its required capital contributions to the fund, it also is required to adhere to the "principles of responsible fiscal management" set out in the Fiscal Responsibility Act 1994. These are [section 4(2), Fiscal Responsibility Act 1994]:

a) Reducing total Crown debt to prudent levels so as to provide a buffer against factors that may impact adversely on the level of total Crown debt in the future, by ensuring that, until such levels have been achieved, the total operating expenses of the Crown in each financial year are less than its total operating revenues in the same financial year.

b) Once prudent levels of total Crown debt have been achieved, maintaining these levels by ensuring that, on average, over a reasonable period of time, the total operating expenses of the Crown do not exceed its total operating revenues.

c) Achieving and maintaining levels of Crown net worth that provide a buffer against factors that may impact adversely on the Crown's net worth in the future.

d) Managing prudently the fiscal risks facing the Crown.

e) Pursuing policies that are consistent with a reasonable degree of predictability about the level and stability of tax rates for future years.

The government is required by the Fiscal Responsibility Act 1994 to establish and articulate its long-term policy objectives in accordance with these principles. The obligation to make contributions to the fund needs to sit alongside these objectives. It was therefore not appropriate for the government to be absolutely bound to make the full capital contribution calculated by the Treasury.[17] However, should it choose to contribute less than the required capital contribution, the government must explain its actions—in the same way that it must explain any departure from the principles of responsible fiscal management [section 44].

Capital Withdrawals

Another way that a future government could seek to divert resources from the fund would be to make capital withdrawals greater than, or in advance of, the rate of withdrawal implied by the capital contribution algorithm. This is dealt with in two ways. First, the legislation only allows capital withdrawals up to the amount implied by the legislated algorithm [section 47(1)]. Second, no capital withdrawal is allowed in any case before 2020 [section 47(2)].

The government also is precluded from requiring the fund to purchase New Zealand government securities, which would amount to a tacit withdrawal.

7

Policy Credibility and Commitment

Most of this policy could have been established administratively without new legislation,[18] but political pressure and other incentives on politicians and officials would then have placed it at continual risk of reversal (Davis 1998). Establishing the fund through legislation enhanced the credibility of the policy and signaled the government's commitment to it. It also strengthened it: only the Parliament can amend or repeal legislation.

The government sought to further enhance the credibility of the legislation by strengthening the process for amending it. In New Zealand the principle of the sovereignty of Parliament means that legislation cannot limit the practice of Parliament, nor can a future Parliament be bound by legislation. It was therefore not seen as practical to try to entrench the legislation (for example, by requiring a super-majority to make amendments), nor to prescribe how Parliament should proceed with amendments. Instead, a requirement was placed on the government, when introducing amending legislation, to report to Parliament on the consultation process that was followed in formulating the proposed amendment [section 73(1) and 73(2)].

"... managed by an independent governing body..."

A separate Crown entity, the Guardians of New Zealand Superannuation, has been established [section 48]. The board of this entity is responsible for investing the fund [section 58(1)]. Several features have been incorporated in the legislation to limit political influence over the board's decisions. These are as follows:

- The board is required to comprise individuals with expertise in investment management, selected by an independent nominating committee. Board members can only be dismissed for good reason.
- The board has full powers to establish a fund management infrastructure. It is permitted no other responsibilities that could create confusion about its role.
- Conflicts of interest are explicitly catered for.
- The Minister's powers of direction of the fund are explicitly limited and must be consistent with the legislated investment objectives.
- Central control or influence over board remuneration and some employment conditions remain with the government.

Separate Crown Entity

To carry out its functions, the governing board of a fund such as the New Zealand Superannuation Fund requires a secretarial infrastructure. One possibility would have been for the board to establish its secretariat as a part of the fund, drawing on fund resources as required. However, the board's expenses would be so small compared to the flows in the fund as a whole that there would be no effective check on the board's direct spending.[19] In particular, some capability was required to ensure that the cost-effectiveness of the board itself could be monitored and the risks of profligacy, or "gold plating," minimized, thus avoiding adverse publicity that could undermine the credibility of the policy. It was therefore decided to establish the board as a separate legal entity—the Guardians of New Zealand Superannuation—with a budget separate from the fund [section 52]. As a Crown entity, this body is subject to an existing well-developed accountability framework under the Public Finance Act 1989. The requirements of this framework include the production of an annual statement of intent prior to the start of each year and an annual report including audited financial statements. These elements of the governance arrangements are discussed further below.

The creation of a separate Crown entity responsible for administration of the fund introduced the likelihood of questions of whether a particular cost should be treated as an expense of the fund or as an expense of the Crown entity. For example, if the board were to carry out a direct fund management function in-house, rather than through a fund manager, this could be considered an expense that should be charged to the fund. Each such instance should be judged on its own merits, however. In any case, all expenses of the Crown entity are required to be met out of money appropriated by Parliament for the purpose [section 52].[20] Leaving this component of cost allocation as a gray area was seen to be an unavoidable implication of obtaining a balance between the independence of the board and its budget accountability.

Expertise Requirements

Board members must, "in the Minister's opinion, [have] substantial experience, training, and expertise in the management of financial investments" [section 55(a)]. This requirement for technical expertise was included for three reasons. First, it makes clear that board appointments are to be made on the basis of individual ability and not simply to secure representation for specific interest groups. Evidence from U.S. state and local pension plans is that nonexpert interest group representation results in lower fund performance (Mitchell and Hsin 1994; Romano 1993). Second, this requirement for technical expertise reiterates the primary objective of the board, which is to invest the fund on a prudent, commercial basis. Third, the effectiveness of the board is critical to the success of this policy. It is therefore essential that board members have a strong understanding of the issues pertaining to investment fund management. The concern of the New Zealand legislators that there be appropriate expertise on the fund's governing body has also been echoed internationally. For example, the British Government has announced that it proposes to legislate to require appropriate expertise and "familiarity with the issues" on the part of pension fund trustees.[21]

In accordance with the practice for appointment to public bodies in New Zealand, there are no requirements regarding New Zealand citizenship or residency. Given the stringent expertise requirements, restricting the board membership to New Zealand citizens and residents in any case could have unreasonably limited the pool of suitably qualified candidates.

7

There also is no restriction on the appointment of individuals who happen to be officials or board executives. This potentially could create situations in which the independence of board members is called into question, but as normal practice in New Zealand is that boards of public bodies do not include ex officio members, such as board employees, ministry officials, or ministers, legislation on this point was not seen as necessary.[22]

Nominating Committee

Partisan appointments to the board potentially could compromise its political independence. To mitigate against this possibility, the Minister of Finance is required to make appointments only from a shortlist of candidates submitted by a nominating committee [section 56]. Adapted from the provisions for appointment of the Canada Pension Plan Investment Board, this is a novel process for Crown entity or state-owned enterprise appointments in New Zealand.[23]

The nominating committee is required to comprise at least four people "with proven skills or work experience that will enable them to identify candidates to the board who are suitably qualified" [section 56(2)]. A determined government conceivably could use its power to appoint a partisan nominating committee, so this procedure is not completely foolproof. It nonetheless is important to the overall effort to ensure the independence of the board.[24]

The nominating committee for the inaugural board members followed the process described on page 36. The nominating committee will need to be reconvened as required for new board appointments and reappointments.

Dismissal

Limitations on the power of the government to dismiss "politically unfavored" board members also help to ensure the independence of the board. However, such limitations must be balanced against the need to be able to replace dysfunctional individuals who may be compromising the board's effectiveness or who otherwise may simply be performing poorly. Provision was therefore included to permit the justifiable removal of an individual for "any reason relating to the member's performance, or ability to perform, his or her duties as a member, the board's performance of its collective duties, or misconduct by the member." [Schedule 3, clause 10][25]

A dismissed board member is not entitled to any compensation relating to removal from office [Schedule 3, clause 10(6)].

Power to Establish Fund Management Structure

The board has wide administrative powers to enable it to carry out its function of investing the fund [sections 49 and 53]. The specific provision was also included that the board may appoint investment managers and custodians [sections 62 and 63]. This may not have been strictly necessary, because the board's broad powers probably already allowed this. However, the provisions already existed in the legislation of another public body with an investment function, so as a matter of drafting practice it was included here to avoid any doubt.

The possibility of requiring an existing agency, such as the Reserve Bank or the Treasury, to act as custodian or fund manager also was considered. There were two reasons for not pursuing this. First, there was a desire to avoid any perception of the government placing constraints on the operation of the fund that could be used as an excuse by the board for poor performance or that could be seen as limiting the independence of the board in its investment decisions. Second, these agencies do not have particular experience as a custodian or fund manager across the range of financial instruments held by the fund and offer no obvious competitive advantage over private sector firms in providing these services.

No Other Responsibilities

The board's sole function is to manage and administer the investment of the fund [sections 51(1) and 58(1)]. It does not administer the benefits payment system, it has no responsibility for determining the levels neither of benefits nor of the Crown's capital contributions or withdrawals, and it does not administer any other funds. This avoids confusion about the board's role and limits the possibility of the board's independence being compromised in carrying out that role.

Conflicts of Interest

In a small capital market like that of New Zealand there is a limited pool of suitably qualified candidates available for appointment to a board such as

7

this. (This is even though there is no residency requirement for appointment to the board.) Conflicts of interest for individual board members inevitably will arise from time to time. The emphasis therefore is not so much on avoiding such conflicts of interest, but more on ensuring that appropriate systems are in place for their identification and management. Examples where conflicts could arise include adviser appointments, manager appointments, and individual investment choices.

The legislation provides for conflicts of interest by requiring board members to disclose any relevant interests as they arise and to stand aside from deliberation and decisions regarding the matter [Schedule 3, clauses 19 to 25]. This was seen as an important requirement for ensuring financial markets have confidence in the integrity of the board. An active conflict of interest also can arise in the use or disclosure to others of inside information that is only available to a board member in his or her capacity as a member of the board. This is also proscribed [Schedule 3, clause 26]. In addition, the board and the fund are subject to securities regulation in New Zealand and in other jurisdictions in which they might invest.

The management of conflicts of interest also is emphasized in the administrative processes surrounding appointments. This is reflected in the appointments process set by the Cabinet Office and in the guidelines published by the State Services Commission.[26]

Ministerial Direction

Given the desire to design the governance arrangements such that the board operates as independently as possible of the government of the day, it may seem strange that the legislation includes a power for the minister to give directions to the board [section 64]. However, this provision is drafted so that a direction cannot be inconsistent with the board's duty to invest the fund on a prudent commercial basis, and the direction is required to be published. The board furthermore is required only to "have regard to" a ministerial direction, and is not obliged to comply with it. Although this arguably renders a direction little different from any comment the minister might care to make, it was seen as an important provision to clarify that, despite the explicit independence of the board, the government is nonetheless entitled to express a view about its expectations as to the fund's performance.

No ministerial directions have been made to date.

Board Remuneration

The level of board members' remuneration is an important issue, because the remuneration needs to be sufficient to attract appropriately qualified individuals without creating a perception of profligacy. It is longstanding government policy in New Zealand that appointments to state bodies follow standard remuneration guidelines and that a responsible minister can depart from those guidelines only after consultation with the State Services Commissioner.[27] The guidelines are relatively detailed and are based on criteria designed to determine the size of the role. This is implemented in the legislation by requiring the minister to approve board members' remuneration [Schedule 3, clause 12].

Having the minister set board members' remuneration raises the potential for the exercise of political influence. An alternative practice could have been to leave the determination of remuneration as a matter for the board. The Canada Pension Plan Investment Board is required to set its own remuneration and benefits "having regard to the remuneration and benefits received by persons having similar responsibilities and engaged in similar activities" [Canada Pension Plan Investment Board Act of 1997, section 10(10)]. This approach was not adopted for the New Zealand Superannuation Fund because of a desire to remain consistent with the standard remuneration guidelines that apply to New Zealand Crown entities.

Employment Conditions

A related constraint on the board is that it must consult with the State Services Commissioner and the Minister of Finance regarding the conditions of employment of its chief executive officer [Schedule 3, clause 46]. Like the requirement for consultation over board remuneration, this is a standard requirement in New Zealand for Crown entities. The chief executive officer can appoint other employees without further external consultation [Schedule 3, clause 47].

The legislation also includes other standard provisions that are applied to New Zealand state sector bodies, such as the requirements to provide safe working conditions and equal employment opportunities [Schedule 3, clause 48]. These are considered to be moral obligations of any good employer.

7

"...with explicit commercial investment objectives..."

The legislated investment objectives for the fund provide a complete basis for the administration of the fund. The fund is subject to the same taxation regime as other privately owned entities, but constraints have been put in place over its ability to borrow money and to take control over companies. There are no constraints, neither maxima nor minima, on domestic investment.

Legislated Objectives

The legislation explicitly sets out the investment objectives for the fund as follows [section 58]:

> The guardians must invest the fund on a prudent, commercial basis and, in doing so, must manage and administer the fund in a manner consistent with
>
> a) best-practice portfolio management,
> b) maximizing return without undue risk to the fund as a whole, and
> c) avoiding prejudice to New Zealand's reputation as a responsible member of the world community.

The board is free to make its own interpretation of these objectives when determining the investment strategy for the fund.

A key element of the policy underlying the fund is that it is not available to the government to use for any other purpose. This requirement places a clear boundary on the scope of investment objectives for the fund: it implies that the investment strategy must be value-maximizing for the fund as a distinct unit and that this is the primary investment objective of the fund. The requirement implicitly excludes other potential objectives for the investment strategy, including:

- broader social outcomes;
- performance of the domestic economy; and
- financial and fiscal management of the Crown as a whole.

The poor performance internationally of public pension funds is largely attributable to investments being directed into these areas (Iglesias and Palacios 2000). This does not imply that these are unimportant areas to which the Crown should not devote resources: they simply are distinct from the purpose of the fund.

Broader Social Outcomes

There is a range of broader social outcomes toward the achievement of which the investment objectives could have been applied. These include:

- Reduced investment in socially undesirable firms and industries, including tobacco, genetic modification of crops, native forest logging, polluters, unsustainable fishing, disfavored nations, weapons, gambling, and alcohol.
- Increased commercial investment in areas such as regional development, hospitals, high technology, and venture capital, and also to reduce foreign ownership of local firms.
- Higher "social" investment. The fund objectives could have mandated investment or spending, through grants, sponsorships, fellowships, or soft loans, in areas in which it would not necessarily achieve a full commercial return but would achieve some social outcome. Topical areas for investment include sport, culture, education, research, ethnic policy, subsidized housing, aid to distressed firms, and public infrastructure.

Specific investment in any of these areas of broader social outcomes is clearly precluded by the fact that the sole purpose of the fund is to finance New Zealand Superannuation. While it may be that there are good commercial reasons for the fund to avoid firms with tobacco interests, for example, it has been determined that any decision to invest must be made purely on a commercial basis and must not compromise the performance of the fund. Within this overarching requirement, it should nonetheless be noted that the fund is required to "avoid prejudice to New Zealand's reputation as a responsible member of the world community" [section 58(2)(c)] and to disclose its policy regarding ethical investment [section 61(d)]. These provisions are discussed further below.

Performance of the Domestic Economy

A large, government-controlled portfolio of financial assets potentially could be used to contribute to active management of the domestic economy: fund investment objectives could be designed to enable a host of economic variables to be affected, including exchange rates; interest rates; levels of investment in the domestic economy generally or in specific sectors; domestic market depth; and liquidity. Setting such objectives for the domestic economy would compromise the primary objective of financing New Zealand Superannuation, however. Other, more transparent instruments are available to the government to pursue these outcomes.

Financial and Fiscal Management of the Crown as a Whole

The third area of potential influence of the investment strategy is its implications for the financial and fiscal management of the Crown as a whole. This area is not as easily excluded as the other areas because the fund is a part of the Crown and its capital and returns ultimately revert to the Crown. The Crown therefore bears the full financial risk of the fund. The fund will comprise a large proportion of the Crown's financial assets for several decades, and there could therefore be significant financial synergies to the benefit of the Crown as a whole if the investment objectives for the fund took into account those Crown-wide interests. Examples of possible financial synergies across the Crown include:

- *Credit risk management.* Investments could be coordinated across the Crown to avoid excessive overall exposure to default on a particular type of investment.
- *Crown portfolio composition.* The composition of the fund's assets could be directed toward construction of a Crown portfolio. The Crown is highly exposed to the domestic economy so there would likely be diversification benefits for the Crown that could be realized by weighting the fund's portfolio more heavily in international assets, for example. The fund is likely to be large relative to other financial stocks and flows of the Crown so its portfolio effect could be significant.
- *Natural hedges.* The financial risks faced in different parts of the Crown that offset one another could be identified, and the Crown

therefore could avoid undertaking extra transactions to manage those risks separately. For example, the exchange rate risk related to foreign-denominated financial assets held in one part of the Crown could be offset by financial liabilities in those currencies in another part of the Crown. There are clearly savings to be made by thus avoiding the costs of separately hedging each item.

- *Risk pooling.* Classes of uncorrelated risks could be self-insured across the Crown, rather than each subentity of the Crown separately insuring its own risks. This may not apply in the case of the fund if the fund is large enough to undertake risk pooling on its own account.
- *Cash management.* Overnight surplus cash balances could be pooled across the Crown to offset against debt. This is already done in respect of the cash balances of government departments.

While it might seem sensible to take advantage of such financial synergies across the Crown, there is a fine line between integrated financial management in the interests of the Crown and raiding the returns on the fund to address short-term priorities other than New Zealand Superannuation. Given this fine line, and given that the long-term financial interests of the Crown are best served by avoiding raiding, it was decided to explicitly state the investment objectives in the legislation and to focus the management of the fund on those objectives, rather than on broader social or economic objectives. As stated above, the ability of the government to direct the fund is limited to its authority to issue nonbinding statements about its expectations for fund performance.

Stability

The fund was established to bring a measure of stability to retirement income policy. The investment strategy adopted could influence whether or not this stability is achieved by affecting the likelihood of policy reversal. This makes stability a potentially relevant investment objective, especially as the fund would very likely be investing in risky capital markets. In adopting a relatively risky portfolio, the chances are significant of the fund performing poorly, especially over the short time horizons over which political performance is invariably judged. This has the potential to compromise the stability of retirement income policy if it raises doubts about the effectiveness and the longevity of the fund. In particular, if there is poor financial performance over the first few years of the fund, political resolve to stay independent of the fund may evaporate, along with public confidence and support. This is recognized in the legislated investment objectives, which require the fund to be managed on a "prudent commercial basis" [section 58(2)]. This term is clearly subjective, but it does give the flavor of the balance of stability that is sought.

Maximizing Return without Undue Risk to the Fund as a Whole

The requirement of maximizing return without undue risk to the fund as a whole recognizes the relationship between risk and return inherent in capital market investment. It is up to the board to determine what constitutes undue risk and to determine the appropriate balance between risk and expected return.

The specification that the risk relates to the fund "as a whole" is important. It recognizes that the fund is to be treated as a portfolio, so the relevant risk of an individual investment is its contribution to overall portfolio risk.

Avoiding Prejudice to New Zealand's Reputation

There was a concern that the independent, commercial flavor of the fund objectives be tempered by recognition that the fund is ultimately a part of the Crown and should behave accordingly. This is reflected in the clause on "avoiding prejudice to New Zealand's reputation as a responsible member of the world community"—which arguably is an implicit requirement of all agencies responsible for public money and public affairs. Including this provision explicitly in the legislation was seen as necessary to ensure that this implicit obligation is not overlooked by a board with an independent mandate explicitly charged to meet commercial objectives.

It has been argued that including this clause is a defect in the policy because it gives the board an excuse for poor performance and thus makes it impossible to hold the board accountable for financial returns (Pozen 2002).[28] There are two reasons to doubt this. First, the legislation requires the statement of investment policies, to include the board's policy regarding the "avoiding prejudice" clause [section 61(d)]. This means that the board cannot use this clause an ex post excuse for poor performance. Second, the sentiment underlying the clause is arguably an implicit requirement of all agencies responsible for public finances.

Taxation

The fund is subject to the same income tax regime as other equivalent privately owned entities [section 76]. This is despite the fact that the fund is property of the Crown. The reason for having the fund subject to tax arises from the strong independence of the board in making its investment decisions. In particular, if the fund was not subject to tax there would be the danger of undesirable outcomes that the government would not be able to mitigate through other controls over the board's activities. There are two main sources of undesirable outcome.

First, if the fund were not subject to tax the fund managers would have a strong incentive to maximize their returns by engaging in avoidance behavior in concert with other taxed entities, effectively cheating the New Zealand tax system. Tax-exempt organizations such as charities have engaged in complicated schemes to take advantage of this kind of opportunity. Fund managers might not see any inconsistency in this kind of activity, as they could argue that their responsibility is to maximize returns to the fund alone, and not to New Zealand as a whole. Taxable entities and their advisers also would have strong incentives to manufacture schemes and encourage the fund to engage with them in joint ventures. Such incentives would increase through time as the fund's resources grow, and the magnitude of the risk to the integrity of the tax base would rise with it. It was not considered possible to implement governance restrictions that would accurately replicate the effect of making the fund taxable. Governance structures that remained robust over the long life of the fund would have been particularly difficult to formulate given the ongoing development of new financial structures and instruments and the ingenuity of professional tax planners.

Second, if the fund were not subject to tax it would have an incentive to avoid investments in entities subject to New Zealand tax. This could encourage it to take outright control of businesses rather than invest in them through a company intermediary,[29] or to favor investments that do not carry the tax imputation credits that taxpayers value (such as fixed interest investments or equities that do not pay New Zealand tax). Neither of these is necessarily favorable as far as the Crown as a whole is concerned.

A consequence of making the fund subject to tax is that since the board's responsibilities only relate to the fund its natural focus would be to maximize the after-tax returns of the fund. However, the Crown benefits not only from the capital withdrawals that ultimately will be made from the

7

fund but also from the tax receipts from the fund over its life. It is therefore the total returns of the fund that are relevant to overall Crown financial management. This begs the question of whether it might be better for the Crown as a whole if the board were to focus on maximizing pre-tax rather than after-tax returns.[30] Even if we assume that the behavioral outcomes described above could be mitigated, it is not self-evident which of the alternative fund objectives would result in a fund investment strategy that would be better for the Crown as a whole. This would require taking into account the financial characteristics of the rest of the Crown's portfolio, including its financial instruments (assets and liabilities), real assets, and expected future tax and benefit flows.[31] It is an issue that has been examined from various dimensions over time (Bradbury, Brumby, and Skilling 1999; Davis 2001; Davis and Fabling 2002; Grimes 2001; and Huther 1998). The main conclusion to arise from this body of work is that public policy is likely to be best served by holding each financial subentity of the Crown responsible for its own strategic asset allocation on the basis of its own assets and liabilities. The decision to have the fund subject to tax was therefore made on the basis of avoiding the potential undesirable outcomes that could arise with a strongly independent, tax-free fund. This does not preclude the board from having an eye to the multiple interests of the Crown in respect of the fund,[32] but it does make it clear that the fund's status as a part of the Crown is not to be traded on.

No Borrowing

The fund ultimately is the property of the Crown [section 40]. Borrowing by the fund, including the incurrence of liabilities or contingent liabilities, is therefore equivalent to Crown borrowing.[33] It was considered that if it was sensible for the Crown as a whole to increase its borrowing, this would be better done in a coordinated fashion by the New Zealand Debt Management Office.

There are various types of transaction that it might be sensible for the fund to undertake as part of a prudent commercial investment strategy that technically are borrowing and that involve incurring liabilities or contingencies. While some examples can be immediately identified (normal credit terms, certain types of financial instrument that are used to manage risks, capital calls, and so on) the full range of such transactions cannot be easily categorized and legislated for in advance. The legislation therefore provided that borrowing (and this was defined widely) is not allowed except with the approval of the Minister of Finance in respect of a transaction or a class of transactions [section 50].

Control over Companies

The fund is intended to be a portfolio of financial investments, not an operator of businesses. There could be wide-ranging consequences if the fund were to end up controlling other entities. There is a range of legislation, including the Public Finance Act 1989, the Public Audit Act 2001, and the Official Information Act 1982, that applies specifically to the Crown and the entities under its control. This places obligations on Crown-controlled entities and constraints on their operations. Under the accounting principles that the Crown is required to follow, all entities ultimately controlled by the Crown must be included in the Crown Financial Statements. If the Crown ultimately were to control an entity, there could furthermore be an implied guarantee by the Crown of the entity's liabilities in the event of financial difficulty.[34] To avoid these consequences, the fund was precluded from taking a controlling interest in other entities [section 59].

A proscription on taking controlling interests is not thought to be a significant constraint on the fund's behavior because it is normal practice for private investment funds to avoid controlling interests. There are two main reasons for this. First, holding a controlling interest in a business limits the liquidity of that investment. Second, the controlling owner inevitably gets drawn into strategic management issues that require a closer operational involvement than that usually sought by a portfolio investor. This provision therefore is not seen as a significant limitation on the ability of the board to administer the investment of the fund.

If it were good public policy (including economic, social, and/or environmental policy) for the Crown to have ownership control of a particular business, it would be better for the government itself to make that ownership decision. The government clearly is better placed than the board to determine what constitutes good public policy; should the decision be made to take control of a business the Crown furthermore should take the necessary action directly and should not act through the fund, to avoid compromising the board's independence.

Limiting control over companies would result in the board having to forego a commercial investment opportunity should that opportunity

7

require taking control of a company. In the context of a large, widely diversified fund this should not be a significant problem. It furthermore does not preclude the fund having investments in particular sectors in which taking a controlling interest is a common investment strategy (for example, venture capital and real estate), because various facilities are available that enable individual investors to jointly invest through an investment manager without any one investor taking a controlling interest in any individual company.

Domestic Investment

Consideration was given to whether there should be constraints, either maxima or minima, on the level of domestic investment by the fund. No such constraints were implemented, for several reasons. First, if legislating to require greater domestic investment by domestic investment funds were good public policy there would be no reason why this constraint should be placed on the fund alone; and there was no political will to place domestic investment constraints on all domestic funds.[35]

Second, the Crown is already heavily exposed to the New Zealand economy through its tax base. It therefore is not clear that a binding minimum on domestic investment would be in the best interests of the Crown. Furthermore, as noted above, the government is better placed to make such investment decisions directly rather than through the fund.

Third, as a practical drafting matter, distinguishing between domestic entities and overseas entities is problematic. New Zealand is a small economy. Its growth and prosperity depends on its interaction with international markets, both suppliers and customers. Many New Zealand-owned entities have significant overseas operations and many significant domestic activities are undertaken by entities that are partly or entirely foreign-owned. Without being specific about what public policy objective is being achieved in each particular instance, it was not possible to draft a definition of "New Zealand entity" that was both narrow enough to be meaningful and broad enough to capture the full range of potential businesses that it could conceivably be good public policy for the Crown to own.

A related issue was whether there should be constraints on the fund owning domestic government stock. One potential way for a government to make a "backdoor" raid on the assets of a public fund would be to require the fund to be invested in domestic government stock.[36] However, as noted above, the provisions for the New Zealand Superannuation Fund do not allow the government to direct the investment strategy. This policy risk is therefore avoided. It was therefore decided not to preclude the fund from owning domestic government stock, should it choose to do so.

"...and clear accountability."

The personal liability of board members is limited and, as noted above, dismissal powers are also limited. The focus is therefore on public accountability. The board is required to establish a statement of investment policies, standards, and procedures. Before the start of each year, the board is also required to include information about its plans for the fund in its statement of intent. At the end of each year, the board is required to produce audited financial statements for the fund that are to be included in the board's annual report to Parliament. This emphasis on self-reporting is balanced by a requirement for a periodic independent performance review of the practice of the board and the performance of the fund. The board is also required to report to the minister on request and to disclose official information publicly on request. Being property of the Crown, the fund and the Guardians of New Zealand Superannuation Crown entity are included in the consolidated Crown financial statements.

Personal Liability of Board Members

There are two aspects to the personal liability of board members: immunity and indemnity.

- *Immunity*. Board members acting in good faith are not personally liable to the fund for any liability of the fund, nor for any deed or misdeed of the board or of its functionaries [Schedule 3, clause 8(1)]. This is a common provision for members of public bodies.
- *Indemnity*. Board members acting in good faith are indemnified by the fund for any civil liability or for the cost of a successfully defended criminal action [Schedule 3, clause 8]. This also is a common provision in recent legislation for New Zealand Crown entity board members. It is similar to the provisions that apply to private sector corporations in New Zealand [Companies Act 1993, section 162].

7

These immunities and indemnities provide important protection for board members who act in good faith; they also underscore the importance of appointing board members who are suitably qualified. These immunities and indemnities also apply to board employees [Schedule 3, clause 8(4)].

As noted earlier, a board member can be dismissed for "any reason relating to the member's performance of, or ability to perform, his or her duties or responsibilities as a member, the board's performance of its collective duties, or misconduct by the member." [Schedule 3, clause 10(2)] In the New Zealand environment this provision is unlikely to be used on a routine basis as a sanction on board members if the fund performs poorly; it nonetheless provides the ultimate backstop against dysfunctional board members.

Statement of Investment Policies, Standards and Procedures

The board is required to establish and adhere to investment policies, standards, and procedures that are consistent with its duty to invest the fund on a prudent commercial basis [section 60(1)]. These must be reviewed at least annually [section 60(2)], a statement of them must be included in the board's annual report [section 68(e)], and the board and chief executive must certify annually whether or not they have been complied with [section 60(f)]. In addition, periodic independent performance reviews (discussed below) must evaluate their appropriateness and the board's compliance with them.

Without limiting what a statement of investment policies, standards, and procedures can cover, the legislation requires it to include [section 61]:

- the classes of investments in which the fund is to be invested and the selection criteria for investments within those classes;
- the determination of benchmarks or standards against which the performance of the fund as a whole, and classes of investments and individual investments, will be assessed;
- standards for reporting the investment performance of the fund;
- ethical investment, including policies, standards, or procedures for avoiding prejudice to New Zealand's reputation as a responsible member of the world community;
- the balance between risk and return in the overall fund portfolio;
- the fund management structure;

7

- the use of options, futures, and other derivative financial instruments;
- the management of credit, liquidity, operational, currency, market, and other financial risks;
- the retention, exercise, or delegation of voting rights acquired through investments;
- the method of, and basis for, valuation of investments that are not regularly traded at a public exchange; and
- prohibited or restricted investments or any investment constraints or limits.

The establishment of investment policies is routine practice in investment fund management. However, the approach taken for the fund has some distinguishing characteristics. First, the legislation makes clear that the board is responsible for setting these policies: the government does not determine them. The listing in the legislation of topics to be covered is simply a disclosure requirement. It is not prescriptive of the particular policies, standards, or procedures to be adopted. A particular example of this is the requirement for the statement to cover "ethical investment, including policies, standards, or procedures for avoiding prejudice to New Zealand's reputation as a responsible member of the world community" [section 61(d)]. This simply requires the board to have a policy regarding ethical investment: it does not prescribe any particular approach to or emphasis on ethical investment.[37] The phrase "avoiding prejudice to New Zealand's reputation as a responsible member of the world community" comes from the investment objectives [section 58(2)(c)]. It was included here to provide explicit disclosure of the board's policies in that regard.

Second, public disclosure of the statement of investment policies, standards, and procedures provides a basis by which the public can judge the board's management of the fund. Third, the disclosure is not simply a statement of good intentions. Both the board and the chief executive are required to certify compliance with the statement of investment policies, standards, and procedures [section 68(f)].

The statement of investment policies, standards, and procedures also provides the vehicle for disclosure of the board's investment strategy for the fund, by requiring coverage of "the classes of investments in which the fund is to be invested and the selection criteria for investments within those classes; and the determination of benchmarks or standards against which the performance of the fund as a whole, and classes of investments and individual investments, will be assessed".

7

The required disclosures are not necessarily all the board would disclose in its statement of investment policies, standards, and procedures. The board's obligation to manage and administer the fund in a manner consistent with best-practice portfolio management [section 58(2)] may well result in additional information being included in this statement.

Statement of Intent

A feature of the accountability requirements for Crown entities of any significant size in New Zealand is the publication of a statement of intent at the start of each financial year [Public Finance Act 1989, Part V]. As noted above, the corporate form of the governing body of the fund is a Crown entity, the "Guardians of New Zealand Superannuation," that is separate from the fund itself. Since it is listed in the Sixth Schedule of the Public Finance Act 1989, this Crown entity is required to produce a statement of intent covering a range of issues relating to the administration of the Crown entity for the coming year, including its objectives, the nature and scope of its activities, its performance targets, and its accounting policies. Some additional disclosure requirements have been added to the requirements for the Guardians' statement of intent to provide ex ante information about the board's intentions for the fund for the period ahead. These are [section 65]:

- a statement of the board's expectations about the performance of the fund over the next financial year, in sufficient detail to enable meaningful assessment against those expectations after the end of that financial year;
- a statement of the key risks to the performance of the fund over the coming year and the actions being taken by the board to manage those risks; and
- the forecast financial statements of the fund for the next financial year, including a statement of accounting policies.

The performance of the fund will depend on the performance of volatile equity markets, so the predictive value of the financial forecasts is limited. They will nonetheless provide information about the board's expectations for the behavior of the fund over the coming year. Forecast financial statements for the next four years for the Crown as a whole, including the fund, are included in the Budget Economic and Fiscal Update and in the December Economic and Fiscal Update.[38]

Audited Financial Statements

The board is required to produce annual financial statements for the fund that follow generally accepted accounting practice [section 66].[39] This is common to all public sector and private sector reporting entities in New Zealand, and mandates full accrual accounting and consistency with financial reporting standards.[40]

Because the fund is property of the Crown, its financial statements are required to be audited by the Auditor General [section 67].[41] The audited financial statements are then required to be included in the board's annual report to Parliament [section 68]. Normal practice is then for a committee of Parliament to scrutinize such reports in public and to call board members or officials to answer questions, usually in public.

The Auditor General has wide powers under the Public Audit Act 2001 to review the performance of any part of the Crown, including both the fund and the Guardians Crown entity.[42]

Annual Report

The accountability requirements of Crown entities in New Zealand include the production of an annual report after the end of each financial year [Public Finance Act 1989, Part V]. In addition to the standard requirements relating to the Guardians Crown entity, the board's annual report is required to include the following information regarding the fund [section 68]:

- the financial statements of the fund for that financial year ,prepared under section 66;
- a statement of responsibility for the financial statements of the fund, signed by the chairperson of the board and the chief executive of the Guardians (if any), and comprising the same statements that are required by section 42(2) of the Public Finance Act 1989 as if the fund were a Crown entity; [43]
- the audit report on the financial statements;
- an analysis and explanation of the performance of the fund over that financial year, including a comparison with the Guardians' expecta-

tions of the performance of the fund that were set out in the statement of intent relating to that financial year;

- a statement of the investment policies, standards, and procedures for
  the fund established by the Guardians under section 60;
- a statement signed by the chairperson of the board and the chief
  executive of the Guardians (if any) certifying whether or not the
  investment policies, standards, and procedures for the fund have been
  complied with throughout that financial year; and
- a schedule of the investment managers and custodians used by the
  Guardians during that financial year and the classes of investments
  for which each was responsible.

The board's obligation to manage and administer the fund in a manner
consistent with best-practice portfolio management [section 58(2)] may
result in additional information about the fund being included in this annual
report. Both the Canada Pension Plan Investment Board and the Norwegian
Petroleum Fund disclose detailed lists of their holdings at year-end.

Normal practice is for the annual reports of Crown entities to be referred
to a select committee of Parliament for its consideration. Board members
or officials may well be called before the committee, usually in public, to
answer any questions about the board's administration of the fund and the
fund's performance.

Performance Review

The main mechanism of the accountability arrangements described above is
self-reporting by the board of its practice and performance, along with scrutiny by a parliamentary select committee. Provision has also been made for
an independent review of the performance of the board to be commissioned
and published at least once every five years [section 71]. The reviewer is
required to form an opinion about:

- whether or not the investment policies, standards, and procedures
  established by the Guardians are appropriate to the fund;
- whether or not the investment policies, standards, and procedures
  established by the Guardians have been complied with in all material
  respects; and
- the investment performance of the fund.

This provision for a regular performance review was included in the legislation despite the fact that the minister already has the power to commission such a review. It was included for two reasons. First, absent specific authority the request for a detailed review such as this might have been interpreted as a challenge to the board's independence. Second, setting a schedule for the process overcomes the political inertia that would result in such a review being avoided until problems are clearly apparent, by which time the review may well be too late to be effective.

Reporting to Minister

There is a range of information requirements to enable the minister and the Treasury to monitor the operation of the fund and to meet broader Crown accountability requirements. For example, regular information on fund performance is required for inclusion in budget forecasts and in the monthly and annual Crown financial statements. There is therefore a general provision to produce information to the minister as required [section 69].

Official Information

The board is subject to the Official Information Act 1982. This legislation applies the principle that all official information is to be publicly available on request unless there is good reason for withholding it.[44] An exception allowed in the legislation is when disclosure could prejudice the commercial activities of the entity or of the Crown, but the general rule is that information is to be made available and when it is withheld a case for withholding must be made in each circumstance. An independent Office of the Ombudsman rigorously investigates complaints against agencies for withholding information.[45]

Crown Financial Statements

The fund is property of the Crown [section 40] and therefore is included in the Crown financial statements.[46] These are required to be produced monthly throughout the year, with audited financial statements produced annually.[47] The financial statements provide an additional layer of information that puts the performance of the fund into the context of the financial management of the Crown as a whole.

7

Policy Development in Public Sector Management

The accountability requirements (and the governance arrangements, generally) regarding the fund are built around and expand on the existing well-developed framework of accountability that applies to all New Zealand Crown entities. This overarching framework is subject to continuous improvement. There notably is interest in increasing the consistency of governance arrangements across the Crown and in ensuring that mechanisms are in place so that "whole-of-government" objectives can be required to be pursued by the individual entities on a consistent basis. This could lead over time to the specific governance arrangements described in this paper being modified.

Implementation Experience

The timeline for the establishment of the fund is summarized in Table 7.1 and is explained in more detail in the following sections.

Development and Passage of Legislation

Establishment of the New Zealand Superannuation Fund was an explicit policy of the Labour Party leading into the 1999 General Election. Following formation of the Labour Coalition Government, in early 2000 a small team was established to fully develop the policy for implementation. This team's location in the Asset and Liability Management Branch of the Treasury reflected recognition at the outset that this was primarily an issue of Crown financial management. The policy was worked up during 2000 and legislation was introduced to Parliament at the end of that year.[49] Following normal parliamentary Select Committee scrutiny, the New Zealand Superannuation Act was passed into law in October 2001. In March 2002, the Treasury undertook an information campaign on behalf of the government. This included a brochure that was mailed to households, a television commercial, internet banner advertisements, and an information website.[50]

Board Appointment

The nominating committee was appointed in October 2001, immediately following the passage of the legislation. It comprised five members chaired

Table 7.1: Timeline of Events

November 1999	Labour Coalition Government formed following General Election
November 2000	New Zealand Superannuation Bill introduced to Parliament
June 2001	Bill reported back from Finance and Expenditure Committee of Parliament
July 2001	The government starts to set aside amounts for capital contributions to the fund: NZ$600 million for 2001/02, in fortnightly installments
October 2001	New Zealand Superannuation Act is passed and becomes law
October 2001	Nominating committee appointed
March 2002	Public information campaign of the fund, including TV adverts, a brochure mailed to households, and an information website
June 2002	Proposed board members announced and consultation commenced
July 2002	The government continues to set aside amounts for capital contributions to the fund. NZ$1,200 million for 2002/03, in fortnightly installments
July 2002	General election. New Labour Coalition Government formed
August 2002	Board of Guardians of New Zealand Superannuation appointed
February 2003	Investment advisor (Mercer) appointed following a competitive selection process
February 2003	Chief executive appointed. Commenced position March 31
Pending[48]	Appointment of advisor for investment manager selection
Pending	Investment managers and custodian(s) appointed
Pending	Capital contributions to date are drawn down by the board and investment strategy is implemented

7

by Vance Arkinstall, chief executive of the Investment Savings and Insurance Association. The committee engaged an international executive search agency to assist it with the identification and selection of suitable candidates. It also advertised widely and consulted with a range of individuals. The committee reported back to the Minister of Finance in March 2002 with a shortlist of 11 nominations for the five to seven board positions. In response to the government's desire to have balanced representation of New Zealand society on public bodies and at the request of the minister, the nominating committee provided a further two names, bringing the final shortlist to 13.[51] The minister decided to appoint six board members from this list, leaving one board position vacant in the meantime. He then consulted

---

Box 7.1: Board Appointees

At the time the inaugural appointments were announced, the Minister of Finance described the appointees as follows:

The chair is **David May**, the deputy chair of the Government Superannuation Fund Authority and the former managing director of the Colonial Group in New Zealand. His term runs until the end of May, 2007.

Sir Douglas Graham is deputy chair and will also serve a five-year term. Sir Douglas was a cabinet minister in the last National-led government and chairs the Lombard Group, a private banking firm with assets under management of around NZ$100 million.

Other appointees are:

- **Dr Michaela Anderson**, director of policy and research for the Association of Superannuation Funds in Australia. [Term expires 31 May, 2006.]
- **Ira Bing**, a private investor with a strong investment banking background in Britain and with Merrill Lynch in Europe. [31 May, 2005.]
- **Brian Gaynor**, a respected independent investment analyst and a director of the New Zealand Investment Trust plc. [31 May, 2006.]
- **Bridget Wickham**: Chief executive of the University of Auckland Development and an experienced senior company executive. [31 May, 2005.]

7

with the other political parties in Parliament [section 56(6)] before recommending the appointments to the Governor General. The appointments were eventually made in August 2002, following a brief delay because of the general election held in July.[52] The appointments were made for staggered terms to provide for continuity when board members' terms expire.

The legislation does not prescribe New Zealand citizenship nor residency for board members. Two of the inaugural members were not New Zealand citizens and one was not a New Zealand resident.

Fund Establishment

The board has been working since its appointment to establish its infrastructure. Consistent with the board's independence from the government and to avoid any perception of government constraint on operational matters of the fund, no "preestablishment" structure was put in place. The board has been entirely responsible for establishing its administrative arrangements.

After engaging an interim secretariat, the board went through a competitive process to select and appoint an investment adviser and other advisers.[53] This process included probity review by the Office of the Auditor General.

The board also undertook a formal executive search process to appoint a chief executive. The plan at this stage is to engage a small executive staff and to outsource investment management.

At the time of writing, the board was about to announce the appointment of an adviser to assist in the selection of fund managers and custodian(s). This selection process will commence once the board has determined the investment strategy and has developed the statement of investment policies, standards, and procedures.

The legislation requires a review of the board's performance to be conducted every five years, with the first review being carried out "as soon as practicable after 1 July 2003" [section 71]. When this provision was originally drafted in 2000 it was envisaged that the fund would be in full operation by that time. Given the slower progress with the implementation, it has not yet been decided when would be the most practicable time for this first review to be undertaken.

Capital Contributions

The government started setting aside capital contributions for the fund from July 2001. The New Zealand Debt Management Office has held these for disbursement to the fund once the Guardians are in a position to start administering it.[54] An amount of NZ$600 million was provided for in the 2001/02 financial year, NZ$1,200 million is being set aside in 2002/03, and NZ$1,800 million is planned to be set aside in 2003/04. After this transitional three-year period the government plans to make capital contributions at the full required rate as set out in the legislation.[55] These amounts are being set aside in fortnightly installments throughout the year. In order to reflect the time value of money, interest has been credited to the accumulating balance at the official cash rate that is set periodically by the Reserve Bank of New Zealand.[56] When the Guardians indicate that they are in a position to take up administration of the fund, the accumulated balance,, including the compounded interest, will be disbursed to the fund as an initial capital contribution. As at the end of January 2003, the accumulated balance amounted to NZ$1,388 million. This is about 1.1 percent of New Zealand's GDP.

Table 7.2: Crown Financial Assets and Liabilities (NZ$ millions)

Year ending 30 June[57]	2002	2003	2004	2005	2006
Financial assets held by core Crown[58]					
RBNZ	5,741	5,735	5,726	5,718	5,709
NZDMO	4,060	2,380	2,613	2,710	2,914
GSF	2,000	3,160	3,160	3,160	3,160
NZSF	600	1,890	3,898	6,277	8,944
Other core Crown	6,336	6,731	7,965	8,871	9,803
Total core Crown	18,737	19,896	23,362	26,736	30,530
Financial assets held by Crown entities					
ACC	3,522	4,019	4,715	5,480	6,303
EQC	4,144	4,417	4,715	5,027	5,353
Other Crown entities	2,164	2,249	2,319	2,391	2,477
Total Crown entities	9,831	10,685	11,749	12,897	14,133
Financial assets held by SOEs	1,001	848	805	973	1,276
Eliminations[59]	-5,213	-5,407	-6,610	-7,195	-7,898
Total Crown financial assets	24,356	26,022	29,306	33,411	38,041
Nonfinancial assets	59,499	60,896	62,592	63,560	63,709
Total Crown assets	83,855	86,918	91,898	96,971	101,750
Borrowings					
Sovereign guaranteed	30,476	31,348	33,579	34,298	34,944
Not sovereign guaranteed[60]	7,147	6,811	6,021	5,979	5,548
Other liabilities	31,994	32,233	32,694	33,153	33,475
Total liabilities	69,617	70,392	72,294	73,430	73,967
NZ gross domestic product					
(nominal)	120,309	124,964	131,293	137,201	143,026

Source: New Zealand Treasury 2002 Budget Economic and Fiscal Update[61]

Other Crown Financial Portfolios

The financial assets that form the New Zealand Superannuation Fund are a subset of the overall financial assets owned by the Crown. Forecasts of the distribution of financial assets and liabilities across the Crown are presented in Table 7.2. Also shown for comparison are forecasts of New Zealand's GDP.

Some of the financial assets are held by entities whose primary role is investment management, and others are held by operating entities for which the management of financial assets is an ancillary activity. These entities each operate under specific legislation that sets out their governance arrangements in detail. They operate with different levels of independence from the government and they have adopted different investment strategies. This partly reflects the different sets of assets and liabilities for which the entities are responsible; it also reflects the history of their establishment. Since the passage of the New Zealand Superannuation Act there has been a move toward lining up governance arrangements with that legislation. The legislation for the Government Superannuation Fund has already been amended and ministerial directions that mirror the legislation in key respects have been made to the Earthquake Commission pending a more fundamental review of its governance arrangements.

Circumstances of the Main Entities

The following sections provide brief descriptions of the circumstances of each of the main entities managing portfolios of financial assets.

Reserve Bank of New Zealand

The Reserve Bank[62] manages New Zealand's foreign exchange reserves. These reserves are included in the government's total portfolio and are integrated into the Debt Management Office's (NZDMO's) asset and liability management process. This is achieved by the NZDMO directly financing the Reserve Bank's foreign exchange reserves through foreign currency deposits with the Reserve Bank. Under this structure, the Reserve Bank's task is to manage its position between its foreign currency liabilities to NZDMO and the foreign-currency assets that make up the foreign exchange reserves.

New Zealand Debt Management Office

The NZDMO[63] is a division of the Treasury that manages the Crown's sovereign borrowings. It holds a substantial portfolio of marketable securities and deposits denominated in foreign currencies to help meet the government's policy of holding no net foreign debt.[64]

New Zealand Superannuation Fund

The New Zealand Superannuation Fund is the subject of the earlier sections of this paper. Table 7.2 shows how it is expected to grow in significance over the next few years. It is the only entity with responsibility solely for investment management.

Government Superannuation Fund

The Government Superannuation Fund[65] is a defined benefit pension scheme for public servants. It was closed to new members in 1992 but there remain about 25,000 employee contributors and 47,000 annuitants. It has an actuarially assessed past service liability of about NZ$12 billion that is reflected in the Crown financial statements. With assets in the region of only NZ$3 billion, it is partly funded, with the Crown guaranteeing any shortfall. This guarantee, combined with the defined benefit nature of the scheme, means that the Crown bears all of the investment risk of the fund. The government's policy is to meet a portion of the unfunded amount each year so that the shortfall is met progressively over the remaining life of the scheme.

The Government Superannuation Fund Authority is responsible for both scheme administration and investment management. Its legislation was amended in 2001 to essentially the same provisions as those described for the New Zealand Superannuation Fund. It has since developed and is implementing an investment strategy diversified across capital markets. It previously held primarily New Zealand Government stock.

Accident Compensation Corporation

The Accident Compensation Corporation[66] administers New Zealand's accident compensation scheme, which provides accident insurance for all New Zealand citizens, residents, and temporary visitors to New Zealand. In return, people do not have the right to sue for personal injury, other than for exemplary damages. The continuing increase in the corporation's portfolio of financial assets over the next few years reflects its movement from a largely pay-as-you-go scheme to full funding of its claims liabilities.

The corporation is required by its legislation to invest its assets as if it were a trustee, and therefore sets its own investment policy. The government retains the power to make policy directions with which the Corporation must comply.

Earthquake Commission

The Earthquake Commission[67] provides natural disaster insurance for residential property in New Zealand. The Minister of Finance has the power to direct the commission regarding its investment and reinsurance policies. Until recently, the commission's Natural Disaster Fund had been required to be invested entirely in nontradable New Zealand Government stock.

In 2001, the minister issued a direction on investment that essentially mirrored the principal provisions described for the New Zealand Superannuation Fund. In particular, the commission must invest the Natural Disaster Fund according to the objectives set out in section 58 of the New Zealand Superannuation Act and it must prepare and adhere to a statement of investment policies, standards, and procedures similar to those required of the New Zealand Superannuation Fund. The direction from the minister also set out some specific requirements surrounding the investment policy, permitting investment in New Zealand Government securities, global equities, and New Zealand bank bills but requiring consultation with the minister should the fund managers wish to go beyond an allocation of 35 percent to global equities or NZ$250 million in bank bills. The issuance of this direction is generally seen as an interim measure pending a more fundamental review of the governance arrangements surrounding the Earthquake Commission.

Other Items

- The other financial assets held in the core Crown include about NZ$4 billion of student loans.[68]
- The financial assets held by state-owned enterprises are primarily marketable securities and deposits held for working capital purposes.[69]

- The main categories of nonfinancial assets are buildings (NZ$17 billion), state highways (NZ$12 billion), and land (NZ$7 billion).
- The "other liabilities" include the accrued past service liability for the Government Superannuation Fund (NZ$12 billion) and the outstanding claims liability of the Accident Compensation Corporation (NZ$8 billion).

Conclusion

The New Zealand Superannuation Fund has been established as a means of smoothing out the impact on the Crown's finances of demographic change. Over the next 50 years or so a permanently higher proportion of the population will become eligible to receive payments of New Zealand Superannuation. Essential to the success of this policy will be the establishment of governance arrangements that ensure efficient management of the financial assets that constitute the fund. The need for such arrangements has been met with legislation establishing the New Zealand Superannuation Fund and its governing body, the Guardians of New Zealand Superannuation. The arrangements were designed around the objective of establishing a clearly defined portfolio of Crown financial resources, managed by an independent governing body with explicit commercial objectives and clear accountability.

References

Bradbury, Simon, Jim Brumby, and David Skilling. 1999. "Sovereign Net Worth: An Analytical Framework." New Zealand Treasury Working Paper 99/3. Available online at www.treasury.govt.nz.

Creedy, John, and Grant Scobie. 2002. "Population Ageing and Social Expenditure in New Zealand: Stochastic Projections." New Zealand Treasury Working Paper 02/28. Available online at www.treasury.govt.nz.

Davis, Nick. 1998. "Governance of Crown Financial Assets." New Zealand Treasury Working Paper 98/2. Available online at www.treasury.govt.nz.

———. 2001. "Does Crown Financial Portfolio Composition Matter?" New Zealand Treasury Working Paper 01/34. Available online at www.treasury.govt.nz.

Davis, Nick, and Richard Fabling. 2002. "Population Ageing and the Efficiency of Fiscal Policy in New Zealand." New Zealand Treasury Working Paper 02/11. Available online at www.treasury.govt.nz.

Grimes, Arthur. 2001. "Crown Financial Asset Management: Objectives and Practice." New Zealand Treasury Working Paper 01/12. Available online at www.treasury.govt.nz.

Huther, Jeff. 1998. "An Application of Portfolio Theory to New Zealand's Public Sector." New Zealand Treasury Working Paper 98/4. Available online at www.treasury.govt.nz.

Iglesias, Augusto, and Robert Palacios. 2000. "Managing Public Pension Reserves: Part I: Evidence from the International Experience." World Bank Social Protection Discussion Paper Series 0003. Washington, D.C.: World Bank. Available online at www.worldbank.org/pensions.

McCulloch, Brian. 2002a. "Estimating the Market Equity Risk Premium." New Zealand Treasury. Available online at www.treasury.govt.nz/release/super/market-risk.pdf.

———. 2002b. "Long-Term Market Return Assumptions for the 2002 December Economic and Fiscal Update." New Zealand Treasury. Available online at www.treasury.govt.nz/release/super/market-assum-defu02.pdf.

McCulloch, Brian, and Jane Frances. 2001a. "Financing New Zealand Superannuation." New Zealand Treasury Working Paper 01/20. Available online at www.treasury.govt.nz/workingpapers/2001/01-20.asp.

———. 2001b. "The New Zealand Superannuation Fund: Comparison with the Irish National Pensions Reserve Fund." *The Actuary*. May 2001 pp. 26-27, Available online at www.the-actuary.org.uk/monthsissues_frames/articles/01_05_01.asp.

Mitchell, Olivia, and Ping Lung Hsin. 1994. "Public Pension Governance and Performance." NBER (National Bureau of Economic Research) Working Paper 4632. Cambridge, Massachusetts: NBER. Available online at www.nber.org.

Palacios, Robert. 2002. "Managing Public Pension Reserves Part II: Lessons from Five Recent OECD Initiatives." World Bank Social Protection Discussion Paper Series 0219. Washington, D.C.: World Bank. Available online at www.worldbank.org/pensions.

Pozen, Robert. 2002. "Arm Yourself for the Coming Battle over Social Security." *Harvard Business Review* 80(11): November 2002 pp 52–62.

7.

Preston, David. 2001. "Retirement Income in New Zealand: the Historical Context." New Zealand Office of the Retirement Commissioner. Available online at www.sorted.org.nz.

Romano, Roberta. 1993. "Getting Politics out of Public Pension Funds and out of Corporate Board Rooms." *American Enterprise* 4(6):42–49.

Stephenson, John, and Grant Scobie. 2002. "The Economics of Population Ageing." New Zealand Treasury Working Paper 02/05. Available online at www.treasury.govt.nz.

World Bank. 1994. *Averting the Old Age Crisis*. New York: Oxford University Press. Available online at www.worldbank.org/pensions.

Notes

1. Note on terminology: The "Crown" and the "Government": New Zealand has a constitutional monarchy. The resources and obligations of the central government sector (or state sector) are therefore generally referred to as being ultimately owned and owed by the Crown. The Executive—the Prime Minister and ministers in power—is referred to as the Government. The Government is accountable to the Legislature, which in New Zealand is a single House of Parliament comprising the elected members of the governing party (or parties, in the case of a coalition government), along with the elected members of the opposition parties.

2. The minimum pension level is formally expressed in terms of a married couple, both eligible, together receiving no less than 65 percent of national average ordinary-time weekly earnings. This can create confusion when attempting to compare notional individual earnings replacement rates across different countries. The rate for an unmarried individual living with others (living alone) is set 20 percent (30 percent) higher than the amount for a married person. For detail of the eligibility for, and amounts of, the New Zealand Superannuation benefit, see www.workandincome.govt.nz/get_financial_assistance/benefits/main_benefits/nz_superannuation.html.

3. The only substantive change was the restoration to 65 percent of the minimum earnings relativity of a married couple's combined entitlement. The previous government had reduced it to 60 percent. Figure 7.1 illustrates this drop in the wage floor in 1998.

4. Unless otherwise noted, all demographic statistics and forecasts stated in this paper are from Statistics New Zealand and use fixed scenarios of fertility, life expectancy, and migration (see www.statistics.govt.nz). Stochastic projections of New Zealand social expenditure are also available (Creedy and Scobie 2002).

5. The total fertility rate in a particular year is the average number of births a woman would have during her reproductive life if she were exposed to the fertility rate characteristic of the various childbearing age groups in that year.

6. New Zealand Superannuation is taxed as income to the recipients. This tax is deducted on payment and returned to the Crown. The "net cost" is the after-tax cost. This is generally treated as the relevant cost to the Crown of NZS.

7. The 40-year horizon was an arbitrary choice. The effects of alternative horizons are illustrated in Figure 4 of McCulloch and Frances (2001a).

8. The government decided to adopt a transitional approach for the first three years to allow the Crown's finances to adjust to making capital contributions. Amounts of NZ$600 million, NZ$1,200 million and NZ$1,800 million were provided for in 2001–02, 2002–03, and 2003–04. This explains the hook at the start of the contribution line in Figure 6.

9. Net public debt amounted to 50 percent of GDP in 1992. It is now in the region of 14 percent of GDP, including zero net foreign currency debt. This achievement is largely attributable to the implementation of the Fiscal Responsibility Act 1994 (www.treasury.govt.nz/legislation/fra/explanation). See Table 2 on page 38 for details of the current and forecast financial position of the Crown.

10. See, for example, Palacios (2002) and McCulloch and Frances (2001b).

11. Without parallel changes to the parameters for NZS, these other policies would not directly reduce the future cost to the Crown of NZS.

12. "Superannuation scheme" is the term used in New Zealand for pension funds. The Superannuation Schemes Act 1989 provides for registration of schemes, implied provisions of trust deeds, financial and actuarial reporting, members' rights to information, and supervision by the Government Actuary. These are largely irrelevant to this fund.

13. In this part of the chapter, references in square brackets are to relevant provisions in the New Zealand Superannuation Act 2001, unless otherwise noted. A copy of this legislation is available at www.treasury.govt.nz/release/super/assent84.pdf.

7

This is the legislation originally enacted. There have since been some routine amendments to the benefits provisions, for example, to implement the annual update of benefit rates listed in Schedule One of the Act. The provisions relating to the fund and its governance can only be changed by Act of Parliament, and at the time of writing are unchanged.

14. However, for tax purposes the fund is treated as if it were a body corporate [section 76(3)].

15. For a detailed analysis of the calculation of the contribution rate, see McCulloch and Frances (2001a).

16. A key assumption is the expected long-term investment returns of the fund (McCulloch 2002b), an important element of which is estimating the market equity risk premium (McCulloch 2002a).

17. Current budget forecasts indicate that the government should be able to meet the required capital contributions for the foreseeable future without compromising its other fiscal objectives.

18. In particular, ministers could have charged a government ministry with responsibility for administering the assets that would be informally designated as belonging to the fund. A parallel arrangement already exists for the management of Crown debt by the New Zealand Debt Management Office, which is a division of the Treasury with no separate legal standing (www.nzdmo.govt.nz).

19. There also is evidence from U.S. state and local pension plans that the practice of permitting administrative expenses to be charged to fund income, rather than to the state or local budgets directly, is associated with reduced average returns (Mitchell and Hsin 1994).

20. "Expense" has a relatively well-defined meaning that is consistent with the generally accepted accounting practice [section 5(2) of the New Zealand Superannuation Act 2001 and section 2(1) of the Public Finance Act 1989].

21. 12 March 2003 speech by Ruth Kelly, Financial Secretary to the U.K. Treasury. (See www.hm-treasury.gov.uk/newsroom_and_speeches/press/2003/press_38_03.cfm.)

22. Cabinet rules state that, in general, public servants should not be appointed to public bodies. See Cabinet Office Minute CO(02)5 or www.dpmc.govt.nz/cabinet/co02/5.html.

23. Appointment of chief executives of New Zealand government departments follows an independent process in which the State Services

Commissioner selects and recommends the candidate. If the government chooses to appoint someone else, this must be disclosed publicly.

24. The legislation does not preclude officials from being on the nominating committee. However, in the New Zealand environment it was taken as given that officials would not normally be appointed to a committee such as this (see also footnote 22).

25. Members' duties include ensuring that the Crown entity acts efficiently and effectively, consistently with its functions and powers, and in a financially responsible manner [Schedule 3, clause 7(2)]. Members are required to act in good faith; with reasonable care, diligence, and skill; and with honestly and integrity [Schedule 3, clause 7(1)].

26. See www.dpmc.govt.nz/cabinet/guide/6.hmtl - 6.27 and www.ssc.govt.nz/board-appointment-guidelines.

27. See Cabinet Office Minute CO(01)8 at www.dpmc.govt.nz/cabinet/circulars/co01/8.html

28. Pozen also asserts that this clause was included "because of legislative pressures." In fact, it was included in the original draft bill that was introduced to the legislature.

29. The provision precluding the fund from taking control over companies [section 59] does not resolve this because the most likely strategy to avoid paying tax altogether would be to dismantle the company structure and then run the business directly as an unincorporated venture of the fund.

30. This issue is particularly relevant in New Zealand, where the tax rules for funds of this type favor a strongly passive investment strategy (because capital gains are not taxed in that situation). However, it requires a ruling from the revenue authority in the case of each taxpayer who seeks to use this tax concession, and it is quite possible that the fund would not be granted a favorable ruling.

31. For example, the Crown already has a significant exposure to domestic capital markets through its tax base; it has a heavy negative exposure to New Zealand government securities; and it has significant exposure to particular industries through its state-owned enterprises.

32. Indeed, the board's performance is likely to be examined publicly along a range of dimensions.

33. Since the fund itself is not a Crown entity or body corporate, section 54 of the Public Finance Act 1989 (regarding the Crown not being liable for the debts of Crown entities) does not apply.

7

34. This implied guarantee could possibly arise despite the provision in section 54 of the Public Finance Act 1989 that states that the Crown is not liable for the debts of Crown entities.

35. This contrasts with some other jurisdictions, such as Canada, where the "foreign property rule" limits the proportion of investment funds that can be allocated to foreign assets.

36. Requiring a public fund to invest in government stock is not necessarily an illegitimate action. It effectively transfers responsibility for risk and investment management of that money to the center. Depending on the relative governance arrangements, this could well be the most efficient means of overall financial management.

37. This is similar to the disclosure requirement placed on private pension funds in the United Kingdom under the Pensions Act 1995.

38. See www.treasury.govt.nz/budgets.

39. In New Zealand, the term "generally accepted accounting practice" is used with the same meaning as the term "generally accepted accounting principles" that is used in other jurisdictions.

40. New Zealand financial reporting standards are largely consistent with the financial reporting standards published by the International Accounting Standards Board (www.iasb.org.uk). The Accounting Standards Review Board (www.asrb.co.nz), which sets financial reporting standards in New Zealand, has announced that it intends to require international financial reporting standards to be adopted in full by all New Zealand reporting entities by 2007.

41. Much of the financial statement audit work of the Auditor General is tendered out to private sector audit firms, especially where specialist industry expertise may be required. This is yet to be determined for the fund.

42. See www.oag.govt.nz for detail about the functions and powers of the Office of the Auditor General, including a copy of the Public Audit Act 2001.

43. In the statement of responsibility, the chairperson and chief executive take responsibility for the preparation of the annual financial statements and the judgments used therein, along with responsibility for establishing and maintaining a system of internal control designed to provide reasonable assurance as to the integrity and reliability of financial reporting. They also make a statement that, in their opinion, the annual financial

7

statements for the financial year fairly reflect the financial position and operations of the fund.

44. For more detail, see www.justice.govt.nz/pubs/other/pamphlets/2001/info_act.html.

45. www.ombudsmen.govt.nz

46. The Guardians Crown entity is also owned by the Crown and therefore also included in the Crown financial statements, along with all other Crown entities.

47. See www.treasury.govt.nz/financialstatements.

48. At the time of completion of this paper, the items marked "Pending" in this table were yet to be completed.

49. The key policy papers are published at www.treasury.govt.nz/release/super/.

50. www.superfund.govt.nz

51. This request was the result of a decision by the Cabinet to seek greater diversity in board appointments generally. See Cabinet Office Minute CO(02)16 at www.dpmc.govt.nz/cabinet/circulars/co02/16.html.

52. It is a convention in New Zealand that significant appointments arising immediately before a general election are held over for the new government to determine.

53. Mercer Investment Consultants (www.merceric.com) was appointed "to provide the board with investment advice relating to the long-term asset allocation for the fund and portfolio construction issues." The board has indicated that additional appointments are expected to be made to provide second opinion advice on these issues.

54. The New Zealand Debt Management Office is a division of the Treasury that manages the Crown's sovereign borrowings and the Crown bank account. See www.nzdmo.govt.nz.

55. These transitional amounts are less than the "required" capital contribution estimated by the Treasury. For example, in the 2002 December Economic and Fiscal Update, the "required" rate for 2003/04 was estimated to be NZ$1,937 million, compared to the NZ$1,800 million that the government has planned to set aside. This relatively small difference might raise a question of why a transitional path was necessary. However, when this transitional path was adopted in early 2000, forecasts at the time predicted that the "required" rate for 2003/04 would be somewhat higher, at about NZ$2,500 million.

7

56. The current official cash rate is 5.75 percent per annum. See www.rbnz. govt.nz.

57. RBNZ=Reserve Bank of New Zealand; NZDMO=Debt Management Office; GSF=Government Superannuation Fund; NZSF=New Zealand Superannuation Fund; ACC=Accident Compensation Corporation; EQC=Earthquake Commission; SOEs=state-owned enterprises.

58. "Financial assets held by the core Crown" excludes holdings of New Zealand Government stock by these subentities.

59. The "eliminations" row nets out the New Zealand Government stock held by the Crown entities and SOEs so that the actual total financial assets of the Crown as a whole (that is, financial claims on parties external to the Crown) is correctly stated. The borrowings and other liabilities are also stated net of eliminations (that is, excluding intra-Crown cross-holdings).

60. The borrowings and other liabilities of SOEs and Crown entities are not guaranteed by the Crown.

61. Refer to www.treasury.govt.nz for more detail.

62. www.rbnz.govt.nz

63. www.nzdmo.govt.nz

64. See footnote 9.

65. www.gsf.govt.nz

66. www.eqc.govt.nz

67. www.eqc.govt.nz

68. Established in 1992, the student loan scheme provides concessionary loans to tertiary students. See www.studylink.govt.nz/student-loan/index. html.

69. State-owned enterprises are limited-liability corporations that operate at arm's-length from the government. See www.ccmau.govt.nz/soe/over view.asp.

Chapter 8

Investment Policies, Processes and Problems in U.S. Public Sector Pension Plans: Some Observations and Solutions from a Practitioner

John H. Ilkiw

Public and private sector pension plans are both subject to the same financing, investment, and organizational principles and both therefore wrestle with the same issues during the establishment and implementation of investment policies.[1] The process that each uses to decide and implement those policies is different, however. Investment policy decisions for private sector pension plans are usually made behind closed doors and by well-paid, full-time individuals with strong investment backgrounds. In contrast, investment policy decisions for public sector plans are usually made in a public forum fishbowl, often by time-pressed individuals receiving honorariums and of limited investment expertise.

Part I of this paper provides some definitions and presents summary statistics to illustrate the important role that public sector pension plans play in the U.S. pension system. The context within which I offer my analysis, findings, and conclusions is then clarified.

Part II discusses the generic investment policy process that implicitly is followed by most private and public sector pension plans in the United States, Canada, and the United Kingdom. The strengths and weaknesses of the process are highlighted and improvements suggested. Adoption of the suggested improvements should result in better-informed and more successful investment policy decisions in both private and public sector pension plans.

Part III begins with a discussion of the impact that ineffective governance structures and procedures have on pension fund investment performance, and continues by identifying seven organizational and behavioral impediments that public sector funds often face when setting and implementing investment policies. These include inadequate understanding by governing fiduciaries of the principles of financing and investment,[2] the inability of governing fiduciaries to separate policy approval from policy implementation, and an overreliance on past performance when making decisions. These impediments are not unique to public sector pension plans, but are usually more visible here than among their private sector counterparts.

Part IV concludes the paper by introducing a one-page performance report designed explicitly for governing fiduciaries. The format is designed to help trustees focus on those investment issues and decisions that ensure plan assets are prudently and profitably managed. The same document provides plan participants with an easy-to-understand report card telling them how well the assets backing their pensions are performing. The reporting format has equal application to private and public sector pension plans.

Part I: Background Information

Distinguishing Public Sector Pension Plans from Other Plans

To avoid confusion, it is useful to distinguish between three types of pension plans: private sector-sponsored plans, public sector-sponsored, and government-sponsored. Private sector-sponsored pension plans are employment-based plans established by firms such as IBM, General Motors, and AT&T. Public sector-sponsored defined benefit pension plans cover employees working for federal, state, and local governments. Government-sponsored pension plans are countrywide, compulsory programs such as the Social Security Retirement System in the United States and the Canada and Quebec Pension Plans in Canada. There is additionally a fourth category of pension plan that may be included with private sector plans: plans established by nonprofit organizations, including colleges, universities, and nongovernmental agencies.

Table 8.1: Sources of Assets for U.S. Retirement System, 2001

Source	$ trillions	% of total
Private sector (DB)	1.85	17
Private sector (DC)	2.11	20
Private insured	1.34	13
State and local government	2.18	20
Federal government (civilian and military)	0.81	8
IRA and Keogh	2.40	22
Total	10.69	100

In some studies, the term "public sector plan" refers to government-sponsored national pension plans. The focus of this paper is defined benefit plans established for public sector employees. It is important to make the distinction between the two, as they can differ significantly in terms of their governance structures, fund sizes, and investment issues.

Importance of U.S. Public Sector Pension Plans

Some 28 percent of the more than US$10 trillion of U.S. retirement assets is in public sector pension funds, including some US$2.2 trillion that is in funds that manage assets on behalf of state and local government employees (see Table 8.1). With 90 percent of state and local government employees participating in defined benefit plans, it is reasonable to conclude that about 90 percent of the US$2.2 trillion comprises assets that are being managed in defined benefit plans.[3] This means that assets in public sector pension defined benefit plans are roughly equal in value to the total assets in all private sector defined benefit plans, which in 2001 totaled US$1.9 trillion.

While their cumulative assets may be equal, individual public sector pension funds are on average larger than their corporate counterparts. For example, nine of the 10 largest U.S. pension funds cover state employees, with California teachers and state employee pension funds having combined assets of more than USS$225 billion (see Table 8.2). The 100 largest U.S. pension funds managed some US$2.9 trillion in assets. Fifty-one of those

8

Table 8.2: Ten Largest U.S. Employee Pension Funds, 2001 (as of September 30, 2001)

Fund	Assets ($ billions)
1. California Public Employees	143.7
2. New York State Common	106.1
3. California State Teachers	95.5
4. Florida State Teachers	88.5
5. Texas State Teachers	75.1
6. New York State Teachers	74.9
7. New Jersey	65.5
8. General Motors	64.6
9. New York City Retirement	54.5
10. Wisconsin Investment	54.5
Total	822.9

Source: Pension and Investments (2002).

8

funds were private and 49 were in the public sector, but the 49 public sector plans held 60 percent of the assets.

While this paper focuses on U.S. public sector pension plans, the analysis, findings, and conclusions presented here apply with little adjustment also to public sector pension plans in Canada and the United Kingdom.

Part II: Toward Better-Informed Investment Policy Setting

Investment Policies Involve Two Big Risk–Return Decisions

All investment policies involve two big decisions: approving a fund's policy exposure to mayor equity and debt asset classes; and establishing the extent to which the selected asset classes are to be actively managed.[4] These policies are termed the "asset allocation policy" and the "active management policy," respectively. It has long been established that the asset allocation policy is the principal determinant of a fund's long-term investment performance: assuming that a reasonable proportion of the assets are being actively managed and not simply managed as index funds, the policy explains about 90 percent of the return volatility.

The balance of the volatility of fund returns is attributable to active management. From a statistical perspective, the active management policy thus appears to be of secondary importance, but setting the policy nonetheless is a key investment decision. Successful active management brings additional returns to a pension fund, making it easier to pay benefits; unsuccessful active management subtracts returns and reduces the amount of assets available to pay those benefits.

Generic AA Decision Process

There are four generic steps in the asset allocation decision: (a) collect inputs, (b) model the behavior of assets and liabilities, (c) evaluate alternative asset allocation combinations, and (d) select the desired asset allocation (see Figure 8.1). The evaluation of alternative asset allocations invariably involves the literal or figurative use of mean-variance optimization procedures to calculate efficient combinations of asset classes (i.e., those weightings that provide the highest expected return for a given level of portfolio volatility, measured in standard deviations).

The optimization decision framework, with its efficient frontier and optimal portfolios, is ubiquitous in the world of financial management. Founded in a concept that earned a Nobel Prize, the framework is routinely used by financial advisory websites, is available in popular and low-cost home computer programs, and is highly regarded by both professional and amateur investors for its precision. Investors worldwide use the framework to establish optimal allocations to domestic and foreign equities, domestic and foreign fixed income, private real estate, private equity, hedge funds, and a host of other exposures, including small capitalization stocks, managed futures, commodities, and even timberland.

Uncertain Parameters and the "Perils of Optimization"

While optimizers are often the centerpiece of the asset allocation policy decision process, they are also its Achilles' heel. Increasingly optimizers

8

Figure 8.1: Generic Asset Allocation Decision Process

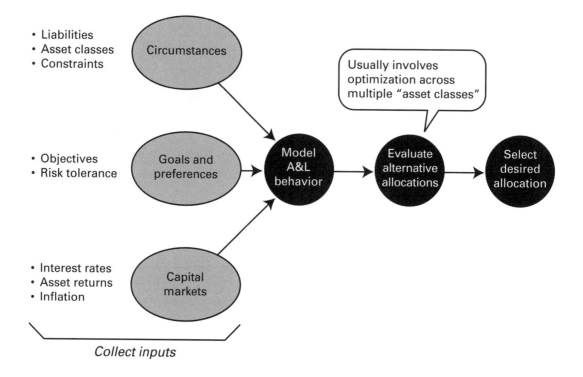

are being recognized as "estimation-error maximizers," because while they provide detailed guidance for making asset allocation policy decisions this guidance is inaccurate. This is because the parameters used by optimizers to calculate efficient combinations of different investments, such as expected returns, standard deviations, and correlations, are unobservable and must be estimated, and these estimates are subject to estimation error.

The answers provided by optimizers are sensitive to even small changes in the value of the estimated parameters submitted by investors, and the weightings of efficient and near-efficient portfolios can vary widely. Experience has shown that a judicious selection of inputs can justify almost any asset allocation policy. If at first the optimization model does not confirm the attractiveness of a favored asset allocation, simply tweaking the inputs or adding a suitable constraint can move the favored policy into the spectrum of efficient portfolios.

Differential Levels of Parametric Uncertainty

All forward-looking estimates of investment parameters are subject to uncertainty, but some parameters are more susceptible to estimation errors than others. The long-term relationships among the major asset classes—stocks, bonds, and cash—are generally well understood and their statistical parameters can be estimated with relative confidence. These asset classes have been studied for decades and their expected relationships have been confirmed using ever-improving historical data. Investors will always debate the magnitude of the parameters summarizing the asset class relationships, but few disagree with the ordinal values of the parameters that capture their long-term relationships. First, equities are expected to outperform bonds, and bonds are expected to outperform cash. Second, equities are more volatile than bonds, and bonds are more volatile than cash. And third, although asset class relationships are firmly interrelated, their behavior is sufficiently uncorrelated to reliably diversify risk.

The behavior of other asset classes or investment opportunities cannot be modeled with the same level of confidence. This notably is true of three performance-enhancing investment opportunities that are the current focus of many public sector pension funds: private real estate, private equity, and hedge funds.

Return series for infrequently traded assets such as private real estate and private equity rely on appraisal pricing procedures, and this introduces a higher level of data unreliability. Parameters derived directly from appraisal-based data underestimate both standard deviations and correlations, thus enhancing the statistical attractiveness of these investment opportunities. Appraisal pricing procedures can be highly subjective, and in some situations purposely misrepresentative. Many hedge fund strategies hold positions in infrequently traded securities and are therefore subject to the same appraisal pricing problems as private real estate and private equity. Verifying actual performance can be further complicated by the lack of transparency that accompanies many hedge fund strategies, because many managers are reluctant to reveal their proprietary ideas and hence compromise their performance advantage.

When considering an allocation to private equity, estimating the magnitude and stability of the illiquidity premium complicates investment modeling. Illiquid assets should pay a premium over their public market counterparts to compensate investors for accepting illiquidity risk (the inability to

8

quickly sell an asset to take advantage of another more compelling investment opportunity), but what magnitude is appropriate? Further, is the risk premium suggested by past experience representative of a future that is more accepting of private equity investing? The illiquidity premium should fall as more institutions embrace private equity investing.

Perhaps the greatest hurdle is the inability to separate the attractiveness of an investment exposure from the success or failure of active management. In the realm of publicly traded securities one can access the returns from the broad market asset class by investing in index funds, and thus avoid the risk of active management. Investors are assured of earning at least the market average return, and in many cases of earning a return that is above the performance of the average actively managed portfolio. With private real estate, private equity, and hedge funds, investors cannot separate the attractiveness of the income stream from the risk of active management. This is especially true of hedge funds, which are not an asset class but are a collection of disparate and unconventional active management strategies that frequently defy clear definition and usually employ leverage (Oberhofer 2001).

When interpreting the results of an asset allocation study that recommends an allocation to private real estate, private equity, and hedge funds it is important to consider to what extent the favorable experience modeled in the study is attributable to successful active management. If investors do not believe they can find or buy the active skills needed to implement a successful private real estate, private equity, or hedge fund exposure they should not accept the asset allocation recommendation. It is possible to replicate the performance of the broad market asset classes by investing in low-cost index funds, but the success of these exposures is driven above all by the investor's ability to employ superior managers (Ilkiw, Scheer, and Payne 2002).

Two-stage AA Recognizes Differential Parametric Uncertainty

Because of the differential uncertainty in capital market estimates, investors should establish their policy portfolios in two stages. Policy exposures to broad market asset classes should be decided at the first stage, using high confidence forecasts. Exposures to performance-enhancing investment opportunities can then be decided in stage two, using lower confidence forecasts and qualitative criteria.

Figure 8.2: Generic Two-Stage Asset Allocation Decision Process

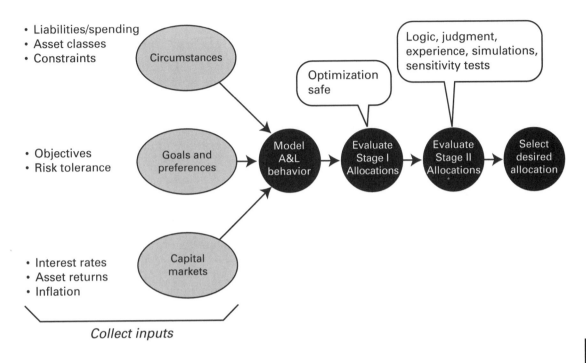

Figure 8.2 illustrates how two-stage asset allocation inserts an additional step into the generic process of selecting an investor-specific allocation policy. Figure 8.3 summarizes the key features of the Frank Russell Company's approach to two-stage asset allocation. This error-reducing approach to asset allocation decision-making finds its origin in research undertaken by Russell and others in the late 1980s and early 1990s. It has been advanced and refined by Russell in concert with clients during its practical application in hundreds of asset allocation studies.

Stage I Allocations

The objective of Stage I is to find a high-confidence asset allocation that best meets client-specific objectives. Stage I thus focuses on finding mathematically optimized allocations to well-understood broad market domestic and foreign asset classes. For U.S.-based investors, this means finding optimal exposures to U.S. equity, non-U.S. equity, and U.S. fixed-income securities.

Figure 8.3: Decide Asset Allocation in Two Stages

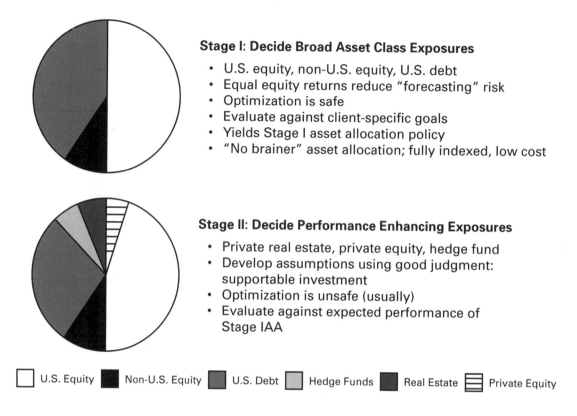

Stage I: Decide Broad Asset Class Exposures

- U.S. equity, non-U.S. equity, U.S. debt
- Equal equity returns reduce "forecasting" risk
- Optimization is safe
- Evaluate against client-specific goals
- Yields Stage I asset allocation policy
- "No brainer" asset allocation; fully indexed, low cost

Stage II: Decide Performance Enhancing Exposures

- Private real estate, private equity, hedge fund
- Develop assumptions using good judgment: supportable investment
- Optimization is unsafe (usually)
- Evaluate against expected performance of Stage IAA

☐ U.S. Equity ■ Non-U.S. Equity ▨ U.S. Debt ▨ Hedge Funds ▨ Real Estate ▤ Private Equity

Because Stage I uses only high-confidence asset class assumptions, investors can assess with relative confidence—but not with certainty—the range of efficient portfolios calculated by an optimization model and the ability of those portfolios to achieve their specific risk–return objectives. Investors also have the comfort of knowing they can implement the Stage I policy portfolio through low-cost index funds. They do not have to accept the additional costs, risks, and uncertainty of active management. Because so little subsequent effort is required to implement a Stage I policy portfolio, they are often referred to as "no-brainer" policy portfolios.

Stage II Allocations

Using the Stage I asset allocation as a high-confidence benchmark, Stage II evaluates the risk and rewards of potentially performance-enhancing

8

investment opportunities. This requires replacing a portion of the "no-brainer" policy portfolio with exposures to investments that increase the likelihood that investors will achieve their objectives. Private real estate, private equity, and hedge funds are among the most frequently referenced return-enhancing investment opportunities. The behavior of these investments cannot however be modeled with high confidence, and any guidance perceived in optimization models can be very misleading.

In the absence of high-confidence forecasts for performance-enhancing investments, investors must rely heavily on their own judgment. In the world of asset allocation studies, this means developing assumptions tied to supportable investment beliefs, logic, experience, and asset–liability simulations and testing the sensitivity of results to changes in the estimated parameters. The various Stage II allocations are evaluated relative to the performance of the higher-confidence Stage I policy portfolio.

Before a Stage II allocation is selected as a policy portfolio, it should satisfy two criteria. First, its expected performance must dominate the performance of the corresponding Stage I policy allocation. This is usually not a difficult criteria to meet because the capital market assumptions used to capture the expected performance of the investment opportunities being assessed invariably are favorable. Second, the investor should be satisfied that the capital market assumptions used to portray the performance have a reasonable expectation of being realized. This criterion is often much more difficult to satisfy. When it comes to evaluating different performance-enhancing investment strategies, experience has shown that investors are usually divided into two camps: those who believe in the future success of a strategy and therefore the robustness of the assumptions used, and those who do not. The movement between the two camps is limited. For those investors in the second camp, the two-stage approach remains a valuable framework because it encourages discussion of issues beyond the simple debating of asset class weightings.

Clarifying Expected Impact on Fund Performance

Figure 8.4 is an example exhibit that summarizes the results of an asset allocation study that employed the two-stage approach to evaluating alternative asset allocations. In the example, an investor with a 10-year investment horizon wanted to understand the impact of different asset allocations, including 5 percent and 10 percent policy exposures to hedge funds. A

Figure 8.4: Two-Stage Asset Allocation Clarifies Projected Impact of Performance-Enhancing Strategies

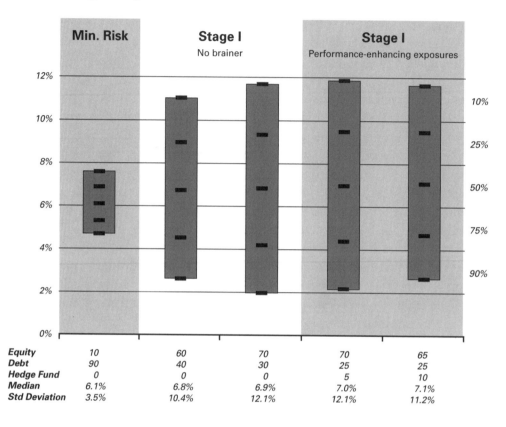

	Min. Risk	Stage I		Stage I	
Equity	10	60	70	70	65
Debt	90	40	30	25	25
Hedge Fund	0	0	0	5	10
Median	6.1%	6.8%	6.9%	7.0%	7.1%
Std Deviation	3.5%	10.4%	12.1%	12.1%	11.2%

single such graphic can illustrate to the investor the projected return–risk trade-offs of multiple asset allocations.

The terms "minimum risk," "Stage I no-brainer policy," and "Stage II performance-enhancing exposures" highlight the investment performance and associated investment implementation implications of each alternative. The implications of each of these alternative allocations would be further underscored as the advisor explained the relative confidence associated with the parameters used to forecast the future performance of different asset allocations. In particular, the advisor should emphasize that the improved performance associated with the hedge fund exposures— i.e., higher returns and lower volatility—assumes first the successful implementation of the modeled hedge fund strategy.

End Result: Higher-Confidence Policy Portfolios

Like other asset allocation models, the two-stage asset allocation approach does not prove that a given investment opportunity will enhance performance. The two-stage decision process does however help investors establish higher-confidence policy portfolios, for two reasons.

First, investors understand clearly why they expect their Stage II policy portfolio to outperform the Stage I alternative of investing in low-cost, broad-market index funds. Second, this improved understanding encourages investors to focus their subsequent management activities on those factors that are critical to realizing their Stage II expectations: that is, manager selection, portfolio construction, and risk management. Because most Stage II investment opportunities require active management, the success of Stage II policy portfolios rests on the investor's ability to select good managers, construct good portfolios, and manage risks effectively.

Part III: Poor Governance Structures and Procedures Impede Successful Implementation of Investment Policies

8

Poor Fund Governance: Costs, Descriptions, and Prescriptions

It has been estimated that ineffective fund governance structures and procedures can reduce investment performance by about 50 basis points annually.[5] While one-half of one percentage point of return may seem small, in the world of pensions it is a large number. With some US$2.2 trillion in state and local pension assets, the 50 basis points translate into some US$11 billion in foregone returns each year—a large amount of money from a beneficiary's perspective. From an actuary's perspective, losing 50 basis points of return increases long-term pension costs by about 8 percent, and from an active money manager's perspective, 50 basis points is often the difference between keeping and losing an investment client.

Descriptions of and prescriptions to resolve governance problems are widely available, for pension funds as for other organizations. Ambachtsheer and Ezra (1998) provide an excellent description of the shortcomings in pension fund governance structures and procedures, provide broad guidance on how effective pension boards operate, and analyze what distinguishes competent from incompetent boards, and Carver and Oliver (2002) are often referenced as governance gurus for both profit and nonprofit organizations.

The collective recognition that fund governance practices need to be improved has spawned a cottage industry of experts providing governance audits, governance recommendations, and governance "best practices" seminars. In practice, however, many of the plans that have used the services of such governance experts are likely to have found that the promised land of governance excellence remains beyond their reach. I would suggest that before they can hope to do their jobs better, governing fiduciaries must first and foremost begin with a better identification and articulation of the hurdles that they face.

Seven Hurdles to Better Fund Governance

The seven hurdles to better fund governance described here are merely the most prevalent and most obstructive—especially when two or more appear in combination—of many. They are of two types: organizational or behavioral. Organizational hurdles are common across most types of organizations, be they pension funds, professional associations, companies, governments, nonprofit organizations, or even church groups. Behavioral hurdles are largely confined to organizations that are responsible for managing financial assets, and in particular financial assets that are held in trust for the benefit of others. The key difference between the two is that in the case of assets held in trust, all decisions are subject to the scrutiny and second-guessing of other interested parties, including the plan sponsor, plan beneficiaries, current contributors, and regulators.

Four Organizational Hurdles

Inadequate Understanding

The transformation of contributions into retirement income is driven by financing, investment, and organizational principles that are well documented but that are not always adequately understood by governing fiduciaries. Individuals find themselves on pension boards for a host of reasons—stakeholder representation, independence, political favors, ex officio status, professional expertise, reputation—but few of these reasons ensure they arrive with an adequate understanding of the workings of a defined benefit pension plan. It is common for members of public sector boards to accept the position knowing that they have an inadequate understanding of financing, investment, and organizational issues but with the expectation that, with the help of incumbent board members, fund investment staff, consultants, and investment managers and by being regularly exposed to the issues, they will learn on the job. Even those members appointed for their expertise and experience often find they are less than fully equipped for the responsibility because their understanding is dated, narrow, or does not translate well into the specialized world of pension management.[6]

Governing fiduciaries do not have to become experts to be effective. However, they do need to have enough knowledge and understanding of issues to be able to assess and challenge advice critically. Decision-making suffers when board members do not have and share an adequate understanding of financing, investment, and organizational principles. For example, should board members start with erroneous and conflicting understandings of one or more basic principles, there inevitably will be disagreements about how best to solve a given issue. Should they start with different premises, disagreement and conflict again will follow. Decision-making will suffer in one of two ways: pressing issues may be deferred until the impasse is resolved, or an incorrect or suboptimal solution may be adopted.

Inability to Separate Policy Approval from Policy Implementation

Boards set objectives, approve policies, delegate policy implementation to management, and then ensure that management runs the business properly. Nothing could be simpler in concept, but few things—and especially the defining, accepting, and enforcing of a clear distinction between policy approval and policy implementation—are more difficult to implement in practice. For most organizations, unequivocally giving management the responsibility and accountability for the implementation of approved policies, subject to board-imposed limitations, is the way most likely to see the objectives of those policies achieved.

From an asset management perspective, boards are accountable for making two big risk-and-return decisions: asset mix policy and active management policy.[7] In setting asset mix policy, the board is expressing a view about what portion of fund assets can be put at risk in order to earn a capital

8

market return premium. When setting active management policy, the board is expressing a view about how many additional assets it is prepared to put at risk to earn additional returns from active management decisions. Once the asset mix policy decision is made almost all boards delegate the implementation of the funds asset mix policy to the managing fiduciaries, subject to the rebalancing of rules, and require periodic reports to confirm that the funds asset allocation has been managed within the specified ranges.

Many boards, however, appear unable to separate the approval of an active management policy from its implementation (Burr 2003). It is a common misconception on many boards that they can only fulfill their fiduciary responsibility for implementation of the fund's active management policy by also deciding which active investment managers to hire and fire. As such, while the board may rely heavily on the guidance and recommendations of its staff and consultants in practice it makes the final decision in the same way that it makes the final decision about asset mix policy.

This is inappropriate and probably counterproductive for three reasons. First, board members seldom have the time, expertise, or experience to evaluate prospective managers with any rigor, and they therefore cannot make truly informed decisions. Most board members consequently end up selecting from shortlisted candidates according to their past performance and the panache with which they present their candidacy—both of which are very poor predictors of future performance. Second, the shortlist of prospective managers will comprise only those that fund staff have decided could do a good job; when the board selects from the shortlist it is thus assuming accountability for the outcome of what is in effect a staff decision. This muddies the accountability between board and management, and ambiguous accountability is a clear indicator of an ineffective governance structure.[8] Third, board and staff will inevitably at times disagree over terminating a manager whose performance record is poor. Board members typically will see only underperformance, whereas management may see a skilled manager whose strategy or style is simply out of favor but who may bounce back with benchmark-beating returns. Disagreements such as this can create mistrust between the governing and managing fiduciaries, with the board questioning management's competence or even the nature of its relationship with the underperforming manager, and management in return developing a suspicion that the board doubts its competence and objectivity.

Poorly Designed Board Performance Reports

The performance reports used by most boards to monitor and evaluate investment returns and investment risk generally provide too much data and too little information—and what information they do provide is usually misleading because of an excessive focus on peer-relative performance. Faced with a constellation of often disjointed data, governing fiduciaries will look for the data that they can most easily understand, will make comparisons that seem logical, and from this will draw conclusions about the success or failure of their pension fund's investment policies. Performance reporting has evolved over the years in an ad hoc fashion, responding to the diverse needs of a host of market participants, each driven by a different agenda. Compounding the profusion of reporting formats is the ever-decreasing cost of computing power, which is making easier and easier the production of reports, exhibits, and diagrams.

Confused performance reports result in confused decision-making. Redesigning board performance reports to meet the explicit needs of governing fiduciaries in an easy-to-understand format would go a long way to improving fund governance. If there is any truth to the axiom "what gets measured, gets managed," board members should demand reports that clearly, crisply, and accurately answer the two questions that should be uppermost in every fiduciary's mind: are plan assets being prudently managed and are they being profitability managed?

By making these two questions the primary focus of board reports and the basis upon which the board evaluates management's ability to implement approved investment policies, the governing fiduciaries can secure a reporting framework that ensures the alignment of management's implementation decisions with beneficiary interests. If either question cannot be answered affirmatively by each board member, the board must call management to account and, if necessary, undertake corrective action.

Ineffective Directors of Investment

Directors of investment (DIs) or chief investment officers (CIOs) are pivotal to the success of an investment program, particularly in public sector pension plans. Many DIs mistakenly believe that they should respond rather than lead, and wait for direction from the governing board. Given that most boards are populated by members with an inadequate understanding of pension financing, investment, and organizational issues this is tantamount to having the blind lead the sighted through an unfamiliar maze. Ineffective DIs also fail to have the board distinguish clearly between policy approval and policy implementation, and do not push for the decision rights and accountability they need to implement board policies.

Taking a nonleadership role is nonetheless an understandable strategy for many DIs of public sector pension funds. Public sector boards can be a hotbed of conflicting political and personal agendas, and trying to exert investment leadership in such an environment can be a career-limiting strategy.

Effective DIs have firm and considered views on what makes an investment program successful and implement their ideas by hiring and managing the right investment staff, by communicating their ideas convincingly to governing fiduciaries, and by managing their expectations accordingly. Most board members would welcome the guidance of a proactive DI, especially one that listens, responds, and when necessary disagrees constructively.

Finally, an effective DI will exhibit a personal commitment to the investment process that he or she has implemented in pursuit of the investment objectives established by the board. In the event of board turnover, the effective DI will become the intellectual flywheel that ensures the fund's investment processes continue to run smoothly.[9] The DI should review with each new board the rationale for the way that assets are managed and should be forthright about what is working well, what is performing below expectations, and what corrective actions are likely to be needed.

Three Behavioral Hurdles

Inability to Specify Risk Tolerance

Risk tolerance—the measure of an investor's willingness to accept a higher probability of loss in exchange for an increase in expected return—is a pivotal parameter in all investment decisions, and is perhaps the most difficult metric for investors to specify, be they individuals or investment committees. Without a clearly articulated statement of risk tolerance, investors inevitability will adopt investment policies and strategies that are unsuitable because they are either too risky or insufficiently risky.[10]

All investors find it difficult to articulate their risk tolerance, but pension fund trustees arguably face a unique combination of challenges. First, they must reach a collective expression of risk tolerance on behalf of not only the plan beneficiaries but also the plan sponsor, and the risk tolerances of these two parties seldom coincide. Second, plan trustees seldom are directly affected financially by success or failure of the investment program they authorize. This means the process of reaching a consensus risk tolerance can easily become an academic trade-off between risk and return. Third, risk tolerances are dynamic, and change not only with changing economic environments but also with changes in board membership, in the funded status of the plan, and in the financial health of the plan sponsor. Fourth, statistical measures of risk and return provided by the asset and liability modeling studies undertaken for trustees cannot convey the emotional pain and regret that accompanies the realization of disappointing investment scenarios. Disappointing outcomes are clinically described as "below-median results," and very disappointing scenarios as "very-low probability single-path events." Finally, and perhaps most significantly, governing fiduciaries tend to underestimate their collective risk tolerance, with respect both to setting a fund's asset mix policy and to setting its active management policy. A statistical assessment usually will accord the same emotional weighting to positive and negative outcomes of equal magnitude, but in reality the disappointment endured as the result of a negative outcome often is more than twice the satisfaction enjoyed from a positive outcome (Kahanmen 2003).

In the absence of a crisp and robust articulation of risk tolerance, governing fiduciaries often will look to see how their peers in other pension funds have made their risk–return policy decisions and will simply adopt similar policies. This is a reasonable approach given that prudence is often judged within the context of what others investors do when faced with similar circumstances, but there is no guarantee that an industry-norm investment policy is the best policy for a public sector pension plan. Trustees should decide their investment policy only after full consideration of the particular circumstances facing the plan for which they have fiduciary responsibility. The circumstances considered must include liability structure, funded status, management resources, and the ability of the sponsor to underwrite poor investment performance should it materialize.

Other governing fiduciaries will seek the guidance of their investment advisors in the belief that the experience and expertise of those advisors gives them a better understanding of the extent to which pension plan assets should be exposed to investment risk. While investment advisors can provide a framework for understanding and evaluating risks, however, few will be willing to assume responsibility for specifying their client's risk tolerance. Advisors are seldom in command of all the facts that trustees use to evaluate their risk tolerance, and an experienced advisor will recognize that risk tolerance ebbs and flows in response to a host of events, including board turnover and market cycles.

This fact notwithstanding, many governing boards will adopt the risk preferences of their advisors, via a process that is subtle and often unrecognized by either party. If the risk preferences of the board and the advisor are a good match, future investment experiences, good and bad, will likely be viewed in their proper context. If the risk preferences are mismatched, problems are inevitable. The advisor will be blamed for any bad news, either in terms of "the fund lost too much money in bad times" or "the fund didn't earn enough money when times were good."

Overreliance on Past Performance

That past performance is an unreliable predictor of future performance is almost universally accepted by governing fiduciaries. Paradoxically, past performance nonetheless is the principal criterion used by governing fiduciaries when they are hiring or firing individual investment managers or evaluating the success or failure of their investment strategies, including their asset mix policies and active management strategies. This paradoxical behavior affects all investors, even the most expert and experienced, but it is legendary among governing fiduciaries—among whom succumbing to the "past performance" temptation produces excessive and expensive turnover of investment managers and the even more expensive and counterproductive turnover of investment policies and strategies.

The willingness of investors to rely on past performance to guide their decisions is readily explained: past performance is easy to measure, cheap to buy, easy to explain, and easy to understand; it is also widely available and regularly referenced by industry participants, including governing fiduciaries, investment managers, investment consultants, and beneficiary groups. We are all subject to the temptation of equating a good outcome with a good strategy and a bad outcome with a bad strategy. We forget, or do not fully appreciate, that the long-term value-generating aspects of most investment returns series are swamped by randomness over shorter timeframes (the same timeframes fiduciaries use to evaluate investment performance). The underperformance of a manager or strategy, for example, can result in external parties drawing an unfavorable comparison with past performance and exerting pressure on the governing fiduciaries. From the point of view of the governing fiduciary, in such situations it is easier to react and be complimented for doing so than it is to endure the criticism for sticking with what may in reality be a perfectly sound manager or strategy.

Despite its flaws, past performance will continue to appeal to governing fiduciaries because the alternatives are usually more expensive and are not foolproof. In-depth research may be a better way to predict the performance of a manager, for example, but requires a significant commitment of resources in terms of quantitative tools and personnel. Perhaps most importantly, however, the alternatives to past performance may not be sufficiently predictive over the sort of time horizon that is important to the governing fiduciary. For example, a research process would be invaluable that over quarterly time periods could identify managers of whom a consistent 55 percent prove to be superior. An investor would simply have to hire from this pool of managers and over long time periods the favorable odds would produce above-benchmark returns.[11] However, because 45 percent of the recommended manager pool under perform there is a significant chance that over shorter time periods performance would be disappointing. Given that many governing fiduciaries have investment time horizons of five years or less, the long-term statistical attractiveness of a 55 percent success quarterly rate loses much of its appeal (Ilkiw 2000).

Tacit Conspiracy of Over Optimism

Various factors combine to instill in the collective mind of trustees active management performance expectations that are unreasonably optimistic. These unrealistic expectations are then used as a yardstick for evaluating investment performance, inevitably resulting in an unproductive and costly turnover of active managers and active strategies.

Four factors conspire to produce unreasonably optimistic performance targets for active management. One is statistical and three are behavioral. The statistical factor is the upward drift in the quartile breaks of a sample of active managers relative to a broad market index, such as the Russell 3000 or Wiltshire 5000 for active U.S. equity managers. This upward drift makes the value-added returns from active management seem larger than if the sample were to be corrected for survivor and backfill bias. Survivor bias refers to the phenomenon of underperforming managers being dropped from the sample, leaving in the sample only those managers that have performed well. Over longer time periods the quartile breaks increasingly measure the value-added of a diminishing number of surviving or successful managers, and are no longer representative of the full community of active managers. Backfill bias refers to the upward shift in quartile breaks if a manager's return history is back loaded into an exiting sample—a consequence of the simple fact that only managers with good track records are motivated to submit historical returns.

The three behavioral factors are the understandable desire of trustees, investment managers, and consultants to help a pension fund earn additional returns from active management. Trustees want higher returns to increase pension assets and are always on the lookout for additional sources of return, and can always find a manager or strategy with a good historical track record to reference as an achievable and reasonable yardstick. Investment managers reinforce this trustee optimism with their ability to highlight those return periods and performance statistics that cast their track record in the best light. Investment consultants provide the third source of reinforcing optimism. Hired by trustees to provide expert investment advice on investment strategies and manager selection, consultants naturally prefer to provide advice that meets their clients' expectations. There is little for them to gain through trying to moderate their client expectations when trustees, investment managers, and competing consulting firms are expecting or selling higher performance expectations—many of which can be supported by pointing to selective performance histories or flawed samples of historical returns.

Governing fiduciaries would make better decisions if the performance criteria used to evaluate outcomes were recalibrated to better represent the upper and lower bounds of what is reasonably achievable for broadly diversified actively managed individual portfolios and broadly diversified total fund investment programs. "Recalibration" is not a code word for lowering expectations to make life easier for investment managers and investment staff: it is a tactful way of asking investors to be more realistic about what is achievable.

A total fund excess return target of 50 basis points net of fees, for example, may to many governing fiduciaries look disappointingly small and not worth pursuing, but this may be because they are harboring unrealistically high performance expectations (Turner and Lert 2003). Fifty basis points of excess return is in reality highly significant: applied to a 60-40 equity–debt asset mix policy it would provide the same expected return as a much more risky passively implemented 75-25 equity–debt policy.[12] From this perspective, it is equivalent to having 15 percentage points more policy exposure to equities, but without the concomitant increase in systematic risk. Over the long term, 50 basis points of increased return lowers the cost of providing a pension by about 8 percent.

Part IV: Trustee-Focused Report for Measuring and Monitoring Fund Performance

To determine if fund assets are being profitability managed, fund and manager performance must be evaluated against established objectives and benchmarks. The three-panel format illustrated in Figure 8.5 answers the three performance questions that should be uppermost in the minds of governing fiduciaries:

- Has investment performance affected benefit security?
- Has the asset–liability mismatch been rewarded?
- Have assets been cost-effectively managed?

Comparing a plan's total fund return with its funding discount rate indicates how benefit security has been affected by investment performance. Benefit security is improved when the total fund return exceeds the funding discount rate, and vice versa. In the example shown in Figure 8.5, the 6.76 percent three-year annualized return was less than the 8.00 percent discount rate by 1.24 percent, thus lowering the plan's funded ratio (assets divided by liabilities) and negatively affecting benefit security. This comparison excludes the favorable or adverse impacts that various noninvestment factors, such as benefit changes, salary growth, mortality experience, termination experience, and retirement rates, have on a plan's funded ratio. Governing fiduciaries should also monitor a plan's solvency ratio during periods of declining interest rates, a requirement that also can be built into the three-panel format.

All plans have a minimum risk portfolio: that combination of assets that best match the year-to-year changes in plan liabilities. This is usually a combination of investment-grade long-bonds, both nominal and real. Subtracting the return of the plan's policy portfolio from the minimum risk

8

Figure 8.5: Three-Panel Trustee-Friendly Performance Report

XYZ Total Fund Performance Report

Three-year returns, ending September 30, 2001

Have returns affected benefit security?	%	
1. Total fund actual return	6.76	Funded ratio declined;
2. Actuarial discount rate	8.00	return below funding
3. Out-performance (1–2)	(1.24)	discount rate
Has plan been rewarded for A&L mismatch?	**%**	
4. Total fund actual return	5.88	A&L mismatch rewarded
5. Minimum risk/high cost policy of 91-day T-bills	5.22	
6. Impact of asset mix policy (4–5)	0.66	
Have assets been cost-effectively managed?	**%**	
7. Active management (1–4)	0.88	Added value
Security selection	1.00	Added value
Asset mix management	(0.12)	Subtracted value

portfolio reveals if the authorized mismatch of assets and liabilities has been rewarded. In the example shown, the plan's minimum risk portfolio is represented by an all-T-bill portfolio. The 5.88 percent policy return exceeded the 5.22 percent T-bill return by a modest 0.66 percent. Over the long term, investors expect to earn a significant premium over T-bills, but over shorter periods the return differences between the minimum risk and risky policy portfolio can be negative—and at times very negative.

(Note that the policy return is the return that could have been earned by investing in the plan's asset mix in indexed portfolios; i.e., the return earned from the capital markets before the impact of active management decisions. This corresponds to the "no brainer" Stage I asset allocation introduced in Part II of this paper.)

The difference between a plan's actual return and its policy return is a measure of the contribution of active management decisions. In this example, active management decisions added 0.88 percent over the three-year measurement period. By subtracting active management investment fees, the net impact of asset management decisions on total fund returns can be estimated. This net value-added return measures the cost-effectiveness of asset management decisions at the total fund level. Performance attribution unbundles value added returns into their asset mix management and security selection components.[13] The negative 0.12 percent value added return from asset mix management decisions suggests the strategies or procedures used to manage the fund's asset allocation exposures should be examined.

The three-panel report does not compare the fund's investment performance relative to the performance of other pension funds because comparisons of total fund returns do not adjust for policies using a different asset mix, and therefore provide potentially misleading information. This is not to say that governing fiduciaries should ignore comparative performance measurement; rather, they should use such measures to address secondary questions. For example, total fund return samples may help explain why a fund with a non-median asset mix policy may be performing significantly above or below its public sector peer group.

The three-panel report provides governing fiduciaries with an easy-to-understand consolidated view of total fund performance relative to established objectives and expectations, and makes clear the accountability for different sources of return. It thus enables time-pressed governing fiduciaries to determine how investment performance has affected benefit security and if fund assets have been cost-effectively managed. Potential problems that may require changes in policies, procedures, or agents are readily identifiable, and the report also provides a convenient, self-explanatory format for the reporting of investment performance to plan sponsors and plan beneficiaries.

Conclusions

The process used by many U.S. public sector plans to develop, decide on, implement, and manage investment policies undoubtedly falls short of the high standards contemplated in state and federal pension legislation. Regulators, plan members, and pension fiduciaries should not necessarily be distressed by this, because perfection in any organization is impossible to achieve. What should be disconcerting is that many pension funds, both private and public, are governed by honest and well-meaning individuals who may have a limited or poor understanding of the principles of pension financing, investment, and organization.

Are fund assets in public sector pension funds exposed to extraordinary or undue risk of loss because governing fiduciaries may be inexperienced or unqualified? In general, the answer is no, because pension assets are protected from undue risk of capital loss by two very effective lines of defense. The first is the entrenched industry practice of diversifying investment across and within asset classes. Diversification is the cornerstone of modern investment practice, and provides significant protection from poor governance by reducing a fund's exposure to any one investment decision.

The second line of defense is the integrity, professionalism, and experience of the internal and external agents that supply services to pension funds: investment staff, actuaries, investment managers, lawyers, auditors, custodians, and consultants, the vast majority of whom work at all times in the best interests of plan members and beneficiaries.

Should either of these lines of defense be breached, however, then a pension plan may be exposed to undue capital losses.

References

Ambachtsheer, Keith P., and D. Don Ezra. 1998. *Pension Fund Excellence Creating Value for Stakeholders*. New York: John Wiley and Sons.

Burr, Barry. 2003. "Delegating Authority in Manager Hiring, Firing Still Rare." *Pensions and Investments*, April 28, 2003, p.35.

Carino, David. 1992. "Performance Calculations", Technical Note, Tacoma, Washington: Frank Russell Company.

Carver, John, and Caroline Oliver. 2002. *Corporate Boards That Create Value: Governing Company Performance from the Boardroom*. San Francisco: Jossey-Bass.

EBRI (Employee Benefit Research Institute). 2002. "An Evolving Pension System: Trends in Defined Benefit and Defined Contribution Plans." EBRI Issue Brief 249, September 2002. Washington, D.C.: EBRI.

Ezra, D. Don. 1998. "Adding Value though Active Manager Selection and Structure: Documenting Russell's Experience." *Conversation Piece*. Tacoma, Washington: Frank Russell Company.

Ilkiw, John. 1998. *Handbook on Asset-Liability Management: A Guide for U.S. Fiduciaries*. Tacoma, Washington: Frank Russell Company.

————. 2000. "Typical Time Periods over Which U.S. Plan Sponsors Evaluate Fund and Manager Performance." Consulting Practice Note 3. Tacoma, Washington: Frank Russell Company.

Ilkiw, John, and Steve Murray. 2002. "Establishing Higher Confidence Policy Exposures Using Two-Stage Asset Allocation." Russell Position Paper. Tacoma, Washington: Frank Russell Company.

Ilkiw, John, Karl Scheer, and David Payne. 2002. "Relative Importance of Manager Selection in the U.S. Private and Public Equity Markets." Consulting Practice Note 56. Tacoma:, Russell Investment Group, Frank Russell Company.

Kahanmen, Daniel. 2003. "Psychology, Risk, and Investment." Presented at the 2003 Russell Global Consulting Conference, Washington, D.C., April 22–26, 2003.

Myners, Paul. 2001. *Institutional Investments in the UK: A Review*. London: HM Treasury.

O'Barr, William, and John Conley. 1992. *Fortune and Folly: The Wealth and Power of Institutional Investing*. Homewood, IL: Business One Irwin.

Oberhofer, George. 2001. "Hedge Funds Are Not a New Asset Class." Consulting Practice Note 25. Tacoma, Washington: Frank Russell Company

Pension and Investments. 2002. "The P&I 1,000." *Pension and Investments*, January 21, 2002.

Por, John. 2003. "Board Governance and the CIOs." *Consultant Connection*, first quarter. Available online at www.investorforce.com.

Shefrin, Hersh. 2002. *Beyond Greed and Fear: Understanding Behavioral Finance and Psychology of Investing*. New York: Oxford University Press.

Turner, Andy, and Randy Lert. 2003. "Don't Be Fooled by Randomness: Use Past Performance Wisely." Presented at 2003 Russell Global Consulting Conference, Washington, D.C., April 22–26, 2003.

8

Notes

1. The views expressed in this paper are those of the author, and are not necessarily shared by Frank Russell Company.
2. When discussing the management of assets held in trust, it is useful to distinguish between the three levels of fiduciary responsibility. Governing fiduciaries have the ultimate responsibility for ensuring assets are man-

aged prudently and profitably. Governing fiduciaries often employ managing fiduciaries—in the form of an investment committee—to provide advice and oversee policy implementation; and managing fiduciaries usually employ a number of operating fiduciaries with specialized skills and knowledge to implement and manage investment policies on a daily basis. In the public sector, the terms "trustees" and "governing fiduciaries" are used interchangeably.

3. In 1998, an estimated 98 percent of full-time state and local employees participated in one or more pension plans. Fully 90 percent participated in defined benefit plans; 14 percent in defined contribution plans; and 33 percent could defer income in a supplementary plan (EBRI 2002).

4. Part II of this paper draws heavily from Ilkiw and Murray (2002). This publication explains in more detail why a two-stage approach to asset allocation produces better- informed investment policy decisions.

5. Ambachtsheer and Ezra (1998). The authors refer to the 50 basis points as the cost of "a serious excellence shortfall" in fund management.

6. This anecdotal observation has statistical support. Trustees often are selected because of their accomplishments in other fields and despite having little or no background training in pension financing, investment, or organizational issues (Myners 2001).

7. Beneficiaries are probably better served if governing fiduciaries see themselves as risk managers, rather than investment managers. "Boards manage risk; management adds value" would be a useful mantra with which to open every meeting of governing fiduciaries.

8. Muddied accountability has some attractive features. If accountability is ambiguous, no one person or group "owns" a bad outcome. Ambiguity allows groups of individuals to manage and deflect blame, which presumably avoids professional embarrassment and manages career risk. Two social anthropologists have in fact concluded that many U.S. pension plans have organized themselves to manage and deflect blame (O'Barr and Conley 1992).

9. Turnover of public sector trustees can be significant. John Por of Cortex Applied Research Inc., a Toronto-based consulting firm specializing in fund governance, observed an annual 25 percent trustee turnover rate among his 75 clients. This equates to a whole new board about every four years (Por 2003).

10. The new field of behavioral finance has provided many examples of human errors in decision-making that stem from perceptual illusions,

238

overconfidence, overreliance on rules-of-thumb and emotions, and incorrect framing of problems and solutions. The behavioral hurdles discussed in this section can be explained by one or more of the psychological phenomenon documented by behavioral economists. See Shefrin (2002).

11. About 55 percent of Russell "buy-ranked" managers outperform their benchmark each quarter. If this 5 percent edge is sustainable, the odds of earning higher than benchmark returns, net of fees, relative to a global benchmark using a multimanager strategy over a 10-year period increases to 95 percent (Ezra 1998).

12. This assumes equity has an expected 300 basis point risk premium over bonds. Each 10 percent increase in equity exposure increases the total fund expected return by 30 basis points. Experience has shown that well-diversified active management programs do not increase total fund risk. The risk of active management is a deadweight loss of returns, not an increase in total fund volatility.

13. Financial analysts routinely scrutinize performance of an investment fund using industry-standard techniques known as performance attribution, which distinguishes between policy returns and active management returns. Active management strategies can be usefully categorized under two rubrics: security selection and asset mix management. Security selection is the buying and selling of assets to earn a return above an investable market index such as the Russell 3000. Asset mix management is the shifting of asset class weights to earn a return above that available from maintaining asset class exposures at their policy weights, such as 60% Russell 3000 and 40% Lehman Brothers Aggregate Bond Index. For an explanation and examples of performance attribution methodologies, see Carino (1992).

8

Chapter 9

The Norwegian Petroleum Fund

Knut Kjær

9

Thank you for inviting me to speak here today. We set out to create the Norwegian Petroleum Fund in 1997, and we were fortunate in those early days to receive a lot of help from the World Bank Pension Fund and Treasury. Perhaps by speaking here I can pay back a little of our debt to the Bank.

Although we are still learning we now have some years of experience behind us. What I am going to do today is give you some background information about the Petroleum Fund and explain what we believe is special about our management model. (We like to think we are competing with Ireland for the title of most transparent fund. They perhaps win, because they are extremely clever, but it is our aim to be as transparent as possible.) I will also give you the background to our investment strategy and will address the issues of how we create excess return in the fund, how we select external managers, and what we see as being most important to the investment process. I will also give you some of our key results. For those of you who are interested, there is more information available on our Web site (http://www.norges-bank.no).

Background

Norway is the third-largest oil exporting country in the world. We believe that our oil production is at its peak, however, and in the coming years we expect it to decline (see Figure 9.1) A key purpose of the Petroleum Fund therefore is to save the oil and gas wealth for future generations. This is not the only reason for the fund, of course; another is that we want to avoid using all of this oil income now, as to do so would introduce the risk of crowding out other sectors of the economy, as has been the case in other countries that have plenty of natural resources. It is worth noting that ours is not the only oil fund in the world: there are similar funds in Abu Dhabi, Alaska, and Kuwait, for example, as well as in other countries and states.

The Petroleum Fund is not formally a pension fund, but it may be important in the future for meeting increasing state pension expenditures. There is a debate underway in Norway about this and there are many who argue in favor of turning the Petroleum Fund into a formal pension fund.

Saving into the Norwegian fund began in the mid-1990s. The size of the fund in 1996 was about US$8 billion and in 2002 was close to US$90 billion

Figure 9.1: Production of Petroleum, Mill. Sm3 Oil Equivalent

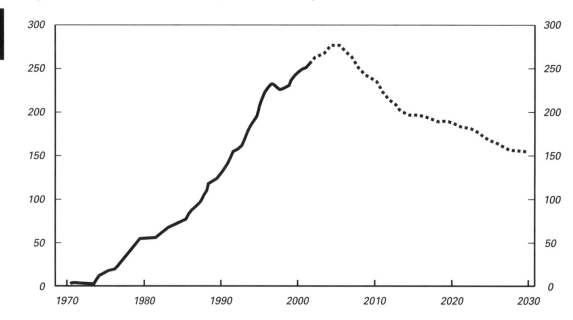

Figure 9.2: Growth of the Petroleum Fund, 1996–2002

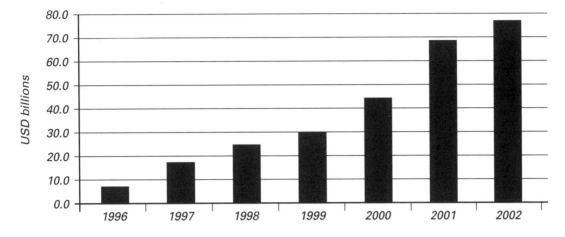

(see Figure 9.2). Today it is more than US$100 billion, helped by the decline in the dollar value as well as by the inflow of oil income.

The fund is managed by Norges Bank, the Norwegian Central Bank, and as we obviously also must manage the central bank reserves the total sum that we manage is more than US$120 billion.

Figure 9.3 shows how we expect pension expenditures in Norway to double as a share of GDP over the next few decades. This represents a tremendous increase in the burden on the state, and particularly so because oil income will fall as production declines. The challenge for the Norwegian Government, and also for the Petroleum Fund, will be to meet this combination of an increase in the pension burden and a decline in oil revenues.

9

Governance

The Petroleum Fund is owned by the Norwegian people and headed by the Minister of Finance. The Ministry of Finance decides all of the main strategic elements of the fund, sets the strategic asset allocation and benchmarks, and sets the risk limits for the manager, Norges Bank. It evaluates the bank using independent consultants and reports to Parliament, mainly through the national budget documents, on the bank's management of the fund.

Figure 9.3: Net Cash Flow from the Petroleum Sector and Pension Expenditures (in percent of GDP)

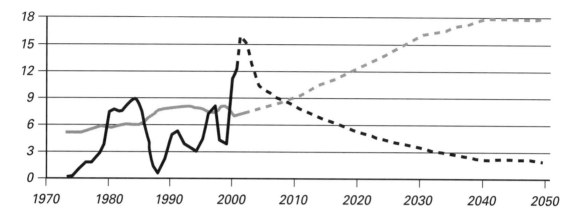

The ministry selected Norges Bank as the operations manager of the fund. Unlike Ireland, which has a 10-year contract for fund management, our contract with the Ministry of Finance binds either party only to giving a notice period of one year if it chooses to end the arrangement. This puts great pressure on my organization to perform well—just like in any business contract, if we do not deliver, we may be sacked. We cannot expect to retain this job simply because we are the central bank.

I was hired from outside the bank in 1997, and was given a large degree of freedom to build up a business unit capable of delivering excellent fund management. We are a part of the bank, but we have a different business culture. Our main goal is to achieve excess return, as measured against the benchmark given by the Ministry of Finance. We have press conferences every quarter at which we must compare our results to the benchmark and explain them. We also disclose information regarding at what cost and at what risk we achieved the results, and so on. Of course, we know that we cannot perform every quarter. We view three to five years as being an appropriate time period for evaluation of returns against the benchmark.

Accountability

The underlying principle of our fund management model is one of account-ability. The role of the politicians is clear: They decide the strategic asset allocation and the benchmark, and such decisions normally determine 90 to 95 percent of the risk and expected return of a fund. The role of the operational manager also is clearly defined. The management of the fund is transparent, as it is in Ireland and other places, and all reports are open to the public. The annual report provides extensive information, and there are additionally on our Web site articles and other information about how we manage the fund.

Investment Policy

Our main investment objective is to maximize the long-term international purchasing power of the Petroleum Fund. The short-term variation in the return is not as important. Parliament has set a guideline stating that 4 percent of the fund can be allocated to the budget every year. This rule preserves the fund capital, by permitting politicians only to use the fund's expected real return. They cannot use the capital itself. The capital further-more cannot be used for strategic investment purposes. The debate on this point continues, but for now it has been decided that the fund will be only a financial investor and will not take the risk of investing large amounts of money in individual companies.

In 1997 the major decision was taken to include equities in the invest-ment universe, benchmark-weighted at 40 percent. This decision was twice debated by Parliament, in the spring session and in the fall session of 1997. Norges Bank advised the Ministry of Finance on the risks and the expected returns of entering the equity markets. It was also decided not to invest in Norway. Norway accounts for only 0.2 percent of the global equity market, and the Petroleum Fund is too large to be invested there. We furthermore have other state funds to invest in Norway, so there is no lack of state capital in the national economy.

The decision on how much to place in equities has been one of the main investment policy issues. I will give you some of the arguments from that discussion. The decisions about expected return and risk relate to the equity portion of the portfolio, and for us the main decision concerned what

9

Figure 9.4: The Mix Between Equities and Fixed Income: Return and Risk in Portfolios

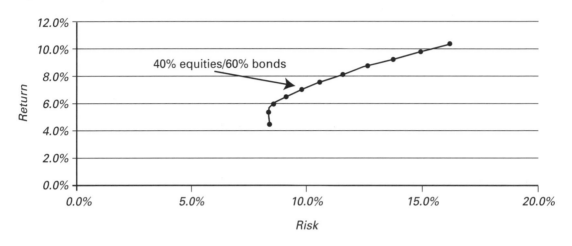

level of risk we should take and what would be the optimal combination of assets. Figure 9.4 provides a simple illustration of the expected risk and expected return in different asset classes, demonstrating that an increase in risk increases the expected return.

The ongoing discussion of course also has addressed the recent poor performance of the equity markets. We lost a lot of money last year due to the decline in these markets. It is important that both politicians and the public understand the reasons why long-term investors should invest in equities, and like others we have tried to make the case for the equity markets. Last week, for example, we invited the authors of *Triumph of the Optimists*[1] to give a presentation at a seminar in Norway about long-term capital market returns. Historical assessments such as this often are limited to U.S. data, take a short time horizon, and assign to the equity risk premium numbers that are too high. *Triumph of the Optimists*, however, covers a period of 101 years and includes data from 16 countries, representing roughly 90 percent of the markets in 1900 (and around 90 percent of the markets today). To me, this book is extremely important for its use of a long historical data series as a guide for the return in the capital markets.

The book points out that annual return fluctuations for equity can be close to 17 percent, which is a large standard deviation (see Figure 9.5) For long-term bonds the fluctuations are one-half of this, indicating that it is

Figure 9.5: Year-to-year Fluctuations in Return

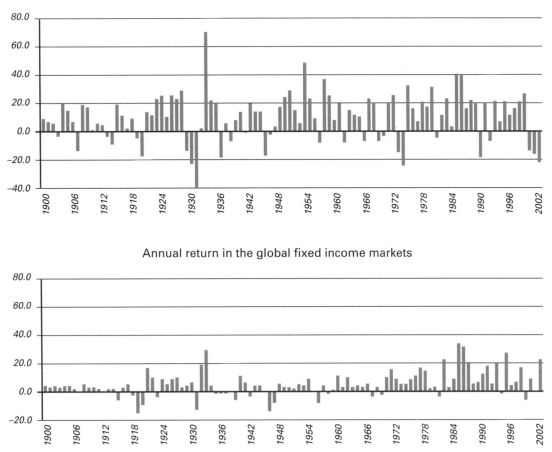

Annual return in the global equity markets

Annual return in the global fixed income markets

less risky to invest in bonds than it is to invest in equities. But if we look at five- or 10-year periods (see Figure 9.6) it becomes apparent that it is in fact less risky to be in equities. Over the course of the 101 years looked at by the book, there is only one 10-year period that shows a negative equity return. (This current decade may be the next one.)

Risk is the downside, but, in annual average, the return on equities is more than 4 percent in excess than the return on money market funds (Figure 9.7). If the 101 years of market history in those 16 countries may be taken as a guide, the extra risk borne by long-term investors pays off.

Figure 9.6: Equity Return—5- and 10-year Horizons

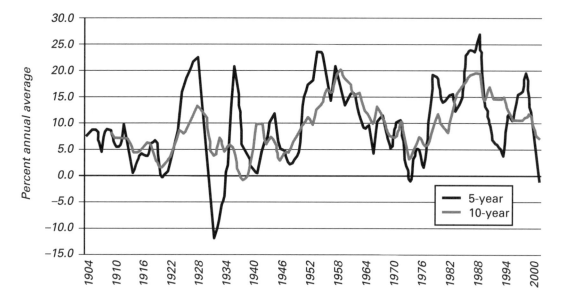

Figure 9.7: Global Capital Market Return, 1900–2002

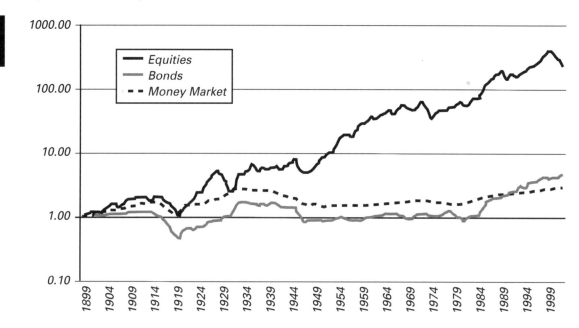

Figure 9.8: The Main Strategic Decision—The Mix Between Equities and Fixed Income

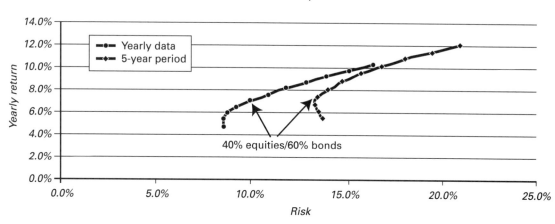

Return and risk in portfolios

The advice given by Norges Bank to the Ministry of Finance is summarized in Figure 9.8. One scale shows risk and the other, the return. For a portfolio comprising 100 percent bonds there is not much risk, but nor is there much return. To increase the return, we must increase the equities content of the portfolio; taking this increase to its limit, the portfolio of 100 percent equities is indicated at the upper right of the graph.

The optimum balance of risk and return will vary with the type of investor, the investor's risk aversion, time horizons, and so on. For the Petroleum Fund the proportion of equities in the portfolio is 40 percent. This 40 percent figure was not arrived at scientifically, it was a political decision taken by the owners of the fund. As mere fund managers it is not our place to go to the politicians and say that 50 percent would be better than 40 percent: they are the ones taking the risk, not us. The guidelines stipulate an equity portion of between 30 and 50 percent, with about 50 percent of the portfolio invested in Europe, 20–40 percent in the United States, and 10–30 percent in Asia (see Figure 9.9). There are 27 countries in which we are permitted to invest.

9

Finally, we are permitted also to do some active management, within a limit defined as 1.5 percent expected tracking error. This may seem to be quite a small risk for active management, but in practice a large majority of active managers fail to create excess net value. It is easy to destroy value by being too optimistic and by doing too much active management. As far as the Petroleum Fund is concerned, we in fact use less than half of our entitled risk limit.

The Ministry of Finance has defined the equity benchmark based on the FTSE (*Financial Times* Stock Exchange) global equity index. The fixed income benchmark is based on the Lehman Brothers global aggregate index. As a result, it is a simple matter for anyone on the outside to calculate the benchmark return. Even before we have our press conferences, the journalists in Norway have calculated the benchmark return that they expect us to report for the previous quarter. This is an indicator of the transparency of our management.

So much for the fund management model, our accountability, and questions of strategy. The rest of my presentation is about how we try to create excess value through active management.

Active Management

We have since 1997 been working on how best to get good returns from active management. We described our investment philosophy and our strategy for achieving excess returns in our 1999 annual report. That article is on our Web site (www.norges-bank.no), but I will describe to you some of the highlights now.

The most important decision that we had to make was how to allocate our risk limits for active management to different areas of management. We chose ultimately to place about 50 percent of the risk with our active equity external managers (see Figure 9.10). We have more than 20 such managers for the portfolio. This diversification of our active management is very important. We delegate our decision-making to both our internal and external managers, and we try to achieve as many independent positions as possible in the total portfolio. (The alternative is to use top-down, macro-based tactical asset allocation, taking only a few large positions each year.) Risk limit of the Petroleum Fund:

Figure 9.9: Benchmark for the Petroleum Fund

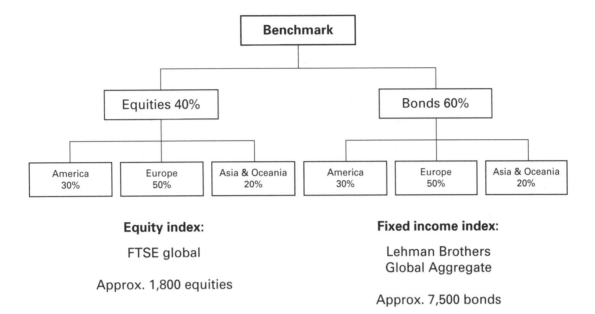

Equity index:

FTSE global

Approx. 1,800 equities

Fixed income index:

Lehman Brothers
Global Aggregate

Approx. 7,500 bonds

We try to specialize, and our operations must be cost-efficient. We have to cost less than 10 basis points. The Ministry of Finance pays our fees up to 0.1 percent of managed funds. If our management costs, excluding performance-based fees, exceed this amount, Norges Bank must cover the excess.

Eighty percent of the portfolio is managed in-house (see Figure 9.11). The cost of this management is less than 50 percent of our overall management costs, and the risk we take in-house similarly is less than 50 percent of our total risk. So although external managers handle only 20 percent of the portfolio, their share of total costs is more than 50 percent and they also are responsible for more than 50 percent of the risk in the portfolio. This apparent inconsistency is in part explained by the fact that our internal management includes enhanced index management and some specialized equity and fixed-income active management.

In-house index management in particular is a cost-efficient way of handling fund management. We try always to allocate a significant portion of the portfolio to the enhanced index mandates. In the early years we used

9

Figure 9.10: Allocation of Risk Units

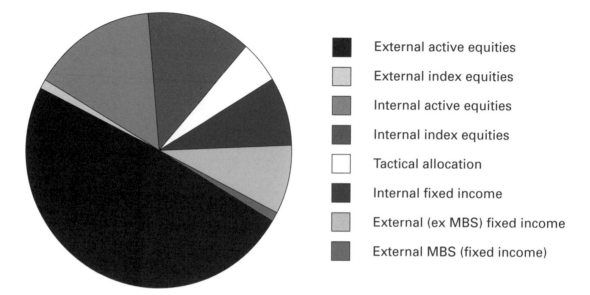

Value at Risk, proportions of total (assumed corr=1)

- External active equities
- External index equities
- Internal active equities
- Internal index equities
- Tactical allocation
- Internal fixed income
- External (ex MBS) fixed income
- External MBS (fixed income)

Figure 9.11: Combining External and Internal Management

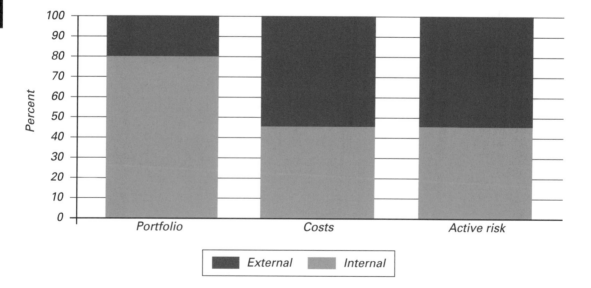

9

external index managers, but we decided in 1999 to try to achieve more return than is usually the case with mandates that aim primarily to have low tracking errors. We are fortunate in that we have the size that is needed to enable us to build up this kind of management in a cost-efficient way.

Another area where careful cost-management is essential is that of transition costs. How much to pay the brokers for execution? How much for market impact? Because we have a huge flow of new money coming into the market every month, we have to be very cost-efficient in our trading.

We delegate decision-making and we try to avoid any decision-making by committee: We much prefer to give investment mandates to individuals, using delegation and clear guidelines. I would never give a committee the task of selecting external managers, and I do not believe in committees taking investment decisions in operational active management. I believe in making people responsible and in making people feel that this is their own money and that they get paid for their success. I may be in a central bank, but every time I see an organization trying to administer fund management through committees, I get afraid.

I have a few comments about external managers. It is difficult these days to be a customer because the marketplace for external management is changing so rapidly with the large number of mergers, acquisitions, and changes in fund management organizations. We have had the experience all too often of our external managers getting new jobs, of teams moving, and so on. Times also are tough for the fund managers themselves. Their costs in general are too high, and with the restructuring that must come it will continue to be difficult to buy services from this industry.

We have one type of mandate that is indexed (*beta*) and other mandates that are pure active mandates (*alpha*). We want our managers to focus on their core ability rather than to just show general competence, which is in part why we always pay the active managers according to their performance. Equity managers, for example, are not allowed to maintain more than a few percent cash in their portfolio, because we do not believe in giving them the market timing decisions. We hire them for picking the right companies for the stock portfolio; market timing is another skill.

Over the last years we have also started to move toward specialized external management. In the beginning our active equity managers would have regional portfolios, for Europe, Asia, and so on. We still have regional managers, but now we also have managers for the health care sector in the United States, managers for energy companies in the global markets, and

9

managers for technology in specific areas. We do not believe in fund managers having skills in all areas. The market for managers is becoming more and more specialized, and we want to hire those fund management companies that are the best in their special fields.

We also try to avoid giving external managers similar mandates. Where this happens they can end up competing against each other, with the position taken by one manager being outweighed by the position taken by another manager. This is another good reason for having different investment universes for different managers.

To summarize, we have different equity mandates: regional mandates, sector mandates, and also small capitalization mandates. In the fixed-income portfolio we have global active mandates and we have specialized, mortgage-based securities mandates for the U.S. markets. (This type of specialization in the fixed-income portfolio will become more common in the future.) And in in-house active management we specialize by basing our managers in Oslo, London, and New York to handle those types of activities that are most likely to realize excess returns in these specific locations. (I should note here also that we have tried asset allocation mandates, managed both internally and externally, but without success.)

We have now around 40 different external mandates and between 20 and 30 different external managers. To select the right managers is of course very difficult: Past performance is not necessarily a good indicator of future results. Our selection process requires that we look closely at the management company's potential information advantage. We look at how the company constructs its portfolios and how many bets it takes. Does it take only three big bets, for example, or does it take 30, 40, or 50 active positions? We naturally prefer managers that have a basket of positions and not only one or two or three big positions. And rather than just look at performance numbers, we look at all portfolio changes that have been made over the course of several years.

We look also at portfolio implementation. What is the company's capability in trading? Does it lose its information advantage by poor trading? We look at the combination of active managers. When we buy in a new manager, we look at that manager's performance compared to the rest of the portfolio. Does his or her capability fit with our total portfolio?

We try in this way to diversify our use of external managers. And having appointed our managers we monitor them daily, and we additionally monitor different aspects of their management on a weekly or monthly basis. Finally,

9

every year we go back to every manager and start again at the beginning as they apply again for the mandates.

We have sacked quite a number of managers, mainly due to changes within their organization. As I mentioned earlier, key people leave and mergers and acquisitions in the industry change their companies. It is essential as we seek to maintain our performance that we monitor changes in these supplier organizations. When we buy services from external managers, we are in effect buying their competence. If people move or if they lose motivation, for example, the performance of their organization will falter. Despite my experience I continue to be surprised by the impact of people on the product offered by even the largest funds management companies. I used to believe that good data systems, infrastructure, and so on were of the greatest importance, but my experience now is that this is very much a people business. Not committees, however: The potential for future excess performance lies primarily with individuals.

To conclude, a few remarks about results. As I have said, the decision to go into equities was taken in 1997. In the years up to 2000, this was a good decision (see Figure 9.12). Since then, it has been not good at all. (Fixed income has been the opposite; since 2000 it has been extremely good.)

The Petroleum Fund has a many-generation perspective, however, and we look at this as a buying opportunity. The fund receives new oil income every month and we are now buying equities that we are going to hold for many years. The timing of the start of our equity investments as a consequence is not important at all—because of the inflow into the fund, we have probably at this point bought only half of the equities that we will hold in 2010.

The debate nonetheless continues. Is it too risky to have 40 percent in equities? There is pressure now on our politicians but I feel sure that because of our long time horizon this construction will survive. People mostly understand that the decision to go into equities entails taking a position for the next 50 or more years, and I am confident that the strategy will be maintained. If we look at the period between 1997 and 2002, the average annual real return furthermore is 2.5 percent. This is despite our having experienced the worst equity market performance since the 1930s. We must look at this in a historical context, and history tells that there normally are many decades between the occurrence of market circumstances such as these we have experienced since 2000.

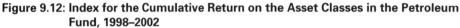

Figure 9.12: Index for the Cumulative Return on the Asset Classes in the Petroleum Fund, 1998–2002

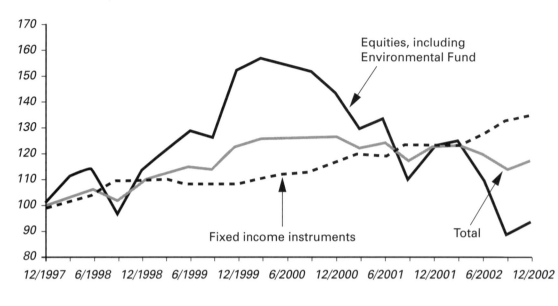

Note: The Fund's currency basket at 12.31.97 = 100.

9

As you know from this presentation, my organization is measured on its performance against the benchmark defined by the Ministry of Finance. Since we started this organization in 1998, we have on average had 0.41 percent of excess return every year. We have beaten the benchmark every year. We additionally have an information ratio (the common measure on the performance of active managers) of 0.94, compared to our minimum target ratio of 0.25. So we have been successful so far, and we are still in our jobs.

Concluding Remarks

Finally, the story of the Norwegian Petroleum Fund is to me very much the story of the organization. There is a clear distinction between the role of the politicians and the role of the operations manager. The operations manager has a very clear mandate, has to report performance every quarter, and is under great pressure to perform. These factors are an important part of the model.

When building up an organization to undertake the management of such an operation, the question inevitably arises of whether it is in fact possible to develop a good fund management group within a public entity. Perhaps the answer is no, because one the necessary investment culture is lacking? But if an investment culture can be built up within the public entity, the advantage of the public entity, as in our case, becomes clear: It is accepted by people as a good brand. The advantage of most public organizations is that they have a solid reputation with respect to reporting, control, the ethics of their people, and the integrity of their people.

Public systems of course are not designed to be investment organizations. What we have tried to do with the Petroleum Fund is simulate a kind of business organization by setting clear goals and clear benchmarks, by putting performance pressure on our people, and by paying people according to their performance.

Thank you.

Notes

1. *Triumph of the Optimists: 101 Years of Global Investment Returns.* Elroy Dimson, Paul Marsh, and Mike Staunton. Princeton, New Jersey: Princeton University Press (2002).

9

Governance and Investment of Provident and Pension Funds: The Cases of Singapore and India

Mukul G. Asher

This chapter examines the governance and investment issues relating to provident and pension funds in Singapore and India.[1]

From the outset I would like to stress that it is my belief that governance and investment are of equal significance in the accumulation phase and the pay-out, or decumulation phase, of provident funds. Many funds are satisfied with the principle that when a member reaches 55 years of age the accumulated balance due to that member should be returned to him or her. To the fund, once the balance is returned its responsibility is over—what the member does with the money is not the fund's concern. From society's viewpoint, however, what the member does with the accumulated balance is of great relevance. By handing over the full balance, the fund also is passing on to its member the responsibility for managing the longevity risk and the inflation risk, as well as the responsibility for meeting the survivor's benefits provisions. Herein lie the governance and investment issues of the decumulation phase of a provident fund.

The Case of Singapore

Singapore is unique among the world's high-income countries with a rapidly aging population in that it relies on a single, state-managed mandatory savings tier to finance its retirement needs. This mandatory savings pillar is administered by the Central Provident Fund (CPF). There are also a government pension fund and an armed forces provident fund, but details concerning these usually are not publicly available. A voluntary tax advantage retirement scheme, SRS, additionally was introduced in April 2001, but its impact has been small. Only about 300 million Singapore dollars (S$) have been put into the scheme, mostly by expatriates working in Singapore. This is in part because of the inherent design limitations of the scheme and in part because of the heavy penalties imposed on preretirement withdrawal.

The assets held by the CPF at end-2002 were about US$55 billion, or about 62 percent of GDP. Fifty-eight percent of the labor force contributes to the fund, a figure that at first glance is misleading as 25 percent of Singapore's work force is foreign and excluded from the CPF. The coverage is regarded as adequate for a city-state.

The CPF falls under the Ministry of Manpower, which has administrative but not policy autonomy over the fund. Policy is determined by the Ministry of Finance. The fund effectively is an agency that undertakes administrative tasks such as the collection of contributions, enforcement, and the administration of different types of schemes. In these areas, it has done an excellent job.

The Manpower Minister has absolute discretion over the appointment of experts and of representatives to the fund of the government, employers, and employees. The minister also appoints the chief executive officer—usually a ruling party member or a former civil servant.

The key governance challenge is to secure the services of competent, independent board members. In Singapore this task is complicated by the country's monocentric power structure and by the fact that information is regarded by those in power as a strategic instrument rather than a public good. While the annual report of the CPF is an excellent public relations document it basically is useless for analytical purposes—it is essential for proper analysis that the analyst dig deeper for hard numbers that are independently verifiable. Further adding to the challenge of governance of Singapore's CPF is the manner in which the investment function of the fund is organized.

The contribution rate structure of the CPF is extremely complex (see Table 10.1). For members who are less than 55 years of age, the contribution to the fund is 33 percent of the member's wages. The wage ceiling currently is $5500. The policy makers have announced that this ceiling will be reduced

10

Table 10.1: CPF Contribution Rates (applicable as of January 1, 2004)

| Employee age | Contribution by employer (% of wage) | Contribution by employee (% of wage) | Total contribution (% of wage) | Credited into: | | |
				Ordinary account (%)	Special account (%)	Medisave account (%)
35 & below	13	20	33	22	5	6
35–45	13	20	33	20	6	7
45–55	13	20	33	18	7	8
55–60	6	12.5	18.5	10.5	0	8
60–65	3.5	7.5	11	2.5	0	8.5
Over 65	3.5	5	8.5	0	0	8.5

Note: The information applies to employees with monthly wages above S$750. Workers included in the categories: (1) Private Sector (2) Government Non-Pensionable employees (3) Non-Pensionable Employees in Statutory Bodies & Aided Schools (4) Singapore Permanent Resident (SPR) employees from their 3rd year onwards.

Source: http://www.cpf.gov.sg/cpf_info/goto.asp?page=/cpf_info/Index_Members.asp

to $4500 by January 2006. Even if this ceiling remains constant, inflation will over time reduce the real value of balances. This in turn will have an important impact on the final replacement rate, as will be shown later.

The contribution rates for members aged 55 and above are considerably lower, and in consequence the wage compensation of this age group is much reduced. This adversely affects retirement income security, and is indicative of the low priority given to income security under the CPF system.

Contributions are channeled into three accounts: the ordinary account, the special account, and the Medisave account. The ordinary account essentially is maintained for housing and other purposes. The special account is for retirement, and receives between 0 and 7 percent of all CPF contributions. This is very low by international standards. In general, a 10 to 15 percent contribution rate, without a wage ceiling, is needed to obtain a reasonable replacement rate of about 40 percent at retirement from this tier. Finally, the Medisave account essentially finances approved medical expenditure, including voluntary health insurance for critical illnesses administered by the CPF.

10

The CPF clearly is not a purely retirement scheme (see Table 10.2), and because it is saddled with multiple objectives it is not able to provide adequately for retirement. This is despite the fact that the contribution rate, at 33 percent, is unusually high. The ratio of withdrawals to contributions has over the recent period been 72 percent, implying that less than one-third of the collected contributions are actually retained by the fund: most contributions are in fact put in and then immediately withdrawn. This results in an extremely regressive type of tax policy, particularly as only one-third of the labor force—a significant proportion of whom are noncitizens who are outside the CPF system—pay income tax. At least two-thirds of the labor force do not earn enough to be subject to income tax and get no tax benefit. The individuals at the upper end, in contrast, get income tax benefit when they

Table 10.2: Various Schemes Under Singapore's CPF System

Type	Scheme	Year introduced
Home ownership	Approved Housing Scheme	1968
	Approved Residential Prop	1981
Investment	Singapore Bus Services (1978) Ltd Share Scheme	1978
	Approved Investment Scheme (AIS)	1986
	CPF Investment Scheme (CPFIS)—replacing AIS	1997
	Approved Non-Residential Properties Scheme (ANRPS)	1986
	Share-ownership Top-up Scheme (SOTUS)	1993
Insurance	Home Protection Insurance Scheme	1982
	Dependents' Protection Insurance Scheme	1989
	Medishield Scheme	1990
	Eldershield Scheme	2002
Others	Company's Welfarism through Employers' Contribution (COWEC) Scheme	1984
	Medisave Scheme	1984
	Minimum Sum Scheme	1987
	Topping-up of the Minimum Sum Scheme	1987
	Loans for Tertiary Education in Singapore	1989
	CPF Top-up Scheme	1995

Source: CPF Board, Singapore.

put in and, should they choose to do so, can withdraw immediately their contribution to invest it in other income-earning opportunities, often with another set of tax benefits. This is a very regressive tax arrangement.

I will not discuss the various schemes outlined in Table 10.2 other than to point to the CPF Investment Scheme (CPFIS), which is of particular relevance to the current discussion. The CPFIS, which has been in existence in one form or another since 1986, permits members to withdraw a certain amount and invest it in approved financial, real estate and other assets.

The member balance of the CPF at end-2002 was S$96.4 billion. This amount is almost wholly invested in nonmarketable government securities. It is a paper transaction, as the interest that is paid on the government securities is a weighted sum of a one-year fixed deposit and of the savings deposit interest rates in local banks, as determined quarterly.

In essence, the government is taking in 35-year, long-term money and paying a short-term interest rate to its members. (The interest rate on these securities is determined retrospectively, after the interest rate on CPF balances has been announced.)

This is not even the full picture. The Singapore government has been consistently enjoying budget surpluses. Therefore, receipts from securities sold to the CPF have not been needed to finance government expenditure. Instead, they are turned over to the Singapore Government Investment Corporation (SGIC). The operations of the SGIC (and other government investment holding companies, such as Temasek Holdings), do not have to be made public. According to the law, nobody, not even the Parliament nor the President, who nominally has the constitutional duty to protect the country's assets, can ask questions about the assets, investment policies, or performance of the SGIC. The absolute lack of transparency of this arrangement means it is almost impossible to know how the proceeds from CPF investments are handled, but they are widely believed to be wholly invested abroad.

There is thus a disconnect between the administered interest rate that is paid on CPF balances and the actual investment and the returns that are obtained. The political risk inherent in this arrangement is obviously extremely high. This arrangement furthermore means that fund members are not realizing the potential power of compound interest (see Figure 10.1).

Figure 10.1 provides calculations of the real returns to members in the periods 1983–2002 and 1987–2002 (the latter to take advantage of an interest rate formula that was introduced in 1986). For the 1987–2002 period,

10

Figure 10.1: Singapore's CPF—Average Annual Compound Growth Rate (AACGR%)

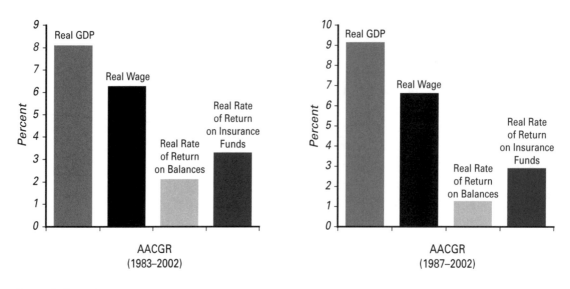

Source: Author estimates.

the real annual rate of return was 1.3 percent. This is obviously too low to realize the potential of compound interest. The rate also is lower than the growth of wages or GDP, adversely impacting the replacement rate.

The CPF also has accumulated about S$3 billion in insurance funds, much of which has been contracted out for investment purposes. The real annual rate of return on investments during the 1987–2002 period was 2.9 percent, more than twice the rate on member balances. This nonetheless is lower than the GDP growth rate.

The nontransparency and nonaccountability of the CPF balances, along with the administered rate of interest, has turned the CPF from nominally a defined contribution, fully funded scheme to essentially a notional, defined benefit scheme financed on a pay-as-you-go basis. There is a universal lesson in this: When considering provident and pension schemes, it is important not to make an assessment on the basis of the label that is given to the scheme; i.e., whether it is a Defined Contribution (DC) or a Defined Benefit (DB) scheme, or a hybrid. The popular belief in Singapore, that the country operates a defined contribution scheme, is mistaken.

To the extent that the government holding companies earn more than is paid to the CPF members, there is an implicit tax on CPF wealth. The

10

International Monetary Fund estimated that the SGIC earned about 10 percent per annum during the 1990s (IMF 2001), but CPF members received only 3.4 percent per annum. The implicit tax over this period therefore was about 6.6 percent per annum. In 2000, this would have amounted to about S$6 billion, equivalent to 42 percent of contributions, or 3.75 percent of GDP.

This implicit tax is recurrent; it is also regressive, because, as stated earlier, those in the upper income groups with higher balances are more likely to take out their money. Among lower-income contributors the share of their total wealth accounted for by CPF wealth therefore is higher, producing this regressivity of tax on CPF wealth.

The cost of a nominal rate-of-return guarantee of 2.5 percent is small, and would not normally counterbalance such a large implicit tax. In times of deflation however, as may be occurring, a 2.5 percent nominal guarantee is not bad, as 1 percent deflation would imply a 3.5 percent real interest rate guarantee.

The replacement rate needs to be analyzed with respect to actual cash balances of the CPF members. Such data however are not available.

A recent study by McCarthy, Mitchell, and Piggott (2001) used simulation to estimate the replacement rate for a new contributor to the CPF (see Table 10.3). For the base case, the replacement rate is estimated to be 28 percent. This rate is based on the wage ceiling of S$6,000. If the wage ceiling is held constant at 0 percent nominal, instead of 0 percent real, the replacement rate reduces to 17 percent. (The actual wage ceiling has since been reduced to S$5,500, so the replacement rate would be even lower.) Given the current 33 percent contribution rate, this is an extremely inefficient way to go about providing for retirement.

The inescapable conclusion is that the replacement rate will be inadequate, even when various parametric reforms are undertaken, and even when only active contributors are considered. This problem is compounded by the fact that active contributors to provident fund systems tend to be a small subset of total members, who may have paid in no more than a single contribution. (Active contributors are those who have been contributing during the current period, however defined.) While inactive members have much lower balances, they also need retirement funding.

In Singapore, a lot of CPF money has gone into housing, so converting property values into retirement income stream is a possibility. This avenue has several technical problems and suffers from high transaction costs, how-

10

Table 10.3: Sensitivity of Results to Potential Policy Changes

	A	B	C	D	E
	Total wealth ($000)	Proportion in housing	Replacement rate		IRR on property
			Earnings	Subsistence	
1. Base case	1774.3	75%	28%	296%	5.82%
CPF Changes					
2. Both CPF Accts ROR up from 0%/1.5% to 5% real	2052.6	65%	34%	359%	4.60%
3. % to Special CPF Acct up from 4% to 8%	1800.3	74%	30%	319%	5.34%
4. CPF contribution ceiling held at 0% nominal instead of 0% real	1598.5	83%	17%	186%	5.23%
5. CPF contribution rates lowered from 40% to 30%	1604.6	83%	14%	148%	4.61%
HDB Changes					
6. ROR on HDB property falls 4% real to 0% real	768.5	36%	32%	339%	0.77%
7. ROR on HDB property 4% real —>10 years, 0% real thereafter	749.1	37%	30%	322%	0.47%
8. ROR on HDB property 0% real—>10 years, 4% real thereafter	1797.6	74%	30%	316%	6.04%
9. HDB resale levy falls from 22.5%/25% to 0%	2296.2	77%	34%	364%	7.42%
10. HDB capital subsidy doubles in nominal terms	2037.8	65%	49%	526%	8.84%

Note: Author's calculation; assumes male head of household married to same age non-working wife.

Source: McCarthy, D., O. Mitchell, and J. Piggott, Table 7, p. 35.

ever. Singapore does not grant either the constitutional or the common law right to own land—the purchase of property confers a user right to property but no right to the land on which it is built, which remains with the state. Most of the inflation hedge of housing comes from higher land values, over time. In Singapore's case, the higher land values are likely to be captured by the government.

The Singapore housing program is only about 30 years old, so this limitation has not been sufficiently recognized. Furthermore, there is no reverse mortgage transaction for the public housing in which 85 percent of the population lives, rendering the reverse mortgage essentially a nonstarter in the Singapore context.

There are several generic reasons for low balances in Singapore, including an unequal wage structure, a high rate of preretirement withdrawals, low returns, and the high transaction costs of investments. It is the rate of return, net of all transaction costs, that is most relevant to the CPF case because it is these returns that are available to members.

The CPFIS scheme permits a member to open an account with any of the approved agent banks, all of which are local. The charges and fees of the agent banks are not regulated. Individual members may invest in a wide variety of investments: as of December 31, 2002 about US$14 billion, one-third of the available amount, was invested under this scheme by about one-quarter of the total members. The average investment was US$19,000. This is too small, and one would therefore expect transaction costs to be extremely high. The transaction costs of unit trust investment in Singapore generally are high, with a 5 to 7 percent spread between the offer (buy) and bid (sell) prices common. There have been some efforts by the CPF to address this issue, but the oligopolistic nature of the asset management industry, relatively low value of investment funds, and the front-loading of the expenses by asset managers may severely constrain these efforts.

It can be shown on the basis of reasonable assumptions specific to Singapore that the difference between the present value of a stream of investments over three decades without transaction costs and the value with transaction costs is about 50 percent. This difference in the two values demonstrates the importance of transaction costs in Singapore's context. The CPFIS scheme does not appear to have been designed with the objective of maximizing the rate of return net of transaction costs.

What Needs To Be Done?

10

Reforms are needed that would require much higher priority to be assigned to the fiduciary responsibility of the CPF Board; that would ensure greater transparency of the investment process and outcome, and that would lower transaction costs.

Serious consideration should be given to the formation of a separate asset management company with statutory requirements for fiduciary responsibility and transparency. The board of such a company should have independent and competent members regulated by the newly constituted Provident Fund Authority (PFA).

Between 10 and 15 percent of contributions should be diverted to this asset management company, with the balance remaining with the current

CPF board to support housing, healthcare, and other objectives. In the medium term (i.e., over two to four years), the accumulated balance of S$96 billion also should be transferred to the new asset management company. This company should publish its investment portfolio on a mark-to-market basis and should follow international best practices in provident and pension fund governance.

The CPFIS scheme should be restructured to restrict individual choice—the funds should be centrally managed, with options only for individuals to allocate funds to different risk–return categories. Each member should be permitted to reallocate his or her portfolio only once every three to four years.

The asset management company should use its expertise and the large pool of funds under its control to reduce transactions and investment management costs and to provide effective diversification with transparency. It also should encourage the funds management industry in Singapore to primarily operate on a wholesale, rather than a retail basis.

The major obstacle to such reforms would likely be resistance from the beneficiaries of the current system. The CPF system also has emerged as Singapore's primary mortgage financing arrangement, and given that the supply of housing is a state monopoly any significant adverse impact on property values would have a serious economic and political impact. This largely explains the lack of boldness in the government's recommendations.

Changing the mindset of Singapore's policymakers—specifically their insistence on relying on a single tier to finance old age—is another major problem. There is substantial analytical evidence that a single tier is inadequate, and that a multi-tier system incorporating a tax-financed redistributive first tier is essential. The parametric reforms in the 2003 and 2004 budgets furthermore have actually limited the role of the CPF in providing retirement income. Developments in the political economy will be crucial in determining the future of social security in Singapore.

The Case of India

India's social security system can be divided into five components.

The first component comprises the civil service pension and provident schemes at state and central government levels. Each state has its own scheme, usually patterned after the central scheme.

The second component comprises the schemes for public sector enterprises, such as the Reserve Bank of India, the public sector banks, electricity boards, oil companies, and various industrial entities. These enterprises manage their own schemes with little supervision and, where regulations are concerned, with considerable ambiguity. Most of the schemes are contributory, but the actuarial and other details and the professionalism with which they are managed is unknown even to the authorities.

The third component comprises the EPF schemes of the Employees Provident Fund Organization (EPFO). The EPFO was set up in 1952, and covers workers in private sector firms with more than 20 employees. It has about 35 million members (the number of active contributors is somewhat lower) and covers more than 340,000 establishments. It provides DC, DB, and life insurance coverage for its members. The key challenge of the EPFO is to ensure that its high contribution rates (about 26 percent of wages, subject to a ceiling), and its operations provide commensurate real benefits to its members and to the economy as a whole.

The fourth component of the social security system is the voluntary tax-advantaged saving schemes, such as post office savings, bank schemes, the individual and group annuities of life insurance companies, and others.

The fifth component comprises the public assistance and other schemes, at the center and in the states. The main determinant of the funding provided for these schemes is the fiscal position of the central and state governments. There is a strong need to improve service delivery.

Governance and Investment Policies and Issues

10

In 2002, the assets of the EPFO schemes amounted to about 6 percent of GDP. The small savings schemes, many of which act as retirement schemes, hold assets equivalent to about 10 percent of GDP, and occupational schemes and the schemes of public sector enterprises additionally hold assets worth an estimated 5 percent of GDP.

These provident and pension assets in total are equivalent to about 20 percent of GDP. As India implements pension reforms this 20 percent will grow very quickly in a relatively short period of time. It is essential therefore that the administration and management of these schemes be rapidly improved. The five components of the social security system also must be integrated into a fiscally, financially, and economically sustainable multi-tier system. These two tasks are vital, and a major challenge for policymakers.

Complicating this challenge is the fact that for most of these schemes the ultimate contingent (or conjectural) liability lies with the central government: the Life Insurance Corporation of India, for example, is explicitly guaranteed by the government. At a time when fiscal consolidation and flexibility are needed to deepen the reform process and help India attain its vision of becoming a developed economy by 2020, the central government is overburdened with all kinds of contingent liabilities. A key reform issue therefore is how to de-link from the fiscal operations of the central and state governments the direct and nonaccountable use of funds generated by the five components, and to ensure that pension and provident funds are able to operate on their own.

EPFO Investment Policies and Performance

One of the main differences between the investment guidelines issued by the EPFO and those issued by the Insurance Regulatory and Development Authority (IRDA) for the pension business of the life insurance companies is that the EPFO guidelines permit only the use of debt instruments—primarily public sector debt instruments.

Not only there is no equity in EPFO's portfolio, but many of the debt instruments also are not allowed to be traded on the market. In other words, they are kept until maturity. This means that the opportunity to build up member balances from the investment returns, rather than from contributions, is being foregone. This is contrary to international practice.

The EPFO, as regulator, furthermore has mandated that these guidelines also apply to exempt funds. It is generally large, financially sophisticated private sector corporations that have in the past received exemption. The EPFO requires that the exempt funds not only follow the same restrictive investment patterns, but also guarantee at least the level of return which is declared by the EPFO. The burden of this guarantee is on the employer. The above arrangements have meant that the exempt funds have an investment portfolio which is similar to that of the EPFO. This precludes the generation of information about the efficiency and returns obtained from alternative investment portfolios. They also artificially increase the demand for public sector debt instruments.

10

Table 10.4a: India—Investment Guidelines of the EPFO

i.	Central Government Securities	25%
ii.	a. State of Government Securities; and/or	
	b. Any other negotiable securities unconditionally guaranteed by the Central Government or any State Government except those covered under (iii)(a) below.	15%
iii.	a. Bonds/securities of "Public Financial Institutions," "Public Sector Companies," Infrastructure Development and Finance Company Limited (IDFC) and/or	40%
	b. Certificates of deposit issued by a public sector bank	
iv.	To be invested in any of the above categories as decided by the Board of Trustees	20%
v.	The Board of Trustees, subject to their assessment of the risk/return prospects, may invest up to 10% out of (iv) above, in private sector bonds/securities that have an investment grade rating from at least two credit rating agencies	20%

Source: EPFO Board, India.

Table 10.4b: India—Investment Guidelines of the IRDA

i.	Government Securities	not less than 20%
ii.	Government Securities or other approved securities (inclusive of (i) above)	not less than 40%
iii.	Balance to be invested in approved investments:	
	a) Equity/Preference Shares of the Company b) Debentures (convertible/partly convertible/non-convertible) c) Short/Medium/Long-term loans d) Any other permitted investments as per the Act/Regulation	not exceeding 60%

Source: IRDA.

10

The IRDA regulates insurance companies, both those that provide annuity products to individuals as well as those furnishing group annuities. The resulting funds are managed in accordance with the IRDA guidelines for pensions. These guidelines are much more consistent with modern portfolio investment management than the EPFO guidelines: they stipulate only the maximum portfolio share that can be assigned to each asset class, giving

Table 10.5: Rates of Contribution for EPFO Schemes, 2001

Scheme	Contribution as percentage of covered wage[a]			
	Employer	Employee	Government	Total
EPF	3.67	12.0	—	15.67
EPS	8.33	—	1.16	9.49
EDLI	0.50	—	—	0.50
Total	12.50[b]	12.0	1.16	25.66

a. The covered wage is Rs6500 per month. Voluntary contributions above this amount are permitted.

b. In addition, employers are levied 1.11% of the wage base on which EPF contributions are made as administration expenses.

Note: EPF=Employees' Provident Fund; EPS=Employees' Pension Scheme; EDLI=Employees' Deposit-Linked Indurance.

Source: Calculated from the Annual Report of the Employees Provident Fund Organization, 2002, Ministry of Labor, Government of India, New Delhi.

some flexibility to the portfolio managers; they also permit investments in more asset classes, including equities, and do not prohibit trading.

India's financial and capital market development is not yet at a stage that would permit the application of the prudent person (or portfolio) norm. This should be kept in mind as a longer-term goal, employable perhaps with the progressive liberalization of the investment regime. What is clear at this point, however, is that the EPFO investment guidelines must move toward the IRDA guidelines for pension funds.

EPFO's Rate of Return

In many countries, the attention paid to the nominal rate of interest declared by a national provident fund can be sufficient to make this rate politically significant. This is becoming true in India, to the extent that even as the whole interest rate structure has been falling there has been a clear reluctance to change the nominal rate. This creates the danger that the real rate can become so high as to be unsustainable, because economic projects funded by the provident fund balances do not generate sufficient returns. What follows is cross-subsidization, distorting the whole interest rate structure and leading to artificial substitution among savings instruments. The efficiency, equity, and fiscal implications of such a distorted rate structure are not always as well understood in India as they ought to be.

The nominal rate declared by the EPFO during 1986–2000 was 11.8 percent per annum, reflecting the lack of investment management and an administered rate of interest. The nominal rate was kept fairly constant, but the annual inflation rate during the period averaged 9 percent, implying a real rate of 2.7 percent. Real GDP growth however, was more than twice this rate. This in turn implies that the replacement rate was likely to be low, particularly when preretirement withdrawals are taken into account. While the 2.7 percent real rate of return is much better than in the case of Singapore's CPF, it could have been considerably better, given the bright prospects of the Indian capital markets and the economy.

Governance Issues

The EPFO falls under the Ministry of Labor. The EPF board of trustees is appointed by the minister, and includes representation by the government, employees, and employers. The tendency is to regard EPFO and its schemes as solely welfare-oriented, a fact that has undermined attempts to apply modern principles of pension economics and management, and international benchmarking. This has also reduced organizational learning and effectiveness.

The EPFO also is unusual in that it combines both defined contribution, fully-funded schemes (at least nominally) and a defined benefit social insurance scheme. The expertise needed for each is very different, and operating the two together has tended to reduce the transparency of the schemes. There are widespread and justifiable concerns about the actuarial sustainability of the Employees Pension Scheme (EPS).

The EPS scheme has a maximum replacement rate of 50 percent, but as there is no inflation indexation the replacement rate available at retirement declines continuously until death. While there is a declining replacement rate in real terms, the cost of providing benefits has been extremely high because of a lack of professionalism in designing and implementing the scheme.[2]

10

EPFO service quality is accurately perceived to be poor, and transaction costs are high. To improve the situation, changes must be made to the governance and organizational structures.

Finally, the EPFO has not developed any in-house investment management expertise because this function has to date been contracted out—and given its portfolio regulations, the EFPO has had no real need for investment expertise. This situation is no longer sustainable. The EPFO must develop its own in-house investment expertise, and to do so will need to pay much greater attention to its human resource practices. It must in particular seek to improve its recruitment of staff with financial management and information technology skills.

To conclude, the primary challenge for the EPFO is to provide benefits to its members, and to the economy as a whole, that are commensurate with its high contribution rates. It is this relationship between input and output that is essentially the crux of any economic analysis.

The EFPO is in the process of implementing a program to reverse these trends. It includes the business reprocessing exercise, including a shift from being an employer-focused organization to one that is employee focused. The service level is being benchmarked to international standards over the next few years, and as the fruits of the initial stages of reform become understood better by policymakers and the public alike, it is to be hoped that there will be an acceleration in this direction. The EPFO schemes and investment guidelines are being modernized and rationalized. The results are likely to be evident in the next two to three years.

The above suggests that the EPFO authorities are aware of this challenge and are trying to address it, but in the end will be judged by results rather than on their good intentions.

Civil Service Pensions

A potentially far-reaching pension reform for civil servants has been implemented since January 1, 2004. Under the initiative, new entrants to the central government (excluding the armed forces) will be placed on a portable DC scheme that stipulates a 10 percent contribution each from the employer and employee. There is no wage ceiling applied to the contributions. This is a radical change from the current DB system, which does not require employee contributions and is unfunded. The initiative permits others to join voluntarily. It is anticipated that some of the states and public sector organizations will also adopt a similar scheme for their new entrants.

Each member has his or her own individual account in a specialized pension organization which is separate from the government. There will be a central record-keeping-cum clearing agency (CRA) which is to be appointed in the second-half of 2004.

The scheme will be regulated by the Pension Fund Regulatory and Development Authority (PFRDA). Initially, the PFRDA will regulate the civil service scheme. It is however anticipated that in due course it will regulate the whole pensions sector. India is the first country in Asia to estab-lish an independent regulator for the pensions sector. An interim regulator has already been appointed. The requisite Act is under preparation and is expected to be approved by the Parliament by end-2004.

Preparations are underway for the regulator to appoint pension fund managers. Initially, the number of such managers is likely to be small. But as business volume increases, more players will be permitted. Each pension fund manager will be required to offer three schemes with differing risk-return profile; and each member will be free to allocate among them. There is likely to be a default option to invest only in debt. The investment guide-lines will be consistent with international best practices and will permit international diversification.

The design of the scheme is such that the pension fund managers will not deal directly with the members. Instead, each day pension fund manag-ers will be given net amounts to be invested in various investment options by the CRA.

The scheme does not permit any pre-retirement withdrawals. There are no government guarantees. The accumulated balances can be withdrawn at age 60. Only a portion however, cab be withdrawn in lump-sum. The rest will be either in the form of an annuity (requiring close coordination with IRDA), or a phased withdrawal option will be devised.

It may be useful to separate the funds of the mandated civil service and the private sector voluntary members. If the states were to join in this type of scheme, separate funds again may have to be kept for each state: merging them together would make administrative tasks more difficult and could reduce transparency and accountability. The separation of funds should not preclude portability, however, as labor mobility is an important advantage of the new system.

10

As the scheme progresses, member balances will begin to grow rapidly. If these are to be invested in a growth and efficiency enhancing manner, financial and capital market reforms, including better corporate governance practices will be necessary. There will also be a need to increase the supply of investible financial assets. This will require fiscal reforms (so that government securities can be rated by the credit rating agencies), increase in the free-float of shares, and listing of more public and private sector firms on India's stock exchanges. India is permitting access to its capital markets to multilateral organizations such as the Asian Development Bank, and to high quality corporates from abroad. These may provide additional avenues for pension fund investments.

There is, however, a need to ensure an adequate replacement rate and reasonable protection against risks for the new entrants to the civil service. It may be worth considering a feature that would provide a basic defined benefit pension, perhaps with a replacement rate of 25 to 30 percent of the average wage of the last 10 years. It may also be useful to consider diverting part of the 20 percent contributions to providing survivors' benefit insurance. This may partly address the longevity risk and gender bias inherent in such schemes.

It is also important to avoid the assumption that the DC system and the regulatory system will operate perfectly all the time. The risk from a single-tier system of pensions is high, and this should be kept in mind as the civil service and other pension reforms progress.

The 2003–04 budget introduced a Varishtha Pension Bima Yojana (VPBY), to be administered by the Life Insurance Corporation (LIC). The VPBY permits any citizen more than 55 years of age to pay a lump sum and get a monthly return in the form of a pension for life. The minimum and maximum pensions are pegged, and these amounts are not indexed to inflation. The pension is also capped. The VPBY to an extent may be a sweetener to ease other reforms through, and the potential cost of supporting it thus the political price to pay for those reforms.

There is a guaranteed return under the VPBY scheme of 9 percent per annum: the difference between what LIC earns and the 9 percent will be made up by the central government. One positive aspect of the scheme is that it is at least an explicit subsidy, but it nonetheless may have been better to have pegged the guaranteed rate at a small premium to the market rate, rather than at an absolute level. Economic literacy is low and political complexity high in India, and it may have been better to start out with rules

10

that are market-consistent and that allow market adjustments than to set up an absolute rate that could be difficult politically to change.

Conclusion

To summarize, the main governance and investment policy challenges confronting India's social security system are as follows. First, the five components of the system are not integrated, but operate independently. Not only does each component operate essentially on its own, but also within each component there are variations in design and administration from state to state and between the states and the central government. There is no systemwide approach to design, implementation, and evaluation.

Second, there has been no overall regulatory authority. It is hoped that the PFRDA will become an effective regulator in a relatively short period of time. In due course, it should also regulate the EPFO and other components of the social security sector. The EPFO could then concentrate on service delivery, which should be its primary role. It is not good practice to have a service deliverer as regulator, as is the case with the EPFO.

The legislation governing provident funds and pension funds is written in the Income Tax Act of 1961, the EPF Act of 1952, and the Indian Trust Act of 1882. All three acts are in need of revision, and the new PFRDA must give priority to pushing through the necessary changes.

Third, the design of pension and provident schemes is not consistent with international good practices in key areas such as benefit and contribution formulas, actuarial studies, administration and compliance, portability, investment policies and management, and stakeholder relations, particularly as regards the provision of information, transparency, accountability, and corporate governance.

Essential reforms in this area include the following:

- Provident and pension funds need to be de-linked from central and state budgetary financing (this does not preclude funds from purchasing marketable government bonds).
- The gradual phasing out of special deposits schemes by the central government is a step in the right direction and should be encouraged.
- The investment guidelines of the EPFO should be made consistent with IRDA guidelines.

10

- Contractual savings and small savings schemes should make a gradual shift from administered interest rates to market rates on.
- The EPFO should be encouraged to increase its investment management expertise, and also should seek to develop expertise in the contracting-out of a portion of the fund on a competitive basis.
- The scope of PFRDA should be widened. There should be greater coordination with IRDA and with the proposed regulator for non-bank financial institutions.

Another measure that would improve the social security of the poor and of others who are not included in these schemes is the fiscal improvement at both the central and state levels. What is needed is a greater drive toward fiscal consolidation and flexibility, with the goal of enabling the state to meet the urgent need to finance social assistance schemes and other social security programs.

India has made remarkable progress since its 1991 reforms, particularly in aligning its economic and political systems. Provident and pension fund reforms are now firmly on the agenda, and India has the capacity to undertake these reforms for the benefit of all stakeholders. Many of the limitations of the current social security system in India are likely to be addressed in the next three to five years. The challenges of providing adequate yet economically and financially sustainable social security benefits to a significantly larger proportion of the elderly than is the case currently will however remain.

References

International Monetary Fund (IMF) (2001), Singapore: Selected Issues, Washington DC: IMF, Country Report No. 01/177.

McCarthy, D., Mitchell, O.S., and Piggott J. (2001), "Asset Rich and Cash Poor: Retirement Provision and Housing Policy in Singapore," Pension Research Council, Wharton School, University of Pennsylvania, Working Paper 2001-10.

Notes

1. The author would like to thank Amarendu Nandy for research assistance. The author can be contacted through e-mail: mppasher@nus.edu.sg, and fax: (65) 6778 1020.

2. As a digression, many people have suggested that what governments in developing countries should do is issue long-term, inflation-indexed bonds. The expectation is that such bonds would be appropriate instruments for developing annuity products that are inflation-indexed, and as a result, inflation protection issue will be addressed. My own view is that such a move would be counterproductive. Inflation indexation of bonds does not reduce the inflation risk: what it does is transfer the risk from bond owners, be they pension funds or individuals, to the taxpayer. The fiscal situation in many developing countries is already weak. To take on the liability that arises from such bonds and that, because future inflation rates is unknown, fiscal consolidation could be adversely impacted. It also would reduce fiscal flexibility because these are the payments that would have to be made first. Such bonds also have a perverse income distribution impact. I have very strong reservations about the efficacy of issuing inflation-indexed bonds in developing countries in general and India in particular.

10

Chapter 11

Supervision of a Public Pension Fund: Experience and Challenges in Kenya

Edward Odundo

I am honored to have been given the opportunity to address this second conference on Public Pension Fund Management.

I propose to speak on the experience and challenges of supervising the public pension fund in Kenya. I will dwell particularly on the National Social Security Fund, which is the only public pension fund under the supervision of the Retirement Benefits Authority. I will also briefly touch on our experience in regulating the other types of schemes that exist in Kenya.

Background

The Kenyan retirement benefits sector dates back to before independence, when it existed in the form of the pioneer Civil Service Staff Pension Scheme and a few occupational schemes set up by large private companies. Prior to the enactment of the Retirement Benefits Act in 1997, however, it was by and large unregulated. There was lack of a harmonized legislative framework and, even with the establishment in 1964 of the National Social Security Fund, a discordant regulatory environment. The only regulations governing the sector were those inscribed in the Income Tax Act and trust laws. These regulations did not encompass developmental objectives.

Between 1964 and 1997 the industry was dominated by retirement benefit schemes run by employers, who typically gave secondary consideration to the interests of scheme members and to matters impacting the country's economy. Many of these schemes furthermore were run through insurance companies whose operations were by and large nontransparent. As a result, the industry was tainted by poor investments, delays and denials of payment to members, and the misuse and outright embezzlement of scheme funds by those entrusted to guard them.

The Retirement Benefit Act

In August 1997 the Kenyan National Assembly enacted the Retirement Benefits Act to address the problems afflicting the industry. The subsidiary Retirement Benefits Regulations were then subsequently passed in 2000 to provide the roadmap for implementation of the Act.

The Act created the Retirement Benefits Authority (RBA), which was charged with implementing the Act and overseeing the industry's management and development. Control of the Authority's operations is vested in an independent board of directors with a majority private sector representation and the autonomy to run the industry without undue government interference.

The Act itemizes five objectives from which the RBA derives its mandate: to regulate and supervise the establishment and management of retirement benefit schemes; to protect the interests of members and sponsors of such schemes; to promote the development of the retirement benefits sector; to advise the Minister for Finance on the national policy for the sector; and to implement all government policies relating to the sector. The RBA has taken as its two priority objectives the protection of funds and the development of the industry.

Several positive changes have been effected in the industry since implementation of the Act. For example, members confidence and involvement in pension scheme affairs has increased tremendously, through board representation, annual general meetings, and the complaints mechanisms mandated by the Retirement Benefits Authority. Pension schemes now operate in a transparent and accountable manner and publish timely audited accounts. At the same time, investment guidelines provided in the law mean that portfolios are now stronger and more diversified, with the result that

11

they have contributed to a significant lengthening in the maturity structure of the government domestic debt and to the successful issue of private sector corporate bonds. Finally, the level of professionalism in pension fund management has risen, as a result of the mandatory use of independent investment advisors and custodians.

In sum, the result of these and other changes has been the accelerated growth and increased diversification of the assets held by the industry. The accumulated assets of the Kenyan retirement benefits industry now have a market value of US$1.8 billion, which translates to 20 percent of GDP. This figure rates far below those of the United States, the Netherlands, and the United Kingdom but compares well with those of Japan and exceeds those of Germany, Italy, and Sweden.

These assets are administered by four different types of scheme, of varying sizes: the Civil Service Pension Scheme, the National Social Security Fund, occupational staff retirement benefit schemes, and individual retirement benefit schemes. The largest of these are the occupational schemes, which account for 61 percent of total industry assets. The National Social Security Fund accounts for 38 percent of assets and the individual schemes for less than 1 percent.

The Civil Service Pension Scheme, created by Act of Parliament in 1942, is noncontributory and nonfunded. It is a typical pay-as-you-go scheme that draws its funding from government tax collection. The scheme's members account for 38 percent of all Kenyans with a pension entitlement, and the government must allocate 5 percent of annual revenues to cover the scheme's liabilities. Because of this overwhelming financial pressure, plans are underway to transform the Civil Service Pension Scheme into a scheme that is contributory.

Occupational staff pension schemes are many in number and continue to multiply. By end-2001 the Retirement Benefits Authority had received application for registration from 1,200 occupational schemes; by March 2003 it had received an additional 180 schemes. Considering that employers are not mandated by law to establish retirement benefit schemes this is an impressive performance. It nonetheless is not what it might be, and the RBA continues to lobby the government to provide incentives to employers to set up more schemes for their employees.

Individual retirement benefit schemes are rare. Currently there are only six schemes, mostly by insurance companies, accredited with the RBA. They nonetheless are valuable, as they are open to all individuals without

11

limitations and therefore are the most readily accessible to those in the informal sectors who wish to save for their retirement.

The National Social Security Fund

The National Social Security Fund, a contributory provident fund, is my main area of discussion. The fund is a workers' saving scheme created by the government to provide a basic retirement benefit. Participation is mandatory for all Kenyans working in private sector businesses with more than five employees. The fund has a registered membership base countrywide of 2.9 million, working for 59,025 registered employers. Contributions to the fund are made jointly by employees and employers. The current contribution per member is US$2.50 per month. Through these contributions the fund has accumulated a book value of US$600 million.

The fund has four specific obligations: to recruit members and identify eligible employers; to collect member contributions; to carry out the administrative functions of the fund; and, most important, to invest the funds received but not required for immediate disbursement.

Main Issues

The fund is faced with numerous challenges that are deeply entrenched in the operations of the scheme and that negatively impact investment returns.

The first challenge is that of an investment profile that is characterized by a lack of diversity: an overwhelming 72 percent of assets—far greater than the recommended 30 percent—is held in real property. Returns from these assets are low, and liquidating them would offer little relief since the property market is depressed and the likelihood of recovering costs is poor. A further 7 percent of assets is invested in bank deposits with 16 financial institutions. Ten of these institutions have collapsed, locking up 4.6 percent of total fund assets. This situation compares badly with that of the country's other occupational schemes, which have only 9 percent of assets invested in real property. These other schemes generally have well-diversified investment portfolios, producing good rates of return: the National Social Security Fund (NSSF) in contrast has been paying a declared interest rate to members that is less than the rate of inflation.

The second challenge is that of poor record-keeping. This has led to delays in determining benefits precipitating a US$100 million unallocated suspense account. Third, the costs of administering the scheme are too high: in 1999–2000, administrative costs amounted to 130 percent of contributions, compared to the International Social Security Association's recommended maximum of 25 percent. The fourth major challenge is that of financial accounting. The fund's accounts have been consistently queried by government auditors: in particular, the pricing of contracts and investments worth as much as 30 percent of the total fund have been queried, raising concerns as to whether or not the stated asset base is in fact realizable.

Diagnosis

The strategy that the RBA has adopted to address these challenges has been to identify their root causes. Four in particular have been established. First, the absence of a regulatory framework has produced an environment that has enabled many of these problems to breed. The absence of guidelines with which to comply and of sanctions for noncompliance means that trustees have had the leeway to do as they wish—including relegating the interests of members to a secondary concern. Second, political interference, particularly in terms of influencing investments and the pricing of those investments, has hampered the operation of the fund. More often than not, managing trustees appointed by the political regime have proven more inclined to serve the interests of their employers than the interests of fund members. Exacerbating this situation, the support of powerful sponsors has meant that trustees that have committed punishable offences have done so with impunity. Third, lack of member involvement and poor understanding of member rights means there has been little or no social audit of the scheme, and therefore again no incentive for proper fund management. Finally, the fund's position as a monopoly in receiving statutory contributions has enabled it to engage in expensive, noncompetitive practices.

Addressing the Issues

The Retirement Benefits Act has been introduced in part to address these issues by requiring the adoption of international fund management practices. The key compliance requirements of the act include the timely preparation and wide publication of audited annual accounts; the outsourc-

11

ing of investments to independent professional fund managers; the placing of assets with reputable and stable custodial institutions; and, in the long term, the diversification of the investment portfolio according to guidelines provided in the law.

Implementation Issues

Progress toward compliance has been painstakingly slow. The political protection of scheme managers in particular has encouraged them to resist the mandated changes. The NSSF in fact has pointedly refused to appoint an independent fund manager or service providers, on the grounds that such appointments would diminish its control over investment decisions and also result in staff retrenchments. Second, the fact that the investment portfolio is skewed toward real property means that it cannot easily be rescheduled to fit the new guidelines—and sale of the fund's real property assets furthermore would incur a loss that would contravene the fund objective of protecting member benefits. Third, the fund and the Retirement Benefits Authority fall under the jurisdiction of different ministries, dissipating direction and control to the detriment of members. Finally, there is a wide disparity between the quoted book value and the market value of the NSSF assets. The book value, is evidently, far higher than the actual value of the physical assets.

Lessons from the Kenyan Experience

Clearly, there are lessons to be learnt from the Kenyan experience. First of these is the need for stakeholder buy-in, and particularly that of politicians. Stakeholder backing is a catalyst for the successful regulation of a public pension fund. Through educational programs targeted at politicians, the public, and other stakeholders, regulators can build the foundation of popular support that is necessary to back up their regulatory efforts. Second, it is important to harmonize the laws and statutes that govern a public pension fund; in particular, the fund and regulator should be put under a single ministerial portfolio as opposed to the Kenyan situation where the fund is in the labour ministry and the regulator at the finance ministry. Third, the historical performance of a fund cannot be disregarded simply because of intergenerational agendas. Difficult and costly decisions about stated assets may have to be faced and made. Finally, it need to be recognized that if they are to

11

achieve the highest possible return at the lowest fiscal cost, public pension funds must be treated the same way as privately run schemes. They must be stripped of the monopolistic practices that act against their members, and for this to happen they must above all be exposed to competition.

Reform Agenda

Cognizance to the above lessons the RBA has a clear vision for the future of the industry in Kenya.

Top of the agenda is the need to bring the National Social Security Fund into full compliance with the Retirement Benefits Act.

Second on the agenda is the transformation of the fund from a provident fund to a pension fund. Current benefit payments by the NSSF do little to assist in the achievement of old-age security. The payment of lump sum benefits is inconsistent with the core objective of a mandatory scheme—to force workers to save for their retirement—because so many of those payments are rapidly squandered. The switch from provident to pension fund will require radical changes, principle among which will be linking pension payments to income, ensuring that returns on investment are significantly higher than the rate of inflation, and possibly also increasing the level of contributions.

Third on the agenda is the creation of competition for statutory contributions through the liberalization of the collection and administration of those contributions. The Retirement Benefits Act seeks to achieve this by providing an option for employers and employees to pay their contributions, including those required by the legislation underscoring the NSSF, to other approved schemes.

Finally, as mentioned earlier, the Retirement Benefits Authority is keen to play a central role in the government's effort to transform the civil service pension scheme to a contributory funded scheme. This will include the nomination of a board of trustees, the appointment of independent fund managers and custodians, and the restructuring of contributions and benefits.

11